A Hand Through The Door For M

MW01698069

دعوة ونصيحة لأختي المسلمة الجديدة

إعداد : ياسمين بنت إسماعيل

A Hand Through The Door For My New Sister

In Accordance with the Qur`ān and authentic Sunnah of the Prophet Muhammad [ﷺ]

by

Yasmine bint Ismail

King Fahd National Library Cataloging-in-Publication Data

Ismail, Yasmine
A hand through the door for my new sister .-
Jeddah.
...p.; ..cm
ISBN 9960-9143-8-0
1- Preaching I-Title
212 dc

4859/21

Legal Deposit no. 4859/21
ISBN 9960-9143-8-0

الطبعة الأولى صفر - ١٤٢٢هـ

عزيزي القارئ:

إذا وجدت أي خطأ في الكتاب نرجو الكتابة:

دار الخير - ص.ب. ٣٢٢٧٤

جدة ٢١٤٢٨ المملكة العربية السعودية

هاتف وفاكس: ٦٨٧٠٦٧٩

We ask all those who can benefit us with corrections or comments etc, to contact us at the following address:

Dar Al-Khair
P.O. Box 32274
Jeddah 21428
K.S.A.
Tel/Fax: 687 0679
Website: www.daralkhair.com

TABLE OF CONTENTS

بسم الله الرحمن الرحيم

INTRODUCTION

All Praise is for Allāh; we praise Him and seek His help and forgiveness. And we seek refuge in Allāh, the Most High, from the evils of our own selves and from our wicked deeds. Whomsoever Allāh has guided, none can misguide him. And whomsoever Allāh has misguided, none can guide him. And I bear witness that there is no god worthy of being worshipped except Allāh, alone, without partner or associate. I further bear witness that Muhammad is His servant and messenger. May Allāh, the Exalted, bestow His peace and blessings on the Final prophet Muhammad, upon his good and pure family, and upon all of his noble companions.

My dear sisters, I find it of paramount importance to write this book for the sea of new sisters whom Allāh, the Most Compassionate, is guiding to the only true path. All praise is for Allāh as much as His Glory and Sublime Majesty rightly deserve as He facilitated this effort. May He reward all those who aided me in any way, especially my loving husband for all his support and help.

This is only a compilation of evidence in accordance with the Qur`ān and authentic *Sunnah* of the Prophet Muhammad [ﷺ]. I must however stress, this is in no way intended to dampen the sisters obligation to seek for herself the knowledge given to us in the Qur`ān and authentic *Sunnah*, according to the understanding of the *Salaf* and the abundance of scholarly works that help to give us a better understanding of the two fundamental sources. There are many treasured collections of books written by the *Salaf* which should be read for one's self.

This is intended to be a quick reference for the new sisters who do not yet have libraries and rely on word of mouth from others with little or no knowledge. I do this as I remember myself and other sisters who reverted to Islām, with a wave of questions and a lot of conflicting answers. This is also for the sisters born in Islām but who were not practicing at all, or not practicing Islām in accordance with the Qur`ān and the authentic *Sunnah* and are in need of a reference.

I have used proofs and evidences from the Qur`ān and tried to use authentic *hadīth* and wherever needed I have also used opinions or explanations from the scholars of the *Salaf*. Most *āyāt* and *hadīths* have been taken from available translations with very few edited as needed and a few *hadīth*s needed translation. May Allāh, the Almighty, have mercy on us and protect all that read this from any flaw herein.

May Allāh, the Almighty, the Exalted, forgive us our sins and shortcomings, and' facilitate good for us and grant us the desired end. May He accept this humble effort for His sake Alone and make it a benefit to all who read it, Āmīn.

Yasmine bint Ismail

Transliteration table

ء	`	ض	<u>d</u>	Vowels	
ب	b	ط	<u>t</u>		a
ت	t	ظ	<u>dh</u>		i
ث	th	ع	'		u
ج	j	غ	gh		
ح	<u>h</u>	ف	f		
خ	kh	ق	q		
د	d	ك	k	Elongations	
ذ	dh	ل	l	اَ	ā
ر	r	م	m	يِ	ī
ز	z	ن	n	وُ	ū
س	s	و	w		
ش	sh	ه	h		
ص	<u>s</u>	ي	y		

FOOD FOR THOUGHT

1. WHY WERE WE CREATED? Allāh the Exalted, the Mighty, said:

﴿ وَمَا خَلَقْتُ ٱلْجِنَّ وَٱلْإِنسَ إِلَّا لِيَعْبُدُونِ ۝ ﴾

﴾And I [Allāh] created not the Jinn and Humans except that they should worship Me [Alone].﴿[51:56]

2. WHY ISLĀM? Allāh, the All- Knowing, said:

﴿ وَمَن يَبْتَغِ غَيْرَ ٱلْإِسْلَـٰمِ دِينًا فَلَن يُقْبَلَ مِنْهُ وَهُوَ فِى ٱلْـَٔاخِرَةِ مِنَ ٱلْخَـٰسِرِينَ ﴾

﴾ And whoever seeks a religion other than Islām, it will never be accepted of him, and in the Hereafter he will be one of the losers.﴿ [3:85]

3. WHAT IF ONE DOUBTS ALL OR PART OF THE LAST REVELATION, THE HOLY QUR`ĀN? Allāh, the All- Encompassing said:

﴿ فَذَرْنِى وَمَن يُكَذِّبُ بِهَـٰذَا ٱلْحَدِيثِ ۖ سَنَسْتَدْرِجُهُم مِّنْ حَيْثُ لَا يَعْلَمُونَ ۝ ﴾

﴾ Then leave Me Alone with such as belie this Qur`ān. We shall punish them gradually from directions they perceive not.﴿ [68: 44]

4. WHY OBEY THE MESSENGER [ﷺ] ALONG WITH ALLĀH, WHY NOT FOLLOW THE QUR`ĀN ONLY? Allāh, the Most High, said:

﴿ وَمَآ ءَاتَىٰكُمُ ٱلرَّسُولُ فَخُذُوهُ وَمَا نَهَىٰكُمْ عَنْهُ فَٱنتَهُوا۟ ۚ وَٱتَّقُوا۟ ٱللَّهَ ۖ إِنَّ ٱللَّهَ شَدِيدُ ٱلْعِقَابِ ۝ ﴾

﴾ And whatsoever the Messenger [Muhammad ﷺ] gives you, take it, and whatsoever he forbids you, abstain [from it], and fear Allāh. Verily, Allāh is severe in punishment.﴿.[59:7]

5. WHAT IS THE LAST DAY? Allāh, the Almighty, said:

﴿ يَوْمَ تُبْلَى ٱلسَّرَآئِرُ ۝ فَمَا لَهُۥ مِن قُوَّةٍ وَلَا نَاصِرٍ ۝ ﴾

﴾ The Day when all the secrets [deeds, prayers, fasting etc.] will be examined [as to their truth]. Then will [man] have no power, nor any helper﴿ [86:9-10]

6. WILL MEN AND WOMEN BE EQUAL IN REWARD [ACCORDING TO THEIR GOOD DEEDS]? Allāh, the Most Merciful, said:

﴿ وَعَدَ ٱللَّهُ ٱلْمُؤْمِنِينَ وَٱلْمُؤْمِنَـٰتِ جَنَّـٰتٍ تَجْرِى مِن تَحْتِهَا ٱلْأَنْهَـٰرُ خَـٰلِدِينَ فِيهَا وَمَسَـٰكِنَ طَيِّبَةً

فِى جَنَّـٰتِ عَدْنٍ ۚ وَرِضْوَٰنٌ مِّنَ ٱللَّهِ أَكْبَرُ ۚ ذَٰلِكَ هُوَ ٱلْفَوْزُ ٱلْعَظِيمُ ﴾

﴾Allāh has promised the believers- men and women gardens under which rivers flow to dwell therein forever, and beautiful mansions in gardens of 'Adn [Eden] Paradise]. But the greatest bliss is the good Pleasure of Allāh that is the supreme success.﴿ [9:72]

CHAPTER 1

THE PILLARS OF ISLĀM

Allāh the Exalted the Mighty, said:

﴿إِنَّ ٱلدِّينَ عِندَ ٱللَّهِ ٱلْإِسْلَـٰمُ﴾

﴾ Truly the religion with Allāh is Islām. ﴿

And what is Islām?

The Messenger of Allāh [ﷺ] said:

" Islām is based on the following five pillars:

1) *To testify that none has the right to be worshipped but Allāh and Muhammad is Allāh's Messenger.*
2) *To offer the [five compulsory congregational] prayers dutifully and perfectly.*
3) *To pay Zakāh [i.e., Obligatory charity]*
4) *To perform Hajj [Pilgrimage to Makkah] to* the *house [Ka'bah]. It is a duty that* mankind *owes to Allāh, those who can afford the* expenses *[for ones conveyance, provision and residence].*
5) *To observe fast during the month of Ramadān.*[1] *"*

1] THE SHAHĀDAH [TESTIFICATION OF FAITH]:

To testify: "*Ashhadu an lā ilāha illa Allāh wa ashhadu anna Muhammadan rasūlullāh*", "None has the right to be worshipped but Allāh and Muhammad is the Messenger of Allāh." This statement is necessary for

---

[1] *Sahīh Al-Bukhārī*, [Eng. Trans. vol. 1 #7].

one to be considered a Muslim and therefore makes one's life and property protected, unless he commits an offence punishable by the laws of Allāh. This is the outward profession and one should strive hard thereafter to act in accordance with this statement, and Allāh knows the affairs of one's heart. This protection is in accordance with the statement of Allāh's Messenger [ﷺ]:

"I have been commanded to fight against people until they testify the fact that there is no god but Allāh, and believe in me [that] I am the Messenger [from the Lord] and in all that I have brought. And when they do it, their blood and riches are guaranteed protection on my behalf except where it is justified by law, and their affairs rest with Allāh."[2]

It is a noteworthy fact that one should take a bath upon entrance into Islām. "It is reported in the *Sahīhayn* [*Sahīh Al-Bukhārī* and *Sahīh Muslim*] that when Thumāmah [رضي الله عنه] wanted to accept Islām he went and took a bath, then came and accepted Islām[3]. This indicates that the *ghusl* [bath] was known [to be prescribed] for those who wanted to enter Islām and a disbeliever is [spiritually] unclean as Allāh mentioned and he is in most cases *junub*[4] and this is a condition not eliminated by a bath while in a state of disbelief. For that reason Imām Ahmad and others took the position that a *ghusl* is mandatory, and that if a disbeliever accepts Islām, no act of worship, such as *salāh*, is acceptable from him until he takes a bath."[5]

---

[2] *Sahīh Muslim* [Eng. Trans. Vol.1 #33].

[3] *Sahīh Al-Bukhārī*, [Eng. Trans. vol. 5. # 658].

[4] *Junub*, a state of ritual impurity caused by ejaculation of semen during intercourse or wet dreams etc. *janābah* as well as purity after menstrual or post-birth bleeding require a complete bath with the intention of ritual purification in order to be able to make *salāh*, recite Qur`ān and perform other acts of worship.

[5] *Legal Rulings of Importance to New Muslims*. Compiled from Fatawa by Shaykh Al-Islām Ibn Taymiyyah, Shaykh Ibn Bāz, Shaykh Ibn Al-'Uthaymīn, and Shaykh Ibn Jibrīn. Besides the *hadīth* on Thumāmah also see *hadīth* #355 in the *Sunan* of Abū Dāwud, the book of Purification.

2] THE *S̲ALĀH* [PRAYER]:

You must offer the five compulsory prayers dutifully and perfectly. Allāh the All-Encompassing, said:

﴿ وَأَقِيمُوا۟ ٱلصَّلَوٰةَ وَءَاتُوا۟ ٱلزَّكَوٰةَ وَٱرْكَعُوا۟ مَعَ ٱلرَّٰكِعِينَ ﴾

﴿ And perform As̲-S̲alāh [Iqāmah As̲-S̲alāh], and give Zakāh , and bow down [or submit yourselves with obedience to Allāh] along with the rāki'ūn [Those who bow down and submit themselves with obedience to Allāh, with Muh̲ammad [ﷺ] as the Muslims do i.e., for Allāh Alone.] ﴾ 2:43

The merit of Prayer:

Many Muslims do not comprehend the importance of *s̲alāh*; *shaykh* 'Abd Al-Muh̲sin Al-'Abbād points out, that of all the *fard̲* [obligatory] duties imposed on mankind, it is only the *s̲alāh* that has been revealed above the Seven Heavens. Allāh summoned His Prophet above the Seven Heavens to reveal the *s̲alāh*, then had him returned back to Earth. There is a long narration in *S̲ah̲īh̲ Al-Bukhārī*, a part of which reads: *"Then he [Jibrā`īl] took my hand and ascended with me to the nearest Heaven..."* They proceeded through to the second Heaven then third etc. till, *"Then Jibrā`īl ascended with me to a place where I heard the creaking of pens...then Allāh enjoined fifty prayers on my followers. When I returned with this order of Allāh, I passed by Mūsā who asked me: 'What has Allāh enjoined on your followers?' I replied: 'He has enjoined fifty prayers on them.' Mūsā said: 'Go back to your Lord [and appeal for reduction] for your followers will not be able to bear it.'* Then it continues in detail until... *"so I returned to Allāh and requested for a further reduction and half of it was reduced. I again passed by Mūsā and he said to me: 'Return to your Lord, for your followers will not be able to bear it. So I returned to Allāh and He said, 'These are five prayers and they are all [equal to] fifty [in reward] for My Word does not change...'*[6]

---

[6] *S̲ah̲īh̲ Al-Bukhārī* [Eng. Trans. Vol. 1, page 211-214].

Originally, **fifty** *salāh* were ordered by Allāh, and the Prophet [ﷺ], at the urging of the Prophet Mūsā [عليه السلام] who he met in the Heavens, went back to Allāh to ask for a reduction in the number of *salāh* offered in a day, till the present **five** *salāh* were ordered. My dear sister it is therefore most improper, to say the least, to complain it takes up a lot of time! I might also remind my sister, that we should not procrastinate using excuses like you are busy with household activities or any other worldly matters thinking that you will make it up later. Allāh warns us:

﴿فَوَيْلٌ لِّلْمُصَلِّينَ ۝٤ ٱلَّذِينَ هُمْ عَن صَلَاتِهِمْ سَاهُونَ ۝٥﴾

﴿ So woe unto those performers of salāh [i.e., hypocrites] who delay their salāh from their fixed times ﴾107:4-5

﴿حَـٰفِظُوا۟ عَلَى ٱلصَّلَوَٰتِ وَٱلصَّلَوٰةِ ٱلْوُسْطَىٰ وَقُومُوا۟ لِلَّهِ قَـٰنِتِينَ ۝٢٣٨﴾

﴿ Guard strictly [five obligatory] As-Salawāt [the prayers] especially the middle salāh [i.e., the best prayer: 'Asr]. And stand before Allāh with obedience [and do not speak to others during the salāh] ﴾2:238

The middle prayer is referred to as the best prayer [i.e., *'Asr*], so one needs to pay special attention to it.

Facts pertaining to her *salāh*:

1) ***Wudū`*** **is necessary [the minor ritual purification necessary, obtained by intention and the washing of the body parts stated below i.e., ablution]**

Allāh, the All-Encompassing, said:

﴿يَـٰٓأَيُّهَا ٱلَّذِينَ ءَامَنُوٓا۟ إِذَا قُمْتُمْ إِلَى ٱلصَّلَوٰةِ فَٱغْسِلُوا۟ وُجُوهَكُمْ وَأَيْدِيَكُمْ إِلَى ٱلْمَرَافِقِ﴾

﴿ O you who believe! When you intend to offer As-Salāh [the prayer] wash your faces and your hands [forearms] up to the elbows... ﴾5:6

And the Prophet [ﷺ] said: *"The Prayer of none amongst you would be accepted in a state of impurity till he performs ablution."*[7]

---

[7] *Sahīh Muslim*, [Eng. Trans. Vol. 1, *hadīth* #435].

How to perform Ablution:

This is found in an authentic *hadīth* narrated by Imām Muslim upon the authority of Humrān [ﷺ] who said:

*"'Uthmān Ibn 'Affān [ﷺ] called for ablution water and this is how he performed the ablution. He washed his hands thrice. He then rinsed his mouth and cleaned his nose with water [three times]. He then washed his face three times; then washed his right arm up to the elbow three times, then washed his left arm like that, then wiped his head; then washed his right foot up to the ankle three times, then washed his left foot like that, and then said: I saw the Messenger of Allāh [ﷺ] performing ablution like this ablution of mine. Then the Messenger of Allāh [ﷺ] said: "**He who performs ablution like this ablution of mine and then stood up [for prayer] and offered two rak'ahs of prayer without allowing his thoughts to be distracted, all his previous sins are expiated.**"* Ibn Shihāb said: Our Scholars remarked: This is the most complete of the ablutions performed for prayer.[8]

It should be noted that the sister should use the toilet first if she is in need of it, as such a pressing need distracts one from the prayer. The Prophet [ﷺ] said:

> *"No prayer can be rightly said when there is food there [before the worshipper] or when he is prompted by the call of nature"*[9]

I found the details of how to perform ablution in Muhammad Ibn Jamīl Zeno's book, *THE PILLARS OF ISLĀM AND IMAN* to be concise and easy for a new sister to follow, by the will of Allāh.

- Before starting it one should intend to enter the state of ritual purity by the action of ablution and say '*Bismillāh*' [In the Name of Allāh].
- Wash your hands up to the wrists three times.

---

[8] *Sahīh Muslim*, [Eng. Trans. vol. 1 #436].

[9] *Sahīh Muslim*, [Eng. Trans. vol. 1 #1139].

- Rinse your mouth by drawing water from your cupped hand and likewise into your nose up to the start of your nose bone- three times for each of these actions.
- Wash your face three times [hairline to chin, ear to ear].
- Wash both arms up to and including the elbows three times starting with the right arm.
- Wipe your wet hands over your hair with a backward then forward motion covering the entire head and wipe the inside and back of the ears with the forefinger and thumb.
- Wash both feet up to and including the ankles three times, starting with the right foot.

After completing the aforementioned, say:

أشهد أن لا إله إلا الله وحده لا شريك له وأشهد أن محمدا عبده ورسوله

"I bear witness that none has the right to be worshipped but Allāh Alone and I bear witness that Muhammad is His slave and His Messenger." [10]

And as for the merit of this *du'ā`*, 'Umar Ibn Al-Khattāb [ﷺ] narrates:

"If anyone amongst you performs the ablution and completes it well and then says, 'I testify that there is no god but Allāh and that Muhammad is the servant of Allāh and His Messenger', the eight gates of Paradise would be opened for him and he may enter by whichever one of them he wishes." [11]

This is the method of ablution in accordance with the *Sunnah* of the Prophet [ﷺ].

---

[10] *The Pillars of Islām and Iman*; Zeno, pg. 60.

[11] *Sahīh Muslim*, [Eng. Trans. Vol. 1 #451]

TAYAMMUM [PURIFICATION WITH DUST]

This is only permissible in certain circumstances as a substitute for *Wudū`* or the *Ghusl* [bath for ritual purification] as Allāh the Most Merciful, said:

﴿ وَإِن كُنتُم مَّرْضَىٰٓ أَوْ عَلَىٰ سَفَرٍ أَوْ جَآءَ أَحَدٌ مِّنكُم مِّنَ ٱلْغَآئِطِ أَوْ لَـٰمَسْتُمُ ٱلنِّسَآءَ فَلَمْ تَجِدُوا۟ مَآءً فَتَيَمَّمُوا۟ صَعِيدًا طَيِّبًا فَٱمْسَحُوا۟ بِوُجُوهِكُمْ وَأَيْدِيكُمْ ۗ إِنَّ ٱللَّهَ كَانَ عَفُوًّا غَفُورًا ﴿٤٣﴾ ﴾

﴿ And if you are ill, or on a journey, or if one of you comes after answering the call of nature, or you have been in contact with women [by sexual relations] and you find no water, perform Tayammum with clean earth and rub therewith your faces and hands. Truly Allāh is Ever Oft-Pardoning, Oft-Forgiving.﴾ 4:43

The method for performing Tayammum is described in the following *hadīth*, in which the Prophet was instructing some of his companions on the correct manner of performing it:

"It would have been sufficient for you to do like this," The Prophet [ﷺ] then stroked lightly the earth with his hands and then blew off the dust and passed his hands over his face and hands "[12]

One who is sick may also perform Tayammum until they heal as long as it is felt that the use of water will increase their illness, delay their healing or kill them. The sick may continue to use Tayammum until they recover from their illness. Tayammum can also be used if no water is available or if there is a severe shortage of water, and Allāh knows best, He said,

﴿ وَلَا تَقْتُلُوٓا۟ أَنفُسَكُمْ ۚ إِنَّ ٱللَّهَ كَانَ بِكُمْ رَحِيمًا ﴿٢٩﴾ ﴾

﴿ Do not kill yourself. No doubt Allāh is most merciful to you.﴾ 4:29.

---

[12] *Sahīh Al-Bukhārī*, [Engl. Trans. vol. 1 #334].

This is the understanding of the *Salaf As-Sālih*[13] and the majority of the scholars. Before performing Tayammum, "*Bismillāh*" is uttered first along with the intention to enter the state of ritual purification just as in ablution with water.

The state of ritual purification is broken by:

i] Events that necessitate *wudū`* [ablution].

Some of the matters that break *wudū`* are: anything that comes out of the genitals or anus such as, urine, stools, urethral discharge [emission before actual semen] and for men: a white discharge at the time of urination and for women: regular discharge from the birth canal that is not related to menses neither is it emotionally based [sexual][14]; deep sleep; direct contact of genitals; losing consciousness; contact upon desire and eating camel-meat.

ii] Events that necessitate a *ghusl* [complete bath[15]].

This includes sexual intercourse [with or without seminal discharge from either partner] as per the *hadīth* upon Abū Mūsā:

"When anyone sits amidst four parts [of a woman] and the circumcised parts touch each other a bath becomes obligatory."[16]

---

[13] *As-Salaf As-Sālih* Our pious predecessors. This refers to the first three generations of *Muslims*. Those who lived at the time of the Prophet [ﷺ] and the next two after them. The Prophet [ﷺ] said in an authentic *hadīth*, **"The best people are those living in my generation, and then those who will follow them, and then those who will follow the latter."** [*Sahīh Al-Bukhārī* Eng. Trans. vol.5 pg. 2 #3] After the death of these generations we [*Muslims*] look to those of our scholars [for guidance] who follow the Qur`ān and authentic *hadīth* of the Prophet [ﷺ] with the correct understanding of the two from these three generations [*As-Salaf As-Sālih*]. It is of great importance for every *Muslim* to understand that we cannot come up with our own understanding of Islām nor can we take the understanding of any scholar unless he is on the correct path in accordance with the *As-Salaf As-Sālih*, and may Allāh make us of the rightly guided, Āmīn.

[14] This discharge is said to be pure, thus if it gets on one's clothing it is not harmful by the will of Allāh, i.e., it is not necessary to wash it of as in the case of urine this is the opinion of *Shaykh* 'Al-'Uthaymīn however she should however wear a panty liner.

[15] See chapter on Menses [point #11] for details on the correct way to perform a complete bath.

[16] *Sahīh Muslim*, [Eng. Trans. vol. 1 pg.196 #684].

Also seminal discharge from the man or woman caused by dreams or thoughts, etc. and menstruation. Purification from one's menstruation can only be done after the end of the period and no prayer is due on her during it.

2) Her dress for the *salāh*.

Once a sister reaches puberty her *salāh* is not accepted unless she sufficiently covers herself. Allāh, the Almighty, said:

﴿ يَـٰبَنِىٓ ءَادَمَ خُذُوا۟ زِينَتَكُمْ عِندَ كُلِّ مَسْجِدٍ ﴾

﴿ O children of Ādam! Take your adornment [by wearing clean clothes] while praying, ﴾7:31

Literally, this verse is directly translated by **scholars** as *"zīnah"* to the *masjid* in reference to beautification in clothing etc. In other words, not only should the clothing cover the aura [private parts] of the worshipper, but it should be clean and the worshipper should increase on this basic covering e.g. for men living in a country where a headdress is worn, he could wear this in addition to a *thawb*. In addition, the worshipper should wear beautiful clothes. This is because you are praying to Allāh and if you were going to see the head of state you would definitely care for your appearance, so who has more right to this than Allāh? A man should also use perfume, however the sister should use perfume only if she is staying at **home**.

Consequently, even at home, it is the opinion of the scholars of the *Salaf* that her entire body and head [except her face if no strange men are present] should be covered for the prayer. 'Ā`ishah [ﷺ] narrated that the Prophet [ﷺ] said:

"The salāh of a woman who has reached puberty is not accepted unless she is wearing a khimār [a long scarf which covers her hair, neck and chest]."[17]

---

[17] Sunan of Abū Dāwud [Engl. Trans. vol. 1 #641] and declared *sahīh* by *Shaykh* Al-Albānī.

The sister should wear a long sleeved dress or cloak that covers her feet and which is neither tight fitting nor transparent, along with a khimār. This covers her basic needs for *salāh* legally. It is also the opinion of a number of respected *Salafī* scholars, including *shaykh Al-Islām* Ibn Taymiyyah, that when a woman is praying where foreign men[18] can see her, she must cover everything i.e., face, hands and feet. However, as mentioned above, even when she is at home she should increase the area covered including her feet [with socks] and hands if possible as Allāh has more right for His servants to be bashful when they talk to Him than to any of His creation.

3) The best place for her *salāh* is at home in her chamber, as we see in the following *hadīth*.

"The Prayer in your chamber is more excellent than that you offer in your apartment, and the Prayer which you say in your courtyard is better than that what you observe in the mosque of your tribe [i.e., which is near your house] and your Prayer in the mosque of your tribe is better than that which you say in my mosque."[19]

4) However if she does want to go to the mosque, her husband [or guardian] should permit her in accordance with the *hadīth*:

"If the wife of anyone of you asks permission [to go to the mosque] do not forbid her"[20]

She should also know, especially in mosques without a section for women, that:

"The best rows for women are the last rows and the worst ones for them are the first ones."[21]

---

[18] See chapter on *nikāh* [marriage] point #2 and chapter on Dress of a Believing Woman.

[19] *Sahīh Muslim* [Eng. Trans. Vol. 1 footnotes on pg.241 #668].

[20] *Sahīh Al-Bukhārī*, [Eng. Trans. vol. 1 #832].

[21] *Sahīh Muslim* [Eng. Trans. vol. 1 #881].

5] She should *never* perfume herself when leaving her home. This includes going to the mosque also.

The Prophet [ﷺ] said:

"When anyone of you comes to the mosque she should not apply perfume"[22]

6] We are prohibited to pray facing a grave.

"Do not pray towards the graves and do not sit on them"[23]

7] One should pray with a *sutra* [an object placed in front of the worshiper indicating their area for prostrating, the purpose being to keep people from crossing directly in front of the worshiper and distracting them in their prayer.].

The Prophet [ﷺ] said: *"When any one of you prays facing something which conceals him from people and anyone tries to pass in front of him, he should be turned away, but if he refuses, he should be forcibly restrained from it for he is a devil."*[24]

8] It is permissible to carry a child during *salāh*.

"I saw the Messenger of Allāh [ﷺ] leading the people in prayer with Umāmah, the daughter of Abū Al-'Ās on his neck and when he prostrated he put her down."[25]

---

[22] *Sahīh Muslim* [Eng. Trans. Vol. 1 #892].

[23] *Sahīh Muslim*. [Eng. Trans. Vol. 2 #2122].

[24] *Sahīh Muslim*, [Eng. Trans. vol. 1 #1024].

[25] *Sahīh Muslim*, [Engl. Trans. vol. 1 #1109]. It was his granddaughter, from his daughter Zaynab.

9] One may shorten the *salāh* on hearing the cries of a child. [Note that this refers to the length of recitation and not the number of *rak'ahs*.]

The Prophet [ﷺ] said: *"Whenever I start the prayer I intend to prolong it but on hearing the cries of a child, I cut short the prayer because I know that the cries of the child will incite the mothers passions."*[26]

This however should not be used as a constant excuse, especially with newborns and first-born babies. My advice is either hold them, try to settle them or put them to sleep when one sees that *salāh* is due. But I know this is not always possible, the rule is 'Fear Allāh as much as you can then if your intention is right, may Allāh the Most Merciful forgive us our short comings.'

10] A question arises with illness including difficult or heavy pregnancies. Is it permissible to sit? The answer is yes *but* bear in mind the following authentic *hadīth*:

'Imrān Ibn Husayn narrates in connection to his sufferance from piles, 'I asked the Prophet [ﷺ] about the praying of a man while sitting. He said:

"If he prays while standing it is better, and he who prays while sitting gets half the reward of the one who prays standing. And whoever prays while lying down gets half the reward of the one who prays while sitting." [27]

11] We have been commanded to eat first if food has already been served.

The Prophet [ﷺ] said:

"When supper is brought and the prayer begins, one should take the food first."[28]

---

[26] *Sahīh Al-Bukhārī*, [Eng. Trans. vol. 1 #678].

[27] *Sahīh Al-Bukhārī* [Eng. Trans. Vol. 2, page 120].

[28] *Sahīh Muslim*, [Engl. Trans. vol., 1 #1134].

12] There is no *ṣalāh* due from the sister during her menses. This includes *nifās* [See chapter on menses]. She is not required to make up for prayers missed during this period.

The Prophet [ﷺ] said:

"Give up your prayer when your menses begin."[29]

13] Should a sister ever forget to perform a *ṣalāh*, she simply makes it up as soon as she remembers regardless of the time period. Also, if she forgets something in the *ṣalāh*, she then makes two prostrations of forgetfulness [*sujūd As-sahwah*].

The Prophet [ﷺ] said:

"If anyone forgets a prayer he should pray that prayer when he remembers it. There is no expiation except the same."[30]

I should point out here that this is if she unintentionally missed it out of sheer forgetfulness and not negligence, for if it is from negligence then she enters the realm of sin. The Prophet [ﷺ] said: *"When one of you stands up to pray, the devil comes to him and confuses him so that he does not know how much he has prayed. If anyone of you has such an experience he should perform two prostrations while sitting down."*[31]

14] During *'Īd* prayers, sisters have to go to the *masjid* and attend the festivities. A frequently asked question is if one is not in the *masjid* itself or there is landscape or space which forces distance between the Imam and the followers, is the *ṣalāh* acceptable?

The Prophet [ﷺ] said: *"All women should participate in the good deeds and in the religious gatherings of the believers."*[32]

---

[29] *Ṣaḥīḥ Al-Bukhārī*, [Eng. Trans. vol. 1 #327].

[30] *Ṣaḥīḥ Al-Bukhārī*, [Eng. Trans. vol. 1 #571].

[31] *Ṣaḥīḥ Muslim*, [Eng. Trans. vol.1 # 1159].

[32] *Ṣaḥīḥ Al-Bukhārī*, [Eng. Trans. vol. 2 # 96].

"We were ordered to go out [for 'Īd] and also to take along with us the menstruating women and mature girls and virgins staying in seclusion."[33]

As far as the space between the Imam and the followers, the *Sahābah* [ﷺ] used to follow the Prophet [ﷺ] in prayer from outside his house, sometimes, while he was in prayer inside. Further, it is the opinion of Al-Hasan [ﷺ] that, 'There is no harm in praying if there is a river between you and the Imam'.[34] It is also the opinion of Abū Mijlāz that, 'One can follow the Imam even if there is a road or wall between the Imam and the followers provided the *takbīr* [i.e., to say *Allāh Akbar*] is audible'.[35]

However, it should be pointed out that according to scholars upon the way of the *Salaf* today, this refers to the one who has left his house to pray in congregation but finds that the *masjid* is full. It does not refer to the one who lives near the *masjid* and is not part of the congregation, who can hear the *salāh* and then chooses to follow the Imam in *salāh* claiming the wall does not stop the sound of the Imam. A sister at home or in a hotel room near the mosque etc. should not follow the sound of the Imam, rather she should either go to the *masjid* and join the congregation or pray by herself in her hotel room, and Allāh, the most High, knows best.

15] The shortening of prayer or the combination of *Dhuhr* and *'Asr* or *Maghrib* and *'Ishā`* is permissible under certain circumstances. For example, danger, travel and illness like the woman in a perpetual state of bleeding as it a hardship on her since she has to bathe before every *salāh*. The length of the prayer in this last example however, stays the same. It is only permissible for her to combine them.

"Allāh has prescribed the prayer by the tongue of your Prophet [ﷺ] as two rak'ahs for the traveler, four for the resident and one in danger."[36]

---

[33] *Sahīh Al-Bukhārī*, [Eng. Trans. vol. 2 # 97].

[34] *Sahīh Al-Bukhārī*, [Eng. Trans. vol., 1 It is part of Chapter 79].

[35] *Sahīh Al-Bukhārī*, [Eng. Trans. vol. 1 Chapter 79].

[36] *Sahīh Muslim*, [Eng. Trans. vol.1 #1463].

"When the Messenger of Allāh [ﷺ] had to set out on a journey hurriedly, he delayed the noon prayer to the earlier time for the afternoon prayer, then he would combine them, and he would delay the sunset prayer to the time when the twilight would disappear and then combine it with the 'Ishā` prayer."[37]

It should be noted that the shortening of the prayers is only for those prayers with four *rak'ahs*[38]. ***Fajr salāh*** is already two *rak'ahs* and stays as such and ***Maghrib salāh*** is three ***rak'ahs*** and stays as such also. While traveling in a car or bus [or on an animal] one should get off and pray in a *masjid* or on the ground for all obligatory prayers.[39] They may pray supererogatory prayers in the car or bus [or on their animal]. As for a plane or train or ship they may pray in them for both obligatory and supererogatory prayers as these modes of transport cannot be stopped during travel.

16] The sister must concentrate and be humble during her *salāh* as she is talking to Allāh.

Allāh the Exalted said:

﴿ قَدْ أَفْلَحَ ٱلْمُؤْمِنُونَ ۝١ ٱلَّذِينَ هُمْ فِي صَلَاتِهِمْ خَـٰشِعُونَ ۝٢ ﴾

﴿ Successful indeed are the believers who offer their salāh [prayers] with all solemnity [calmness] and full submissiveness [humility]. ﴾ 23:1-2

17] In our times of trials, Allāh, the Majestic, the Mighty, has ordered us to turn to Him for help. The way we do this is through prayer. His Prophet [ﷺ] also taught us that whenever we have decisions to make we should ask Allāh through the *salāh of Istikhārah* for guidance to arrive at a correct decision.

Allāh the Almighty, said:

﴿ يَـٰٓأَيُّهَا ٱلَّذِينَ ءَامَنُوا۟ ٱسْتَعِينُوا۟ بِٱلصَّبْرِ وَٱلصَّلَوٰةِ ۚ إِنَّ ٱللَّهَ مَعَ ٱلصَّـٰبِرِينَ ۝١٥٣ ﴾

[37] *Sahīh Muslim*, [Engl. Trans. vol.1 #1514].

[38] *Rak'ah*: The part of prayer which consists of one standing, one bowing and two prostrations.

[39] *Sahīh Al-Bukhārī*, [Eng. Trans. vol. 2 pg.117 #210].

﴾O you who believe! Seek help through patience and prayer. Truly Allāh is with the patient.﴿ 2:153

The companions of the Prophet [ﷺ] reported in a *hadīth*:

"The Messenger of Allāh [ﷺ] used to teach us the supplication for Istikhārah [seeking what is beneficial from Allāh] as he would teach us a Sūrah."[40]

We go through many trials in this world, the new sisters find amongst these, non Muslim families or countries and sadly Muslim families who do not want her to practice her religion in accordance with the Qur`ān and authentic *Sunnah.* She has to remember none can help but Allāh and she should always turn to Him first for guidance. He is the Protecting Friend and Guardian, *Subhānallāh wa bihamdih*! He created us to worship Him yet He tells us He is our Protecting Friend and Guardian! How compassionate and merciful He is.

18] We [Muslims] have a prayer for every aspect of our lives. This is because Islām is a complete way of life.

Allāh, the Almighty, said:

﴿ ٱلْيَوْمَ أَكْمَلْتُ لَكُمْ دِينَكُمْ وَأَتْمَمْتُ عَلَيْكُمْ نِعْمَتِى وَرَضِيتُ لَكُمُ ٱلْإِسْلَـٰمَ دِينًا ﴾

﴾This day, I have perfected Your religion for you, completed My favor upon you, and have chosen for you Islām as your religion.﴿ 5:3

These prayers are called *Du'ā`s.* There are *du'ā`s* when one awakens, or goes to the bathroom, eats, sleeps, approaches one's spouse, leaves or enters ones house etc. Success, by the will of Allāh, can be attained through constant remembrance of Allāh; it keeps one away from committing evil actions [by the will of Allāh]. Allāh, the Almighty said:

---

[40] Sunan of Abū Dāwud, [Eng. Trans. vol.1 #1533] and declared *sahīh* by *Shaykh* Al-Albānī.

﴿ وَٱذۡكُرُواْ ٱللَّهَ كَثِيرًا لَّعَلَّكُمۡ تُفۡلِحُونَ ﴾

﴾ ...and remember Allāh much that you may be successful. ﴿ 62:10

Remember dear sisters, Allāh said:

﴿ فَخَلَفَ مِنۢ بَعۡدِهِمۡ خَلۡفٌ أَضَاعُواْ ٱلصَّلَوٰةَ وَٱتَّبَعُواْ ٱلشَّهَوَٰتِۖ فَسَوۡفَ يَلۡقَوۡنَ غَيًّا ﴾

﴾ Then there succeeded a generation who have given up As-Salāh [prayers][i.e., made their salāh to be lost, either by not offering them or by not offering them perfectly or by not offering them in their proper times etc.] and have followed lusts. So they will be thrown in Hell. ﴿ 19:59

The Prophet [ﷺ] said:
"Between a man and Shirk and kufr [disbelief] is abandonment of salāh."[41]

"If there was a river at the door of any one of you and he took a bath in it five times a day would you notice any dirt on him? They said, ' not a trace of dirt would be left'. The Prophet [ﷺ] said, 'This is the example of the five prayers with which Allāh blots out [annuls] evil deeds."[42]

THE TIMES FOR THE *SALĀH*.

Allāh, the Most Majestic, informs us in His Book:

﴿ إِنَّ ٱلصَّلَوٰةَ كَانَتۡ عَلَى ٱلۡمُؤۡمِنِينَ كِتَٰبًا مَّوۡقُوتًا ﴾

﴾ Verily, As-Salāh [the prayer] is enjoined on the believers at fixed hours. ﴿ 4:103

And His Prophet [ﷺ] tells us:
"The time for the morning prayer [lasts] as long as the first visible part of the sun does not appear, and the time of the noon prayer is when the sun declines from its zenith and there is not a time for the afternoon prayer and

[41] *Sahīh Muslim*, [Eng. Trans. vol.1 #147].

[42] *Sahīh Al-Bukhārī*, [Eng. Trans. vol.1 #506]. It should be noted this refers to minor sins not major sins.

the time for the afternoon prayer is so long as the sun does not become pale and its first visible part does not set and the time for the evening prayer is that when the sun disappears and the time for the night prayer is to the middle of the night." [43]

If one is in an area where the *adhān* cannot be heard, then they should ask about prayer times at the main *masjid* in their area. Most areas have the prayer timetables for the different times of the year.

THE FIVE *FARD* [OBLIGATORY] *SALĀH*.

a) *Fajr salāh.*
The Morning Prayer before sunrise. It comprises of two *rak'ahs* , before these, there are two very stressed *Sunnah rak'ahs* if one wishes to do so. About these *Sunnah rak'ahs* the Prophet [ﷺ] said:
"They are dearer to me than the whole world."[44]

b) *Dhuhr salāh.*
The noon prayer. This consists of four *fard rak'ahs*. With two or four *rak'ahs* [*Sunnah*] before and two *rak'ahs* after the *fard salāh* if one wishes to do these in addition to the *fard*.

c) *'Asr salāh.*
The after noon [and most stressed] prayer has four *rak'ahs* [*fard*] with two *sunnah rak'ahs* before the *fard*. The intentional missing of this [*fard*] *salāh* is equated to the loss of ones entire family and wealth[45] or to all his good deeds being annulled.[46]

d) *Maghrib salāh.*
The evening prayer. It comprises of three *fard rak'ahs* with two *sunnah rak'ahs* after the *fard*.

e) *'Ishā` salāh.*

---

[43] *Sahīh Muslim*, [Eng. Trans. vol.1 #1276].
[44] *Sahīh Muslim*, [Eng. Trans. vol. 1 #1574].
[45] *Sahīh Al-Bukhārī*, [Eng. Trans. vol. 1 #527].
[46] *Sahīh Al-Bukhārī*, [Eng. Trans. vol.1 #528].

The night prayer, it is four *rak'ahs* [*fard*] with two *sunnah rak'ahs* after the *fard*. It is worth noting that these two *sunnah* ***rak'ahs*** after *'Ishā`* *salāh*, are different from late night or *tahajjud* prayer. These [i.e., *tahajjud*] are also *sunnah* prayers and they are offered anytime after *'Ishā`* *salāh* up until the time for *Fajr salāh*. One may go to sleep for part of the night, then arise and offer them and sleep again till it is time for *Fajr salāh*, or offer them before they sleep if they do not want to miss them but fear they may not arise. By arising one can catch the last third of the night, the time when Allāh descends in a manner befitting His Majesty to the lowest heaven to accept repentance from His slaves [It is more rewarding to sleep then arise]. This *sunnah salāh* may be offered in sets of two until one is satisfied or as much as they are capable of [i.e., in case they are weak, sick etc.].

There are a lot of good books on *salāh* available in English like *Shaykh* Al-Albānī's, "*The Prophet's Prayer described from the beginning to the end as though you see it*." I found it to be a wonderful description, may Allāh, the Most Compassionate, shower His abundant mercy on him and forgive him. Therefore, I will leave out the description of the *salāh* itself. I would however like to point out again that one needs to follow the Qur`ān and the authentic *sunnah* in their *salāh* and in all other matters of their religion. They should beware of committing *bida'* [innovations] and blind following of *madhhabs* [schools of thought] and rather stick to what the Prophet [ﷺ] left us. As such, I recommend the aforementioned book.

Other than these *salāh*, one should try to engage in other *sunnah salāh* some of which are; *Duhā* [forenoon prayer], *Witr* [odd number of *rak'ahs* after all the night prayer one is going to offer, one *rak'ah* suffices], *Tahajjud* [late night prayer], *Tarāwīh* [late night prayer during the month of *Ramadān*] a most stressed *sunnah* and if one catches [i.e., is praying on] *Laylah Al-Qadr* [the blessed night] in the last ten days of *Ramadān* [said to be the 23rd, 25th, 27th or 29th] there is a tremendous blessing for them, also the funeral and Eclipse prayers.

3] THE *ZAKĀH* [OBLIGATORY CHARITY].

Allāh the Exalted, the Mighty said:

﴿ وَأَقِيمُوا۟ ٱلصَّلَوٰةَ وَءَاتُوا۟ ٱلزَّكَوٰةَ وَمَا تُقَدِّمُوا۟ لِأَنفُسِكُم مِّنْ خَيْرٍ تَجِدُوهُ عِندَ ٱللَّهِ إِنَّ ٱللَّهَ بِمَا تَعْمَلُونَ بَصِيرٌ ﴾

﴿ And perform As-Salāh and give Zakāh, and whatever of good [[deeds] that Allāh loves] you shall send forth for yourselves before you, you shall find it with Allāh, Allāh is All-Seer of what you do.﴾ 2:110

Nobody is doing any one else a favor by paying the *Zakāh* on his wealth. This is simply an obligatory duty and the world's wealth [in reality] belongs to Allāh. Allāh, the Exalted said:

﴿ ءَامِنُوا۟ بِٱللَّهِ وَرَسُولِهِۦ وَأَنفِقُوا۟ مِمَّا جَعَلَكُم مُّسْتَخْلَفِينَ فِيهِ فَٱلَّذِينَ ءَامَنُوا۟ مِنكُمْ وَأَنفَقُوا۟ لَهُمْ أَجْرٌ كَبِيرٌ ﴾

﴿ Believe in Allāh and His Messengers and spend of that over which He has made you trustees; and those of you who believe and spend [in charity] - for them is a great reward.﴾ 57:7

﴿ وَٱلَّذِينَ يَكْنِزُونَ ٱلذَّهَبَ وَٱلْفِضَّةَ وَلَا يُنفِقُونَهَا فِى سَبِيلِ ٱللَّهِ فَبَشِّرْهُم بِعَذَابٍ أَلِيمٍ ﴾

﴿ And those who hoard gold and silver and do not spend it in the way of Allāh, announce to them a painful torment.﴾ 9:34

Zakāh is due on property that:

1) One has had in possession for a year.
2) And, it has reached the minimum amount for that type of property, of which there are four types:
   a) Gold, silver, money: 2.5 percent in the annual savings or at least 85 grams in gold or the equivalent in silver or money.
   b) Livestock that grazes freely without being fed grain or commercially.

c) Agricultural products, grain and fruit which becomes due when the crop is ripe [this is so the amount of actual yield is calculated in case of loss etc.].

d) Business inventory- goods owned for the purpose of sale.

Other facts she should know about *Zakāh*.

1) She should consult her husband before giving from his property. Should there be a situation whereby she is unable to do this then the following *hadīth* pertains to her:

"It is not permissible for a woman to present a gift from her husbands property except with the permission of her husband."[47]

"When a woman gives in charity from her husbands meals without wasting the property of her husband, she will get reward for it and her husband to will get a reward for what he earned and likewise the storekeeper will have the reward likewise."[48]

2) The merit of charity.

"Everyday two angels come down from Heaven one says, 'O Allāh! Compensate every person who spends in your cause,' and the other [angel] says,' O Allāh! Destroy every miser'."[49]

"Do not shut your money bag; otherwise Allāh will withhold His blessings from you spend [in Allāh's cause] as much as you can afford."[50]

"A mans afflictions [wrong deeds] concerning his wife, children and neighbors are expiated by [his] prayers, charity and enjoining good."[51]

---

[47] Sunan of Abū Dāwud, [Eng. Trans. Vol.2. #3540]. Declared *hasan sahīh* by *Shaykh* Al-Albānī.

[48] *Sahīh Al-Bukhārī*, [Eng. Trans. vol. 2 #518].

[49] *Sahīh Al-Bukhārī*, [Eng. Trans. vol.2 #522].

[50] *Sahīh Al-Bukhārī*, [Eng. Trans. vol.2 #515].

"Seven people will be shaded by Allāh under His shade on the day when there will be no shade except His [the Day of Judgment]. They are:

1) a just ruler;
2) a young man who has been brought up in the worship of Allāh [[alone] sincerely from his childhood];
3) a man whose heart is attached to the mosque[who offers the five compulsory congregational prayers at the mosque];
4) two persons who love each other only for Allāh's sake, and they meet and part in Allāh's cause only;
5) a man who refuses the call of a charming woman of noble birth for illegal sexual intercourse with her and says:' I am afraid of Allāh';
6) a person who practices charity so secretly that his left hand does not know what his right hand has given[i.e., nobody knows how much he has given in charity];
7) a person who remembers Allāh in seclusion and his eyes get flooded with tears."[52]

It should be noted that in this ***hadīth***, even though the wording refers to males, it also encompasses the women who are characterized with those same qualities.

3) We should not belittle those who can only afford to give in small amounts for charity as Allāh has said:

﴿ وَٱلَّذِينَ لَا يَجِدُونَ إِلَّا جُهْدَهُمْ فَيَسْخَرُونَ مِنْهُمْ سَخِرَ ٱللَّهُ مِنْهُمْ وَلَهُمْ عَذَابٌ
أَلِيمٌ ﴿٧٩﴾ ﴾

---

[51] *Sahīh Al-Bukhārī*, [Eng. Trans.vol.2 #516].

[52] *Sahīh Al-Bukhārī*, [Eng. Trans. vol 2 #504].

﴾ And those who could not find to give charity [in Allāh's cause] except what is available to them so they mock at them [believers], Allāh will throw back their mockery on them, and they shall have a painful torment. ﴿9:79

It is incumbent on every slave of Allāh, man and woman, to give *Zakāh*. Therefore at the end of each year this should be calculated from her property [jewelry, bank accounts etc.]. I must point out that the lady has to pay *Zakāh* on **her** property, from her property and not from her husbands. The exception being *zakāh Al-Fitr* for example where the head of the family [usually] gives food out to the needy on behalf of his family. But as long as the sister owns property falling into the categories stated before, she is responsible to Allāh for the *Zakāh* owed on it. However if any other family member willingly pays it for her the scholars are of the opinion that it is permitted. A sister should not limit herself to giving only in obligatory *Zakāh* but should regularly give charity. I might remind her that even without riches she can do this, as a smile is charity, a kind word is charity, fulfilling the needs of ones spouse or children can be charity, especially when she makes her intention for the sake of Allāh. Remember that it is an expiation for sins! Here is a *hadīth* for us to ponder over which is narrated by 'Ā`ishah [رضي الله عنها], the wife of the Prophet [ﷺ]:

"A poor woman came to me with her two daughters [for charity], I gave her three dates. She gave one to each girl and wanted one for herself. The two girls asked her for this also. So she divided it into two parts and gave one to each of the girls. I was much impressed by her action and mentioned all this to the Prophet [ﷺ]. He said: *'Allāh has ordained Paradise for her in consequence of this action: or Allāh freed her from Hell on account of this gesture'.*"[53]

[53] Sahīh Al-Bukhārī, [Eng. Trans.Vol.2 #499]. Wording from *Riyād As-Sālihīn* [pg. 176].

4] *HAJJ* [the pilgrimage to Makkah].

Allāh, the Majestic, said:

﴿ وَلِلَّهِ عَلَى ٱلنَّاسِ حِجُّ ٱلْبَيْتِ مَنِ ٱسْتَطَاعَ إِلَيْهِ سَبِيلًا ﴾

﴾ And Hajj [pilgrimage to Makkah] to the House [Ka'bah] it is a duty that mankind owes to Allāh, those who can afford the expenses [for ones conveyance, provision and residence.﴿ 3:97

This dear sister, means that if you can afford to travel on vacations especially to other countries, you can therefore afford *Hajj* before your vacation. Any one who can afford transportation expenses, food and residence expenses and has no reason like ill health stopping them, they are incurring a sin and Allāh knows best. It is to be done once in your lifetime however, you still get reward should you manage to do it more times than that.

Other facts she should know.

1] The merits of *Hajj* and *'Umrah* [minor pilgrimage].

The Prophet [ﷺ] said:

"Whoever performs Hajj to this house [Ka'bah] and does not approach his wife for sexual relations nor commits sins [while performing Hajj] he will come out as sinless as a newly born child [just delivered] by his mother."[54]

"[The performance of] 'Umrah is a expiation for the sins committed [between it and the previous one]. And the reward of Hajj Mabrūr [the one accepted by Allāh] is nothing except Paradise."[55]

"'Umrah during the month of Ramadān would suffice for Hajj or Hajj with me."[56]

[54] *Sahīh Al-Bukhārī*, [Eng. Trans. vol.3 #45].

[55] *Sahīh Al-Bukhārī*, [Eng. Trans. vol.3 #1].

[56] *Sahīh Muslim*, [Eng. Trans. vol. 2 #2885].

This statement of the Prophet [ﷺ] does not remove the once in a lifetime obligation from the sister for *Hajj*, rather it refers to the great reward of an *'Umrah* in *Ramadān*.

2] She is exempted from *Hajj* if she has no *mahram* [guardian whom she cannot marry or her husband].

Ibn 'Abbās [ﷺ] said:

"I heard Allāh's Messenger [ﷺ] delivering a sermon and making this observation: 'No person should be alone with a woman except when there is a mahram with her, and the woman should not undertake journey except with a mahram.' A person stood up and said: Allāh's Messenger, my wife has set out for pilgrimage, whereas I am enlisted to fight in such-and-such a battle, whereupon he said: You go and perform Hajj with your wife."[57]

3] It is the Jihad of a woman.

'Ā'ishah [ﷺ] asked Allāh's Messenger [ﷺ]:

"Is Jihad incumbent on women? He replied, **'Yes Jihad which does not include fighting is incumbent on them, it is the *Hajj* and *'Umrah*.'** "[58]

4] Her dress for pilgrimage.

Women assume Ihram in their normal attire. They can wear socks, however they may not wear gloves nor can they wear their face veils. The Prophet [ﷺ] said:

"A woman [pilgrim] does not cover her face with a veil nor does she wear gloves."[59]

However the rule about a lady who happens to be in the presence of strange men still applies, as it is impossible to make a pilgrimage without

---

[57] *Sahīh Muslim*, [Eng. Trans. vol. 2 #3110].

[58] Wording from *Bulūgh Al-Marām*. Origin found in *Sahīh Al-Bukhārī* [Eng. Trans. vol.4 #128.]

[59] *Sahīh Al-Bukhārī*, [Engl. Trans. vol. 3 #64].

vast numbers of strange men in extreme close proximity to every lady, in this day and time. Most scholars of the *Salaf*, are of the consensus that it is *wājib* [obligatory] for women to cover their faces when strange men are present [especially in this day and time as *fitnah* is rampant], with obvious strong evidence like verse 24:31 in the Book of Allāh. And 'Ā`ishah [ﷺ] said:

"May Allāh bestow His Mercy on the early emigrant women. When Allāh revealed, ***'They should draw their veils over their necks and bosoms, '*** they tore their aprons and covered their faces with it."[60]

No face veils, made for that purpose, can be used, she may however use a portion of the garment on her head pulled over her face or throw a large cloth covering her entire head over her, and Allāh knows best.

4) The shortening of the hair.

During *Hajj* or *'Umrah*, men shave their heads while women trim of about an inch [from their entire head] of hair. A woman wearing plaits should remove an inch from every plait.[61]

[60] ***Sahīh** Al-Bukhārī*, [Eng. Trans.Vol.6. #220].

[61] Hajj, Umrah and Ziyara, by Dr. V. AbdurRahim, Islāmic Univ. Medinah Munawara, pg. 32.

5] SAWM [FASTING].

Allāh, the Almighty, said:

﴿ يَـٰٓأَيُّهَا ٱلَّذِينَ ءَامَنُوا۟ كُتِبَ عَلَيْكُمُ ٱلصِّيَامُ كَمَا كُتِبَ عَلَى ٱلَّذِينَ مِن قَبْلِكُمْ لَعَلَّكُمْ تَتَّقُونَ ﴿١٨٣﴾ ﴾

﴾ O you who believe! Observing As-Sawm [fasting] is prescribed for you as it was prescribed to those before you, that you may become Al-Muttaqūn [pious].﴿ 2:183

The Prophet [ﷺ] said in a *hadīth Qudsi*[62]:

"Every good deed of the son of Adam is multiplied in reward ten to seven hundred times except for fasting, for it is for Me and I will grant the reward for it, he leaves his passion and his food for my sake. The fasting person has two moments of happiness; one moment when he ends his fasting for the day [iftār] and the other when he meets his Lord. And the smell which issues from the mouth of the fasting person is more pleasant to Allāh than the smell of musk [fragrance]."[63]

This pillar of Islām involves the abstinence of food, drink and sexual intercourse from dawn to dusk.

---

[62] These are *hadīths* whereby the narrator says that the Prophet [ﷺ] said that,' Allāh said '. It's chain of narration can be traced all the way back to Allāh. It should be noted that because it is a *hadīth Qudsī* that does not mean it is *sahīh* rather it is to be graded and checked like a regular *hadīth* as it could have been fabricated. The difference between this kind of *hadīth* and the Qur`ān is that a] the Qur`ān is the Word of Allāh in actual words and in meaning, while the *hadīth Qudsī* it is the speech of Allāh only in meaning **b]** also the Qur`ān is narrated to us from large numbers of people, whereas the case is not necessarily the same for a *hadīth* .c] also Allāh promised to protect the Qur`ān whereas He did not promise to protect the *hadīth Qudsī* thus some have fabricated them on their way to us **d]** One who is impure [ritually] may not touch the Qur`ān whereas such a person may touch books of *hadīth* e] and reciting the Qur`ān is a form of Worship while reading *hadīth Qudsī* is not necessarily so.

[63] *Sahīh Muslim*, [Eng. Trans. Vol. 2 #2568].

Other facts she should know about fasting.

1) Merits of the fast.

"When the month of Ramadān arrives the gates of heaven are opened and the gates of Hell are closed and the devils are chained."[64]

"Sawm [fasting] is a shield [or screen or shelter] from the Hell-Fire."[65]

"Whoever observed fasting in the month of Ramadān out of sincere faith and hoping for a reward from Allāh, then all his previous sins will be forgiven."[66]

"Every servant of Allāh who observes fast for a day in the way of Allāh, Allāh would remove, because of this day, his face further from the Fire [of Hell] to the extent of seventy years' distance."[67]

2) She should guard her *Salāh*.

The sister should guard her *salāh* by praying on time, and not sleep till time to prepare *iftār* [the meal taken at the time to break fast] or any like behavior for example watch television to kill time so as not to feel the fast. Rather she should be even more adamant about all her forms of worship and increase them, especially her *salāh* and more so in the last ten nights.

"'Ā`ishah [ﷺ] reported that when the last ten nights began Allāh's Messenger [ﷺ] kept awake at night [for prayer and devotion], wakened his family and prepared himself to observe prayer [with more vigor]."[68]

---

[64] *Sahīh Al-Bukhārī*, [Eng. Trans. vol. 3 #123].

[65] *Sahīh Al-Bukhārī*, [Eng. Trans. vol.3. #118].

[66] *Sahīh Al-Bukhārī*, [Eng. Trans. vol. 3 #125].

[67] *Sahīh Muslim*, [Eng. Trans. vol. 2 #2570].

[68] *Sahīh Muslim* [Eng. Trans. vol. 2 #2643].

3) She should refrain from sins.

The Prophet [ﷺ] said:

"If a person does not refrain from lying and evil actions, Allāh is not in need of his leaving his food and drink [i.e., Allāh will not accept his fasting]."[69]

I must point out that this includes backbiting and foul language, which should be avoided all year long at any rate.

4) She should take a meal [*suhūr*] before starting the fast.

The Prophet [ﷺ] said:

"Take a meal a little before dawn, for there is a blessing in taking a meal at that time."[70]

I would like to point out to the sister the portion of the *hadīth*, " a little before dawn"; this is approximately 10-20 minutes before the Adhān for *Fajr salāh*, not hours before. She should neither skip it intentionally nor should she over eat, but should eat in moderation.

5) She should break fast immediately and not wait.

The Prophet [ﷺ] said:

"The people will continue to prosper as long as they hasten the breaking of fast."[71]

Breaking the fast is done at the time of the Adhān for *Maghrib salāh*.

6) She may break fast when on a journey.

The Prophet [ﷺ] said:

" Fast if you like, break it if you like."[72]

The Prophet [ﷺ] also said:

"It is not righteousness that you fast on a journey."[73]

---

[69] *Sahīh Al-Bukhārī*, [Eng. Trans. vol. 3 #127].

[70] *Sahīh Muslim*, [Eng. Trans. vol. 2 #2412].

[71] *Sahīh Muslim* [Eng. Trans. vol. 2 #2417].

[72] *Sahīh Muslim*,[Eng. Trans. vol. 2 #2487].

[73] *Sahīh Al-Bukhārī*,[Eng. Trans. vol. 3 #167].

Narrated Anas Ibn Mālik [ﷺ]: *"We used to travel with the Prophet [ﷺ] and neither did the fasting persons criticize those who were not fasting, nor did those who were not fasting criticize the fasting ones."*[74]

However the fast is to be made up before the next *Ramadān* [the following year] as is the case with sick or weak individuals who would do themselves more harm than good as Allāh has forbidden us to intentionally harm ourselves especially if chances of death are possible.

7) When on her menses, she is forbidden to fast.
[See chapter on menses.]

8) If she is in the state of junub or ends her menses and cannot take a bath before dawn she must nevertheless begin the fast and then bathe later.

'Ā`ishah [ﷺ] the wife of the Prophet [ﷺ] said:

"He [the Prophet, ﷺ] [woke up in the] morning in a state of junub which was not due to a wet dream and then observed fast."[75]

If a sister ends her menses before dawn or is in the state of junub the fast for that day is still upon her and she should start her fast and then take a bath after the Adhān for *Fajr salāh* and then pray. [For more details see chapter on menses]

9) One may kiss or embrace one's spouse provided it is not because of and will not produce a sexual desire that could break the fast through sexual intercourse.

'Ā`ishah [ﷺ] the wife of the Prophet [ﷺ] said:

"Allāh's Messenger [ﷺ] used to kiss [his wives] while fasting and embraced [them] while fasting; but he had the greatest control over his desire compared to you."[76]

---

[74] *Sahīh Al-Bukhārī*, [Eng. Trans. vol. 3 #168].

[75] *Sahīh Muslim*, [Eng. Trans. vol. 2 #2451].

10] Like food and drink, sexual intercourse is completely forbidden in the daytime.

A person came to the Prophet [ﷺ] and said:

"Messenger of Allāh, I am undone. He said, 'What has brought your ruin?' He said; I have had intercourse with my wife during the month of Ramadān. Upon this he [the Holy Prophet ﷺ] said, 'Can you find a slave to set him free?' He said, 'no.' He said, 'Can you observe fast for two consecutive months?' He said,' no.' He [the Prophet ﷺ] said: 'Can you provide food to sixty poor people?' He said, ' no.' then he sat down and [in the meanwhile] there was brought to the Messenger of Allāh [ﷺ] a basket which contained dates. He [the Prophet ﷺ] said: 'Give these [dates] in charity.' He [the man] said: 'Am I to give one who is poorer than I? There is no family poorer than mine between the two lava plains of Medina.' The Prophet [ﷺ] laughed so that his molar teeth became visible and said: 'Go give it to your family to eat'."[77]

It is imperative that the sister be aware of the fact that this does not mean it is permissible as long as the *fidyah* is paid. Rather, should it happen in dire circumstances, then one compensates. Also, the first option is to be followed if impossible then the second alternative is to be pursued etc. before the final option is used, and Allāh is the All- Seer, All-Knower of all that we do.

11] Should the sister be insulted or if someone tries to pick a fight with her, she should avoid this and say to the person:

As instructed by the Prophet [ﷺ]:

" I am fasting."[78]

May Allāh protect us from such a plight.

---

[76] *Sahīh Muslim*, [Eng. Trans. vol. 2 #2439].

[77] *Sahīh Muslim*, [Eng. Trans. vol. 2 #2457].

[78] *Sahīh Al-Bukhārī*, [Eng. Trans. vol. 3 # 128].

12] When a member of her family dies and she is an heir of the deceased, she should make up any fasts the person owed to Allāh.

This includes fasts for *Ramadān* or oaths taken before death.

"If anyone dies in a state [that he had to complete] some fasts his heir must fast on his behalf."[79]

13] The fast of a pregnant or nursing woman.

If she can fast she should do so. If she finds it impossible or difficult she may break it and make it up later or feed a poor person for each day. There are two opinions on the subject and she can read more on this in the chapter on Making up missed Fasts.

"Allāh has remitted half the prayer to the traveler, and fasting to the traveler, the woman who is suckling an infant and the woman who is pregnant. [To delay the observance of fast]."[80]

14] On intentional and unintentional vomiting.

"If one has a sudden attack of vomiting while one is fasting, no atonement is required of him, but if he vomits intentionally he must make atonement."[81]

15] *I'tikāf* in *Ramadān*.

I'tikāf is the seclusion in the *masjid* to devote that time to the worship of Allāh, one does not leave the *masjid* except in cases of necessity such as to relive oneself. It is usually done in the last ten days of *Ramadān*.

---

[79] *Sahīh Muslim*, [Eng. Trans. vol. 2 #2553].

[80] Sunan of Abū Dāwud, [Eng. Trans. vol. 2 #2402] and declared *hasan sahīh* by Sheik Al-Albānī.

[81] Sunan of Abū Dāwud, [Eng. Trans. Vol.2 #2374] Declared *sahīh* by *Shaykh* Al-Albānī. Atonement here is compensatory payment for missed acts of worship in this case of fasting. These atonements are not made up but instead proofs from authentic *hadīths* or the noble Qur`ān, are used to find out what and how this is done e.g. feeding a poor person for a day of missed fasting for a pregnant woman.

The sister should not be on her menses and should have the permission of her husband or guardian, also there should be no chance for problems, for example the *masjid* should have a secluded section for women as obvious problems from mixing of sexes may arise. At the time of the Prophet [ﷺ], tents were set up in the *masjid*, in this day and time no such thing is done as the floors back then in the *masjid* were the actual ground. If she is a *mustahādah* [woman who perpetually bleeds even off her menses] she may perform *I'tikāf* so long as there is no chance of there being cleaning problems. Also no sexual relations are to be indulged in by one doing *I'tikāf* until they come out of this state. However a wife may visit her husband in the mosque. Allāh said:

﴿ وَلَا تُبَٰشِرُوهُنَّ وَأَنتُمْ عَٰكِفُونَ فِى ٱلْمَسَٰجِدِ ۗ تِلْكَ حُدُودُ ٱللَّهِ فَلَا تَقْرَبُوهَا ﴾

﴾ While you are in I'tikāf in the mosques, do not have sexual relations with your wives; these are the limits set by Allāh; so, do not approach them.﴿ 2:187

"The Prophet [ﷺ] used to practice *I'tikāf* in the last ten days of *Ramadān* till he died and then his wives used to practice *I'tikāf* after him."[82]

"One of the wives[83] of the Prophet [ﷺ] practiced *I'tikāf* with him while she had bleeding in between periods and she would see red [blood] or yellowish traces and some times we would put a tray beneath her when she offered prayer."[84]

"Safiyyah [رضي الله عنها] went to [visit] the Prophet [ﷺ] while he was in *I'tikāf*. When she returned, the Prophet [ﷺ] accompanied her walking."[85]

---

[82] *Sahīh Al-Bukhārī*, [Eng. Trans. vol. 3 #243].

[83] It was Umm Salamah.

[84] *Sahīh Al-Bukhārī*, [Eng. Trans. vol. 3 #253].

[85] *Sahīh Al-Bukhārī*, [Eng. Trans. vol. 3 #254].

CHAPTER 2

THE PILLARS OF ĪMĀN [FAITH]

Allāh, the Exalted, said:

﴿ وَمَن يَكْفُرْ بِالْإِيمَانِ فَقَدْ حَبِطَ عَمَلُهُ وَهُوَ فِي الْآخِرَةِ مِنَ الْخَاسِرِينَ ﴾

﴾ And whosoever disbelieves in īmān [i.e., in the Oneness of Allāh and in all the other Articles of Faith i.e., His Angels, His Holy Books, His Messengers, the Day of Resurrection and Al-Qadar [Divine Preordainment]], then fruitless is his work; and in the Hereafter he will be among the losers.﴿ 5:5

In the *hadīth* of Jibrā`īl [ﷺ], the Prophet [ﷺ] was asked the meaning of *īmān*. He answered:

"That you affirm your faith in Allāh, His angels, His Books, His meeting, His Messengers and that you believe in Resurrection and that you believe in Qadar [Divine Decree] in all its entirety [the good and the bad of it]."[86]

In another wording of this *hadīth*, it reads: '...the Last Day' [i.e., the Day of Resurrection].

---

[86] *Sahīh Muslim*, [Eng. Trans. vol. 1 #1].

1]- BELIEF IN ALLĀH.

The first pillar of *Īmān* is the belief in Allāh, the Creator of everything, in the manner in which He has described Himself either in the Qur`ān or through His Prophet Mu<u>h</u>ammad [ﷺ]. Allāh, the Exalted, said:

﴿قُلْ هُوَ ٱللَّهُ أَحَدٌ ۝١ ٱللَّهُ ٱلصَّمَدُ ۝٢ لَمْ يَلِدْ وَلَمْ يُولَدْ ۝٣ وَلَمْ يَكُن لَّهُۥ
كُفُوًا أَحَدٌۢ ۝٤﴾

﴾ Say [O Mu<u>h</u>ammad ﷺ] He is Allāh, [The] One. Allāh A<u>s</u>-<u>S</u>amad [The Self -Sufficient Master, whom all creatures need, He neither eats nor drinks]. He begets not nor is He begotten. And there is non co-equal or comparable unto Him.﴿ 112:1-4

Allāh Akbar! And:

﴿ٱللَّهُ لَآ إِلَـٰهَ إِلَّا هُوَ ٱلْحَىُّ ٱلْقَيُّومُ ۚ لَا تَأْخُذُهُۥ سِنَةٌ وَلَا نَوْمٌ ۚ لَّهُۥ مَا فِى ٱلسَّمَـٰوَٰتِ وَمَا
فِى ٱلْأَرْضِ ۗ مَن ذَا ٱلَّذِى يَشْفَعُ عِندَهُۥٓ إِلَّا بِإِذْنِهِۦ ۚ يَعْلَمُ مَا بَيْنَ أَيْدِيهِمْ وَمَا خَلْفَهُمْ ۖ
وَلَا يُحِيطُونَ بِشَىْءٍ مِّنْ عِلْمِهِۦٓ إِلَّا بِمَا شَآءَ ۚ وَسِعَ كُرْسِيُّهُ ٱلسَّمَـٰوَٰتِ وَٱلْأَرْضَ ۖ وَلَا
يَـُٔودُهُۥ حِفْظُهُمَا ۚ وَهُوَ ٱلْعَلِىُّ ٱلْعَظِيمُ ۝٢٥٥﴾

﴾ Allāh! Lā ilāha illa Huwa [none has the right to be worshipped but He] the Ever living, the One who sustains and protects all that exists. Neither slumber, nor sleep overtakes Him. To Him belongs whatever is in the heavens on earth. Who is he that can intercede with Him except with His permission? He knows what happens to them [His creatures] in this world, and what will happen to them in the Hereafter. And they will never compass anything of His Knowledge except that which he wills. His Kursī extends over the heavens and the earth, and He feels no fatigue in guarding and preserving them. And He is the Most High, Most Great.﴿ 2:255

Sub<u>h</u>ānallāh! This āyah is called Āyah Al-Kursī [footstool]. It is the greatest āyah in the Qur`ān[87], the Kursī is the footstool of Allāh, the Exalted, the Mighty. His Prophet [ﷺ] informs us that:

---

[87] *<u>S</u>a<u>h</u>ī<u>h</u> Muslim*, [Eng. Trans. vol. 2 #1768].

"The Kursī compared to the 'Arsh [Throne of Allāh] is nothing but like ring thrown out upon open space of the desert. If the Kursī extends over the entire universe, then how much greater is the 'Arsh. Indeed Allāh the Creator of both the Kursī and the 'Arsh is the Most Great."[88]

2]- BELIEF IN HIS ANGELS.

The second pillar of *Īmān* is the belief in Allāh's angels.

﴿ وَمَا يَعْلَمُ جُنُودَ رَبِّكَ إِلَّا هُوَ وَمَا هِيَ إِلَّا ذِكْرَىٰ لِلْبَشَرِ ﴾

﴾ And none can know the forces of your Lord but He. And this is nothing other than a warning [reminder] to mankind.﴿ 74: 31.

Some things she should know about them.

- **What are they?**

a) They are messengers of Allāh. Allāh the Almighty said:

﴿ ٱلْحَمْدُ لِلَّهِ فَاطِرِ ٱلسَّمَٰوَٰتِ وَٱلْأَرْضِ جَاعِلِ ٱلْمَلَٰٓئِكَةِ رُسُلًا أُو۟لِىٓ أَجْنِحَةٍ مَّثْنَىٰ وَثُلَٰثَ وَرُبَٰعَ ﴾

﴾ All the praise and thanks be to Allāh, the [only] Originator [or the [only] Creator] of the heavens and the earth, Who made the angels messengers with wings-two, or three or four...﴿ 35:1.

We shall examine the *hadīth* concerning the following verse,

﴿ فَكَانَ قَابَ قَوْسَيْنِ أَوْ أَدْنَىٰ ۝ فَأَوْحَىٰٓ إِلَىٰ عَبْدِهِۦ مَآ أَوْحَىٰ ۝ ﴾

﴾ And was at a distance of two bows length or [even] nearer. So [Allāh] revealed to His slave [Muhammad ﷺ through Jibrīl] whatever He revealed.﴿ 53:9-10

[88] Fatwā of Ibn Taymiyyah, [vol.5 pg. 54, 55].

Within it, we also find more of a description for the angel Jibrā`īl [the greatest angel of them all]. Narrated Abū Is<u>h</u>āq Ash-Shaybānī: "I asked Zirr Ibn <u>H</u>ubaysh regarding the Statement of Allāh:

﴿ فَكَانَ قَابَ قَوْسَيْنِ أَوْ أَدْنَىٰ ۝ فَأَوْحَىٰٓ إِلَىٰ عَبْدِهِۦ مَآ أَوْحَىٰ ۝ ﴾

﴾ And was at a distance of two bows length or [even] nearer. So [Allāh] revealed to His slave [Mu<u>h</u>ammad ﷺ through Jibrīl] whatever He revealed. ﴿ 53:9-10

On that, Zir said, "Ibn Mas'ūd informed us that the Prophet [ﷺ] had seen [the Angel] Jibrā`īl having 600 wings."[89]

b) They are a special creation of Allāh created from light and they were created before humans to worship Allāh. Allāh the Almighty said:

﴿ وَإِذْ قَالَ رَبُّكَ لِلْمَلَٰٓئِكَةِ إِنِّى خَٰلِقٌۢ بَشَرًا مِّن صَلْصَٰلٍ مِّنْ حَمَإٍ مَّسْنُونٍ ۝ ﴾

﴾ And [remember] when your Lord said to the angels: ' I am going to create a man [Adam] from dried [sounding] clay of altered mud'. ﴿ 15:28

"Angels were created from light, Jinn were created from a smokeless fire, and Adam was created as was described to you [i.e., from clay]."[90]

c) When so ordered they can appear in the shape of man as we see in the following <u>*hadīth*</u>.

"It was Jibrā`īl [عليه السلام] who used to come to the Prophet [ﷺ] in the figure of a man, but on that occasion, he came in his actual and real figure and [he was so huge] that he covered the whole horizon."[91]

- **What they are not.**

The Quraysh and even present day Christians, among others call angels children of Allāh, they call them daughters of Allāh. About this Allāh said:

---

[89] <u>*Sahīh*</u> *Al-Bukhārī*, [Eng. Trans. vol.4 #455].

[90] <u>*Sahīh*</u> *Muslim*, [Eng. Trans. vol.4 #7134].

[91] <u>*Sahīh*</u> *Al-Bukhārī*, [Eng. Trans. vol. 4 #458].

﴿ وَجَعَلُواْ لِلَّهِ شُرَكَآءَ ٱلْجِنَّ وَخَلَقَهُمْ ۖ وَخَرَقُواْ لَهُۥ بَنِينَ وَبَنَٰتٍۭ بِغَيْرِ عِلْمٍ ۚ سُبْحَٰنَهُۥ وَتَعَٰلَىٰ عَمَّا يَصِفُونَ ﴾

﴿ Yet, they join the Jinn as partners in worship with Allāh, though He has created them [the Jinn]; and they attribute falsely without knowledge sons and daughters to Him. Be He Glorified and Exalted above all that [evil] they attribute to Him.﴾ 6:100

﴿ وَجَعَلُواْ ٱلْمَلَٰٓئِكَةَ ٱلَّذِينَ هُمْ عِبَٰدُ ٱلرَّحْمَٰنِ إِنَٰثًا ۚ أَشَهِدُواْ خَلْقَهُمْ ۚ سَتُكْتَبُ شَهَٰدَتُهُمْ وَيُسْـَٔلُونَ ﴾

﴿ And they make the angels who themselves are the slaves of the Most Gracious [Allāh] females. Did they witness their creation? Their testimony will be recorded and they will be questioned!﴾ 43:19.

In a *hadīth* we find more proof of their misconceptions:

"The infidels of Quraysh said, ' The angels are Allāh's daughters whose mothers are the mistresses among the Jinn'."[92]

"Allāh said, ' The son of Adam tells lies against Me although he has no right to do so, and he abuses Me although he has no right to do so. As for his telling lies against Me, he claims that I cannot re-create him as I created him before; as for his abusing Me: it is his statement that I have a son [or offspring] No! Glorified be Me I am far from taking a wife or son [or offspring]'."[93]

Far above is Allāh, the Exalted, the Mighty, from such evil that they associate with Him. We seek refuge with Him from the cursed Satan, who causes man to entertain such evil notions.

---

[92] *Sahīh Al-Bukhārī*, [Eng. Trans. vol.4 Chapter 11].

[93] *Sahīh Al-Bukhārī*, [Eng. Trans. vol. 6. #9].

iii] Some of their names and tasks that we know of.

Some of the angels' names we know of, like Jibrā`īl, Mīkā'īl, Isrāfīl and Mālik. Allāh said:

﴿ وَمَا يَنظُرُ هَـٰٓؤُلَآءِ إِلَّا صَيۡحَةً وَٰحِدَةً مَّا لَهَا مِن فَوَاقٍ ﴿١٥﴾ ﴾

﴿ And these only wait for a single sayhah [shout [i.e., the blowing of the Trumpet by angel Isrāfīl]]. There will be no pause or ending thereto [till everything will perish except Allāh [the only God full of Majesty, Bounty and Honor]].﴾ 38:15

The Prophet [ﷺ] said:

"Last night I saw [in a dream] two men coming to me. One of them said, ' The person who kindles the Fire is Mālik, the gatekeeper of the [Hell] Fire and I am Jibrā`īl, and this is Michael.'[94]

Jibrā`īl is the greatest of Allāh's angels, and he brings down revelation to the messengers of Allāh, Allāh said of him:

﴿ عَلَّمَهُۥ شَدِيدُ ٱلۡقُوَىٰ ﴿٥﴾ ﴾

﴿ He [the Prophet ﷺ] has been taught this [Qur`ān] by one mighty in power [Jibrā`īl].﴾ 53:5

There are two guardian angels assigned to every servant of Allāh.

﴿ إِذۡ يَتَلَقَّى ٱلۡمُتَلَقِّيَانِ عَنِ ٱلۡيَمِينِ وَعَنِ ٱلشِّمَالِ قَعِيدٌ ﴿١٧﴾ مَّا يَلۡفِظُ مِن قَوۡلٍ إِلَّا لَدَيۡهِ رَقِيبٌ عَتِيدٌ ﴿١٨﴾ ﴾

﴿ [Remember] that the two receivers [recording angels] receive [each human being after he or she has attained the age of puberty] one sitting on the right and one on the left [to note his or her actions] not a word does he [or she] utter, but there is a watcher by him ready to record it.﴾ 50:17-18

[94] Sahīh Al-Bukhārī, [Eng. Trans. vol.'4 #459].

There is an angel in our wombs.

"Allāh has appointed an angel in the womb and the angel says, 'O Lord! A drop of discharge [i.e., semen] O Lord! A clot. O Lord! a piece of flesh. And then if Allāh wishes to complete the child's creation the angel will say, O Lord! A male or a female? O Lord! Wretched or blessed [in religion]? What will his livelihood be? The angel writes all this while the child is in the womb of its mother."[95]

There is an angel who pushes the clouds. Part of a longer *hadīth* reads:

"[Then] they said: 'Tell us what thunder is? 'He [ﷺ] replied: ' [It is] an angel from the angels of Allāh the Mighty and the Majestic, who has been given the task of [pushing] the clouds with his hand or in his hand is a whip made of fire which he uses to drive the clouds wherever Allāh commands.' They [the Jews] said: 'So what is the sound [of thunder] that is heard?' He [ﷺ] replied: 'His voice [i.e., the voice of the angel or the sound of the whip]'."[96]

iv] The angels worship Allāh.

In the Book of Allāh, the Almighty, we find;

﴿ وَمَا مِنَّآ إِلَّا لَهُۥ مَقَامٌ مَّعْلُومٌ ۝ وَإِنَّا لَنَحْنُ ٱلصَّآفُّونَ ۝ وَإِنَّا لَنَحْنُ ٱلْمُسَبِّحُونَ ﴾

﴾ There is not one of us [angels] but has his known place or position. Verily, we [angels] stand in rows for prayers [as you Muslims stand in rows for your prayers]. Verily we [angels] are they who glorify [Allāh's praises i.e., perform prayers]. ﴿ 37:164-166

And in the *hadīth* of the night journey of the Prophet [ﷺ]:

"Then I was shown Al-Bayt Al-Ma'mūr [i.e., Allāh's house said to be the Ka'bah equivalent in Paradise]. I Asked Jibrā'īl about it, and he said, 'This is Al-Bait-al-Ma'mūr Where 70,000 angels perform prayers daily, and when they leave they never return to it [a new batch comes each time]."[97]

---

[95] *Sahīh Al-Bukhārī*, [Eng. Trans. vol.4 #550].

[96] *Musnad* of Imam Ahmad vol.1 pg. 284. Declared *hasan* by Ahmad Al-Madkhalī in his checking of *I'lām As-Sunnah Al-Manshūrah*.

[97] *Sahīh Al-Bukhārī*, [Eng. Trans. vol.4 #429].

3] BELIEF IN HIS MESSENGERS.

All Praise is for Allāh Alone, who in His Infinite Wisdom and Mercy, did not create us and leave us without guidance. Rather He sent guidance and instruction with His Messengers and Prophets. Not all Prophets were Messengers but all Messengers were Prophets, this is because only Messengers were sent with Books. Allāh said:

﴿ وَلَقَدْ بَعَثْنَا فِى كُلِّ أُمَّةٍ رَّسُولًا أَنِ ٱعْبُدُوا۟ ٱللَّهَ وَٱجْتَنِبُوا۟ ٱلطَّٰغُوتَ ﴾

﴾ And verily, We have sent among every ummah [nation, community] a Messenger [proclaiming] Worship Allāh [Alone] and avoid [or keep away from] Tāghūt [all false deities etc. i.e., do not worship Tāghūt besides Allāh].﴿ 16:36

Allāh then warns us:

﴿ وَمَن يَكْفُرْ بِٱلْإِيمَٰنِ فَقَدْ حَبِطَ عَمَلُهُۥ وَهُوَ فِى ٱلْءَاخِرَةِ مِنَ ٱلْخَٰسِرِينَ ﴾

﴾ And whosoever disbelieves in Faith [i.e., in the oneness of Allāh and in all the other Articles of faith i.e., His Angels, His holy Books, His Messengers, the Day of Resurrection and Al-Qadar [Divine Preordainment's]], then fruitless is his work; and in the Hereafter he will be among the losers.﴿ 5:5

Therefore it is imperative that one believes in all the Messengers of Allāh. We know of twenty five Prophets mentioned in the Qur`ān, in English their names are: Elishia, Job, David, Dhul-Kifl, Āron, Hūd, Abraham, Enoch, Elias, Jesus, Isāc, Ishmael, Lot, Moses, Noah, Sālih, Shuaib, Solomon, Ezra, Jacob, John, Jonah, Joseph, Zachariya, Muhammad or Ahmad. Ibn Al-Qayyim said: "Allāh, Glorified be He, chose 124,000 Prophets from the children of Adam, may the peace and blessings of Allāh be upon them all. And He chose the Messengers from amongst them [i.e., the 124,000] and they were 313 in number - according to a *hadīth* narrated by Ahmed and Ibn Hibbān in his *Sahīh* upon the authority of Abū Dharr"[98].

[98] Refer to *Zād Al-Ma'ād* by Ibn Al-Qayyim [1/43].

Muhammad [ﷺ] was the last and final Prophet and none will come after him. And he was also the best of creation. Allāh, the Almighty, said of him:

﴿ مَّا كَانَ مُحَمَّدٌ أَبَآ أَحَدٍ مِّن رِّجَالِكُمْ وَلَٰكِن رَّسُولَ ٱللَّهِ وَخَاتَمَ ٱلنَّبِيِّـۧنَ ۗ وَكَانَ ٱللَّهُ بِكُلِّ شَىْءٍ عَلِيمًا ﴿٤٠﴾ ﴾

﴾ Muhammad [ﷺ] is not the father of any of your men, but he is the Messenger of Allāh and last [end] of the Prophets. And Allāh is Ever All-Aware of everything. ﴿ ***33:40***

The Prophet [ﷺ] said:

"I have been sent [as a Messenger] in the best of all generations of Adam's offspring since their creation."[99]

The Prophet [ﷺ] was the seal of the Prophets and as such had a seal on his back.

As-Sā`ib Ibn Yazīd narrated: "My aunt took me to Allāh's Messenger[ﷺ] and said, O Allāh's Messenger! My sister's son is sick." So he passed his hand over my head and invoked for Allāh's blessing upon me and then performed the ablution. I drank from the water of his ablution and I stood behind him and looked at his *khatam* [the seal of Prophethood] between his shoulders [and its size was] like the button of a tent."[100]

It is incumbent on every Muslim to send *salāms* [the Peace and Blessings of Allāh] on the Prophet Muhammad [ﷺ] whenever they hear his name mentioned.

Allāh said in His Book:

﴿ إِنَّ ٱللَّهَ وَمَلَٰٓئِكَتَهُۥ يُصَلُّونَ عَلَى ٱلنَّبِىِّ ۚ يَٰٓأَيُّهَا ٱلَّذِينَ ءَامَنُوا۟ صَلُّوا۟ عَلَيْهِ وَسَلِّمُوا۟ تَسْلِيمًا ﴿٥٦﴾ ﴾

---

[99] *Sahīh Al-Bukhārī*, [Eng. Trans. vol. 4 #757].

[100] *Sahīh Al-Bukhārī*, [Eng. Trans. vol.8 #363].

﴾ Allāh sends His salāh [Graces and Honors, Blessings, Mercy, etc.] on the Prophet [Muhammad ﷺ] and also His angels too [ask Allāh to bless and forgive him]. O you who believe! Send your salāh on [ask Allāh to bless] him and you should greet him with the Islāmic way of greeting [salutation i.e., As-Salām 'Alaykum].﴿ 33:56

In part of a longer narration by Al-Hākim we find that the Prophet [ﷺ] said: *"When I climbed the second step Jibrā`īl stated: May the person suffer humiliation when your name is recited before him and he fails to send you salutations. In answer, I stated, Āmīn."*[101]

One may do this by saying, " O Allāh! Send your *salāh* [Grace and Honor] on Muhammad and on Muhammad's family as You sent *salāh* on Ibrāhīm's family. O Allāh! Send Your Blessings on Muhammad and on Muhammad's family as You sent Your Blessings on Ibrāhīm's family. You are indeed worthy of all praise, full of glory."[102] And also saying the greeting of the Muslims, *As-Salām 'Alaykum wa Rahmatullāh wa Barakātuh* except adding to the end [or beginning] a title of his like, *Yā Rasūlullāh* [O Messenger of Allāh].

---

[101] The Book of Fasting by Muhammad Iqbal Kilani, pg. 19. Al-Hākim, with a *sahīh* chain of narrators

[102] *Sahīh Al-Bukhārī*, [Eng. Trans. vol. 8 #369].

4] BELIEF IN HIS BOOKS.

The fourth Pillar of *Īmān* is the belief in all the Books Allāh revealed to his Messengers. The belief here is that at the time they were revealed they were truly the message of Allāh, the Almighty. However the only Book left in its true and unadulterated form is the Qur`ān in its entirety. This is because it is the last revelation Allāh will send to us and He promised to protect it. Allāh said:

﴿ إِنَّا نَحْنُ نَزَّلْنَا ٱلذِّكْرَ وَإِنَّا لَهُۥ لَحَٰفِظُونَ ﴾

﴿ Verily, We, it is We Who have sent down the Dhikr [i.e., the Qur`ān] and surely, We will guard it [from corruption].﴾ 15:9

﴿ إِنَّهُۥ لَقُرْءَانٌ كَرِيمٌ ۝ فِى كِتَٰبٍ مَّكْنُونٍ ۝ لَّا يَمَسُّهُۥٓ إِلَّا ٱلْمُطَهَّرُونَ ۝ تَنزِيلٌ مِّن رَّبِّ ٱلْعَٰلَمِينَ ۝ ﴾

﴿ That [this] is indeed an honorable recitation [The Noble Qur`ān]. In a Book well- guarded [with Allāh in the heaven i.e., Al-Lawh Al-Mahfūdh]. Which [that Book with Allāh] none can touch but the purified [i.e., the angels]. A Revelation [This Qur`ān] from the Lord of the 'Ālamīn [mankind, jinn and all that exists].﴾ 56:77-80

﴿ كِتَٰبٌ أَنزَلْنَٰهُ إِلَيْكَ لِتُخْرِجَ ٱلنَّاسَ مِنَ ٱلظُّلُمَٰتِ إِلَى ٱلنُّورِ بِإِذْنِ رَبِّهِمْ إِلَىٰ صِرَٰطِ ٱلْعَزِيزِ ٱلْحَمِيدِ ﴾

﴿ [This is] a Book which We have revealed unto you [O Muhammad [ﷺ] in order that you might lead mankind out of darkness [of disbelief and polytheism] into light [of belief in the Oneness of Allāh and Islām Monotheism] by their Lord's leave to the Path of the All-Mighty, the Owner of All Praise.﴾ 14:1

There are four Books we know of;

a) The Torah sent with the Prophet Mūsā [Moses عليه السلام].
b) The Psalms sent with the Prophet Dāwud [David عليه السلام].
c) The Gospel sent with the Prophet 'Īsā [Jesus عليه السلام].

And finally, the Qur`ān, which confirms and fulfills the ones before it, with the Prophet Muhammad [ﷺ], [or Ahmad, [Ahmad is the name Allāh inspired 'Īsā to call him in the Injīl [Gospel], who foretold his advent]]. Allāh the Mighty, the Exalted said:

﴿ وَمَا كَانَ هَٰذَا ٱلْقُرْءَانُ أَن يُفْتَرَىٰ مِن دُونِ ٱللَّهِ وَلَٰكِن تَصْدِيقَ ٱلَّذِى بَيْنَ يَدَيْهِ وَتَفْصِيلَ ٱلْكِتَٰبِ لَا رَيْبَ فِيهِ مِن رَّبِّ ٱلْعَٰلَمِينَ ﴿٣٧﴾ ﴾

﴾ And this Qur`ān is not such as could ever be produced by other than Allāh [Lord of the heavens and the earth], but it is a confirmation of [the Revelation] which was before it [i.e., the Tawrāt [Torah], and the Injīl [Gospel]], and a full explanation of the Book [i.e., laws, decreed for mankind]- wherein there is no doubt - from the Lord of the 'Ālamīn [mankind, jinn and all that exists]. ﴿ 10:37

Some Merits of the Qur`ān from hadīth.

"The most superior among you [Muslims] are those who learn the Qur`ān and teach it."[103]

"Whoever recites Āyah Al-Kursī[104] *following every obligatory prayer, nothing prevents him from entering Paradise except dying."*[105]

"Whoever recites the last two verses of Sūrah Al-Baqarah at night they will suffice him [To ward off the Satan]."[106]

The Prophet [ﷺ] said to his companions: "Is it difficult for any of you to recite one third of the Qur`ān at night?" This suggestion was difficult for them so they said, 'Who amongst us has the power to do so, O Allāh's Messenger?' Allāh's Messenger replied, "Allāh [the] One the Self Sufficient Master Whom all creatures need.'[Sūrah Al-Ikhlās to the end 112:1-4], is equal to one third of the Qur`ān."[107]

---

[103] *Sahīh Al-Bukhārī*, [Eng. Trans. vol. 6 #546].

[104] Qur`ān 2:255.

[105] At-Tabarānī, Ibn Hibbān and others. *Shaykh* Al-Albānī grades it *sahīh*.

[106] *Sahīh Al-Bukhārī*, [Eng. Trans. vol. 6 #530].

[107] *Sahīh Al-Bukhārī*, [Eng. Trans. vol. 6 #533].

5] BELIEF IN THE LAST DAY.

Belief in the Last Day is the fifth Pillar, and this day has a number of other names like; The Day of Standing, The Day of Grief and Regret or The Striking Hour. We seek refuge with The King of the Day of Judgment, from this fearsome Day, Āmīn. Allāh refers to it in detail in several places in the Qur`ān. Sūrah Al-Qāri'ah [or the striking hour] for instance is devoted entirely to it.

بِسْمِ ٱللَّهِ ٱلرَّحْمَٰنِ ٱلرَّحِيمِ ﴿ ٱلْقَارِعَةُ ۝١ مَا ٱلْقَارِعَةُ ۝٢ وَمَآ أَدْرَىٰكَ مَا ٱلْقَارِعَةُ ۝٣ يَوْمَ يَكُونُ ٱلنَّاسُ كَٱلْفَرَاشِ ٱلْمَبْثُوثِ ۝٤ وَتَكُونُ ٱلْجِبَالُ كَٱلْعِهْنِ ٱلْمَنفُوشِ ۝٥ فَأَمَّا مَن ثَقُلَتْ مَوَٰزِينُهُۥ ۝٦ فَهُوَ فِى عِيشَةٍ رَّاضِيَةٍ ۝٧ وَأَمَّا مَنْ خَفَّتْ مَوَٰزِينُهُۥ ۝٨ فَأُمُّهُۥ هَاوِيَةٌ ۝٩ وَمَآ أَدْرَىٰكَ مَا هِيَهْ ۝١٠ نَارٌ حَامِيَةٌۢ ۝١١ ﴾

﴿ Al-Qāri'ah [the striking Hour i.e., the Day of Resurrection]. What is the Striking [Hour]? And what will make you know what the Striking Hour is? It is a Day whereon mankind will be like moths scattered about, And the mountains will be like carded wool, Then as for him whose balance of [good deeds] will be heavy, He will live a pleasant life [in Paradise] But as for him whose balance [of good deeds] will be light, He will have his home in Hāwiyah [pit in Hell]. And what will make you know what it is. [It is] a hot blazing Fire!﴾ 101:1-8

It will be the Day of:

﴿ فَسَوْفَ يُحَاسَبُ حِسَابًا يَسِيرًا ۝٨ وَيَنقَلِبُ إِلَىٰٓ أَهْلِهِۦ مَسْرُورًا ۝٩ وَأَمَّا مَنْ أُوتِىَ كِتَٰبَهُۥ وَرَآءَ ظَهْرِهِۦ ۝١٠ فَسَوْفَ يَدْعُوا۟ ثُبُورًا ۝١١ وَيَصْلَىٰ سَعِيرًا ۝١٢ إِنَّهُۥ كَانَ فِىٓ أَهْلِهِۦ مَسْرُورًا ۝١٣ إِنَّهُۥ ظَنَّ أَن لَّن يَحُورَ ۝١٤ ﴾

﴿ ...then as for him who will be given his Record in his right hand, he surely will receive an easy reckoning, And will return to his family in joy! But whosoever is given his Record behind his back [in his left hand from behind] he will invoke his destruction, And shall enter a blazing Fire, and made to taste its' burning. Verily, he was among his people in joy! Verily, he thought that he would never come back [to Us]!﴾ 84:7-14

It will be a Day of accounting for every tiny good or bad deed. We need to live our lives remembering that we shall see then what we do now, living each day like it was our last one as far as deeds are concerned, the questions are, 'Do I have enough good deeds yet , am I sure I haven't nullified them? Is someone going to take from my good deeds on that Day because I have done something bad to them, am I sure? A lengthy *hadīth* to give more insight on that Day:

"The people said, 'O Allāh's Messenger! Shall we see our Lord on the Day of Resurrection?' The Prophet [ﷺ] said, *"Do you have any difficulty in seeing the sun and the moon when the sky is clear?" We said, "No." He said, "So you will have no difficulty in seeing your Lord on that Day as you have no difficulty in seeing the sun and the moon [in a clear sky]." The Prophet [ﷺ] then said, "Somebody will then announce, 'Let every nation follow what they used to worship' So the companions of the cross will go with their cross, and the idolaters [will go] with their idols and the companions of every god [false deities] [will go] with their god, till there will remain those who used to worship Allāh, both the obedient ones and the mischievous ones, and some of the people of the Scripture. Then Hell will be presented to them as if it were a mirage. Then it will be said to the Jews, What did you use to worship?' They will reply, 'We used to worship Ezera, the son of Allāh.' It will be said to them, 'You are lairs, for Allāh has neither a wife nor a son. What do you want [now]?' They will reply, 'We want You to provide us with water.' Then it will be said to them, 'Drink,' and they will fall down in Hell [instead]. Then it will be said to the Christians, 'What did you use to worship?' They will reply, 'We used to worship Messiah, the son of Allāh.' It will be said, 'You are lairs, for Allāh has neither a wife nor a son. What do you want [now]?' They will say, 'We want you to provide us with water.' It will be said to them, 'Drink,' And they will fall down in Hell [instead]. When there remain only those who used to worship Allāh [Alone], both the obedient ones and the mischievous ones, it will be said to them, 'What keeps you here when all the people have gone?' They will say, 'We parted with them [in the world] when we were in greater need of them than we are today, we heard the call of one proclaiming, 'Let every nation follow what they used to worship,' and now we are waiting for our Lord. Then the Almighty will come to them in a shape other than the one which they saw the first time, and he will say, 'I am your Lord,' and they will say, 'You are not our Lord.' And none will speak to Him except the Prophets, and then it will be said to them, 'Do you know any sign by which you can recognize Him?' They will say, 'The Shin,' and so Allāh will then uncover His shin whereupon every believer will prostrate before Him and there will remain those who used to prostrate before Him just for showing off and for gaining good reputation. These people will try to prostrate but their backs will be rigid like one piece of wood [they will be unable to prostrate]. Then the bridge will be laid across Hell." We, the companions of the Prophet [ﷺ] said, "O Allāh's Messenger! What is the bridge?" He said, "It is a slippery bridge on which there are clamps and [Hooks like] a thorny seed that is wide at one side and narrow at another and has thorns with bent ends. Such a seed is found in Najd and is called As-Sa'dān. Some of the believers will cross the bridge as quickly as the wink of an eye, some others as quick as lightening, a strong horse, fast horses or she camels. So some will be safe without any harm; some will be safe after receiving some scratches, and some will fall down into the Hell [Fire]. The last person will cross by being dragged [over the bridge]." The Prophet [ﷺ] said, "You [Muslims] cannot be more pressing in claiming from me a right that has been clearly proved to be yours than the believers in interceding with Almighty for their [Muslim] brothers that day, when they see themselves safe. They will say, 'O Allāh [save] our brothers for they used to pray with us, fast with us and also do good deeds with us.' Allāh will say, 'Go take out [of Hell] anyone in whose heart you find faith equal to the weight of one [gold] dīnār.' Allāh will forbid the fire to burn the faces of those sinners. They will go to them and find some of them in Hell [Fire] up to their feet, and some up to the middle of their legs. So they will take out those whom they recognize and then they will return, and Allāh will say [to them], ' Go take out anyone in whose heart you find faith equal to the weight of one half dīnār.' They will take out whomever they will recognize and return, and then Allāh will say,*

'Go and take out anyone in whose heart you find faith equal to the weight of an atom [or small ant], and so they will take out all those whom they will recognize.' Then the Prophets and the angels and the believers will intercede, and [last of all] the Almighty [Allāh] will say, 'Now remains My intercession.' He will then hold a handful of the fire from which He will take out some people whose bodies have been burnt, and they will be thrown into a river at the entrance of Paradise, called the water of life. They will grow on its banks, as a seed carried by the torrent grows. You have noticed how it grows by a rock or beside a tree, and how the side facing the sun is usually green while the side facing the shade is white. Those people will come out [of the river] like pearls, and they will have [golden] necklaces, then they will enter Paradise whereupon the people of Paradise will say, ' These are the people emancipated by the Magnificent. He has admitted them into Paradise without them having done any good deeds and without them sending forth any good [for themselves].' Then it will be said to them, 'For you is what you have seen and it's equivalent as well." [108]

[108] Sahīh *Al-Bukhārī*, [Eng. Trans. Vol. 8, page 395-399].

6] BELIEF IN AL-QADAR [PRE-DESTINATION].

Allāh said in His Book:

﴿إِنَّا كُلَّ شَيْءٍ خَلَقْنَٰهُ بِقَدَرٍ ﴿٤٩﴾﴾

﴿ ***Verily We have created all things with Qadar [Divine Preordainments of all things before there creation, as written in the Book of Decrees- Al-Lawh Al Mahfūdh].*** ﴾ ***54:49***

His Prophet [ﷺ] said:

"The pen has dried after writing what you will surely encounter."[109]

We shall use excerpts from *'Fate in Islām'* by Dr Saleh As-Saleh.

There are four levels of *Qadar*:

a) Allāh's knowledge.

He knew what had occurred, what will occur, as well as that which did not occur [past, present and future].

b) The writing.

This was done fifty thousand years before creation i.e., about the provisions and deeds etc. of all creation. In this level we find the *Taqdīr* [books] covering a persons life span i.e., his livelihood life span, deeds and religious status [believer or unbeliever] which is written while he is in the womb. The Annual Taqdīr, that takes place on the Night of Decree [*Laylah Al-Qadar*]. And the Daily Taqdīr, here the majority of scholars of Tafsīr said that:" Everyday, Allāh gives life and causes death, creates and provides; lifts some in honor and humiliates others; cures an ill person and releases a captive; relieves from hardship and answers a supplicate; gives the one who asks Him and forgives a sin. His actions and creations are infinite."

The writing in the Preserved Tablet is Preserved: it is not subject to any change whatsoever because it is based upon Allāh's Knowledge. In other books, however, changes may occur, as in the books handled by the angels.

---

[109] *Sahīh Al-Bukhārī*, [Eng. Trans. vol. 8 Chapter 1].

Allāh said:

﴿ يَمْحُواْ ٱللَّهُ مَا يَشَآءُ وَيُثْبِتُ وَعِندَهُۥٓ أُمُّ ٱلْكِتَـٰبِ ﴾

﴿ Allāh blots out what He wills and confirms [what He wills]; and with Him is Umm Al-Kitāb [The Preserved Tablet].﴾ 13:39

Ibn Taymiyyah explains: " Provisions and life terms are of two kinds: The unchanged record written in *Umm Al-Kitāb*, and another, subject to increase and decrease, made known to the angels by Allāh. Allāh commands the angels to write a certain life span in the book they have, for example, and if that person does join ties of kinship then He orders them to write an extension [as per the *hadīth* on the benefit of joining ties of kinship]. However Allāh Knew if the person would do so or not.

c) The Will of Allāh.

i.e., whatever He wills will occur.

d) The Creation.

Allāh is the Sole creator of everything including man's deeds.[110]

Some things to know on *Qadar*.

1) Simply because things have been written it is not permissible to blame sins on *Qadar*.

In other words, one commits evil with no remorse claiming if it wasn't written they wouldn't have done it, for the Prophet [ﷺ] said:

"There is not of you but has his place assigned either in the Fire or in Paradise.' Thereupon a man from the people said, ' Shall we not depend upon this, O Allāh's Messenger? [Shall we abandon our deeds since the fate of everyone has already been decided?]. The Prophet [ﷺ] said: ' No, but

---

[110] End of excerpt from Dr. Saleh As-Saleh's, *Fate in Islām.*

carry on and do your deeds, for everybody finds it easy to do such deeds [as will lead him to his place].'The Prophet [ﷺ] then recited the verse 92:5."[111]

﴿ فَأَمَّا مَنْ أَعْطَىٰ وَاتَّقَىٰ ۝ وَصَدَّقَ بِالْحُسْنَىٰ ۝ فَسَنُيَسِّرُهُ لِلْيُسْرَىٰ ۝ وَأَمَّا مَنۢ بَخِلَ وَاسْتَغْنَىٰ ۝ وَكَذَّبَ بِالْحُسْنَىٰ ۝ ﴾

﴾ As for him who gives [in charity] and keeps his duty to Allāh and fears Him, And believes in Al-Husnā. We will make smooth for him the path for ease [goodness]. But he who is a greedy miser and thinks himself self-sufficient. And belies Al-Husnā. We will make smooth for him the path for evil.﴿ 92:5-10

Therefore strive hard for the desired end. May Allāh, the Compassionate make our paths smooth to goodness, Āmīn.

2] Beware one may do deeds of the person from Paradise but his last deed may be of the people of the Hell, thus he may end in the Fire!

One may do righteous deeds all his life then change before he dies to evil deeds, or likewise, one may not look like the people of Paradise but when death is close he does deeds of the ones of Paradise and he then attains it. Don't let the cursed *Shaytān* make you comfortable in your deeds. Constantly strive, you don't know which will be the hour Allāh recalls your soul, and remember that your intention for these good deeds should be for the sake of Allāh alone. Consider the following *hadīth*:

"O Allāh's Messenger! Do you know what the man you described as of the people of the Fire has done? He has fought very bravely for Allāh's cause and has received many wounds.' The Prophet [ﷺ] said: *But he is indeed one of the people of the Fire.* Some of the Muslims were about to have some doubt about that statement. So while the man was in that state, pain caused by the wounds troubled him so much that he put his hand into his quiver and took out an arrow and committed suicide with it. Off went some men of the Muslims to Allāh's Messenger [ﷺ] and said, O Allāh's Messenger! Allāh

[111] *Sahīh Al-Bukhārī*, [Eng. Trans. vol. 8 #595].

made your statement true. So and so has committed suicide.' Allāh's Messenger[ﷺ] said, *'O Bilāl! Get up and announce in public: None will enter Paradise but a believer, and Allāh may support this religion [Islām] with a wicked man.''*[112]

Also;

"There was a man before you who had killed ninety-nine people and he asked about the one with the most knowledge in the country. He was directed to a monk and he then went to him and asked: 'If one killed ninety-nine people is there a chance for him to repent? He replied: No. So he killed him and completed one hundred. He then asked about the one with the most knowledge in the country. He was directed to a scholar and he asked: If one has killed one hundred people is there a chance for him to repent? He replied: 'Yes, the only thing stopping you is by you not going to such and such a land where there are some people who are worshiping Allāh, so worship Allāh with them and do not return to your land; it is an evil land. So he left and when he was half way there death came to him and then the angel of mercy and the angel of punishment argued. The angel of mercy said that he came sincerely, hoping and seeking repentance from Allāh. The angel of punishment said that he never did any good. Then an angel came to them in the form of a man and stood between them and said: 'Measure the distance between the two lands and whichever one was closer then that is for him. It was found that the land which he was going to was the closest so the angel of mercy took his soul.'"[113] In another version still in Sahīh Al-Bukhārī and Sahīh Muslim, the additional wording is included; *"so Allāh directed one land to come closer and directed the other land to go further away and he said; 'Now measure the distance between them.' It was found that he was nearer to his goal by a hand span so he was forgiven."*

---

[112] *Sahīh Al-Bukhārī*, [Eng. Trans. vol. 8 #603].

[113] *Sahīh Muslim*, [Eng. Trans. vol. 4 #6662/ #6664].

3] All good is from Allāh and all the bad or evil that happens to us is from ourselves.

Allāh said:

﴿ مَّآ أَصَابَكَ مِنْ حَسَنَةٍ فَمِنَ ٱللَّهِ ۖ وَمَآ أَصَابَكَ مِن سَيِّئَةٍ فَمِن نَّفْسِكَ ﴿٧٩﴾ ﴾

﴾ Whatever of good reaches you, is from Allāh, but whatever of evil befalls you, is from yourself.﴿ 4:79

Therefore we should be patient with our trials and ask Allāh to forgive us, and know that what has happened, never could have missed us and what has missed us, never could have happened to us. And that is the *Qadar* of Allāh, the Almighty.

4] Some kinds of *Qadar* are changeable with good deeds or *du'ā`s*, by the will of Allāh.

Examples of this are found in the *hadīths*:

"Whoever loves that he be granted more wealth and that his lease on life be extended, then he should keep good relations with his kith and kin." [114]

"Take refuge with Allāh from the difficulties of severe calamities, from having an evil end and a bad fate and from the malicious joy of your enemies." [115]

Remember *Qadar* is preordained, however that should in no way influence your efforts to accomplish as much good [deeds] as possible in your life, because Allāh said:

﴿ فَمَن يَعْمَلْ مِثْقَالَ ذَرَّةٍ خَيْرًا يَرَهُۥ ﴿٧﴾ وَمَن يَعْمَلْ مِثْقَالَ ذَرَّةٍ شَرًّا يَرَهُۥ ﴿٨﴾ ﴾

﴾ Whosoever does good equal to the weight of an atom [or a small ant] shall see it. And whosoever does evil equal to an atom [or a small ant] shall see it.﴿ 99:7-8

So strive, O servants of Allāh, strive for a good end.

---

[114] *Sahīh Al-Bukhārī*, [Eng. Trans. vol. 8 #15].

[115] *Sahīh Al-Bukhārī*, [Eng. Trans. vol. 8 #613].

CHAPTER 3

TAWH̲ĪD

[BELIEF IN THE ONENESS OF ALLĀH, MONOTHEISIM]

Allāh, the Almighty, the Exalted said:

﴿ وَإِلَٰهُكُمْ إِلَٰهٌ وَاحِدٌ ۖ لَّا إِلَٰهَ إِلَّا هُوَ الرَّحْمَٰنُ الرَّحِيمُ ﴾

﴾ And your Ilāh [God] is one Ilāh [God-Allāh], La ilāha illa Huwa [there is none who has the right to be worshipped but He], the Most Gracious, the Most Merciful.﴿ 2:163

This is encompassed in the statement, *Lā ilāha illa Allāh*; There is none worthy of worship in truth except Allāh. By saying this, one negates, *Lā ilāha*- there is no deity, then affirms, *illa Allāh*- except Allāh, [worthy of worship, in truth]. Saying it and acting on it every single day of your life. The weight of the statement of *Tawh̲īd*:

"Mūsā [ﷺ] said:' Rabb, teach me something with which I can remember You and supplicate to You.' Allāh answered: 'Say, O Mūsā, La ilāha illa Allāh! Mūsā said: 'O my Rabb [Lord], all Your slaves say these words.' Allāh said: ' O Mūsā, if the seven heavens and all they contain other than Me [Ghayriy] and the seven earths as well, were all put in one side of a scale and La ilāha illa Allāh put on the other then the latter would outweigh them." [116]

We have also been informed in another *h̲adīth* that from it's merit is:

"Indeed Allāh has forbidden for Hell the person who testifies: There is nothing worthy of worship in truth but Allāh, seeking thereby nothing but Allāh's Face." [117]

---

[116] *Kitāb At-Tawh̲īd*, by Muh̲ammad Ibn 'Abd Al-Wahhāb pg.24. The *h̲adīth* is reported by Ibn H̲ibbān and declared *sah̲īh̲* by Al-H̲akim.

[117] *Sah̲īh̲ Al-Bukhārī*, [Eng. Trans. vol. 8 pg. 373].

Yet one should not rely solely on this ignoring their duties and good deeds. If one testifies to this [statement], it will be in their heart and show through their limbs and mouth by the observance of prayer, fasting, charity, jihad or can be through enjoining the good and forbidding the evil and restraining from evil like neglecting the rights of ones brothers or sisters in Islām by back-biting, oppression etc.

a) What is worship?

All sayings and acts loved by Allāh, like prayer or fasting. Allāh, the Exalted, the Mighty said:

﴿ قُلۡ إِنَّ صَلَاتِى وَنُسُكِى وَمَحۡيَاىَ وَمَمَاتِى لِلَّهِ رَبِّ ٱلۡعَٰلَمِينَ ﴾

﴿Say [O Muhammad ﷺ]: Verily, my salāh, my sacrifice, my living and my dying are for Allāh, the Lord of the Ālamīn [mankind, jinn and all that exists].﴾ **6:162**

The origin or basis of performing an act of worship, is that it is *harām* or forbidden, until Allāh Himself, the Self-Sufficient, the Master, legislates that for us. We *cannot* invent any other methods with which to worship Him nor may we worship any other created thing along with Him. May Allāh keep us on His straight path.

b) Why must we worship Allāh [Alone]?

Allāh said:

﴿ وَمَا خَلَقۡتُ ٱلۡجِنَّ وَٱلۡإِنسَ إِلَّا لِيَعۡبُدُونِ ﴾

﴿ And I created not the Jinn and Humans except that they should worship Me [Alone].﴾ **51:56**

And His Prophet Muhammad [ﷺ] informed us that:

"Mankind's duty to Allāh is to worship Him Alone and not to associate partners with Him in anything." [118]

---

[118] *Sahīh Al-Bukhārī*, [Eng. Trans. vol. 9 #470].

c) How do we worship Allāh?

This is achieved through obedience to Allāh and His Messenger [ﷺ], i.e., using the Qur`ān and Authentic *Sunnah* [hadīth] with the understanding of the *Salaf* [our pious predecessors]. Allāh said:

﴿ يَـٰٓأَيُّهَا ٱلَّذِينَ ءَامَنُوٓا۟ أَطِيعُوا۟ ٱللَّهَ وَأَطِيعُوا۟ ٱلرَّسُولَ وَلَا تُبْطِلُوٓا۟ أَعْمَـٰلَكُمْ ﴾

﴾ O you who believe! Obey Allāh and obey the Messenger [Muhammad ﷺ] and render not vain your deeds. ﴿ 47:33

His Messenger informed us:

"Whoever does a deed [in religion] which we have not commanded, it is rejected." [119]

"The best people are those living in my generation, and then those who will follow them, and then those who will follow the latter." [120]

Therefore both the Qur`ān and Authentic *Sunnah* [hadīth] should be followed according to the understanding of the *Salaf*, to the exclusion of all other additions or innovations. Such additions may stem from groups of *bida'* or offshoots from the blind following of *madhhabs* or *shaykhs*, which will lead to the most feared sin, *Shirk* [associating others in worship with Allāh]. The Prophet of Allāh, Muhammad [ﷺ] said:

"By Him [Allāh] in whose Hand Muhammad's soul is, there is none from amongst the Jews and the Christians [of these present nations] that hears about me and dies without believing in the message with which I have been sent [i.e., Islāmic monotheism] but he will be from the dwellers of the Hell Fire." [121]

Allāh the Exalted, the Mighty said,

﴿ إِنَّ ٱلَّذِينَ فَرَّقُوا۟ دِينَهُمْ وَكَانُوا۟ شِيَعًا لَّسْتَ مِنْهُمْ فِى شَىْءٍ ۚ إِنَّمَآ أَمْرُهُمْ إِلَى ٱللَّهِ ثُمَّ يُنَبِّئُهُم بِمَا كَانُوا۟ يَفْعَلُونَ ﴾

[119] *Sahīh Muslim*, [Eng. Trans. vol.3 pg. 1025-1026]

[120] *Sahīh Al-Bukhārī*, [Eng. Trans. Vol.5 #3].

[121] *Sahīh Muslim*, [Eng. Trans. vol. 1 #284].

﴾ Verily, those who divide their religion and break up into sects [all kinds of religious sects], you [O Muhammad ﷺ] have no concern in them in the least. Their affair is only with Allāh, Who then will tell them what they used to do. ﴿ 6:159.

"The Jews and the Christians were divided into seventy one or seventy two religious sects, and this nation will divide into seventy three - all in the Hell except one and that is the one in which I and my companions are today [i.e., the Qur`ān and Sunnah]." [122]

Islām is a complete way of life, and contained within the Qur`ān and the Authentic *Sunnah* [with the correct understanding of these from the *Salaf* as-Sālih[123]] are the solutions to every aspect of man's existence, from worship to politics, from etiquette on how to use the bathroom to treatment of guests. Therefore one need not look to other than the Qur`ān and *Sunnah* to find what they consider a better way to reach or worship their Lord as He already informed us in clear detail of how to worship Him in a manner pleasing to Him. Allāh said:

﴿ ٱلْيَوْمَ أَكْمَلْتُ لَكُمْ دِينَكُمْ وَأَتْمَمْتُ عَلَيْكُمْ نِعْمَتِى وَرَضِيتُ لَكُمُ ٱلْإِسْلَٰمَ دِينًا ﴾

﴾ This day, I have perfected your religion for you, completed My Favour upon you, and have chosen for you Islām as your religion. ﴿ 5:3

To put it bluntly, He created us, gave us the religion He intended for us and gave us the rules, sustenance and abundant beauty around us. Allāh told us in addition to this that we can call on Him for help, if we sin, [breaking the rules He gave us] and out of fear of Him, repent, He will forgive us [by the will of Allāh]. And after this life of tests, if we worship Him as ordered following the rules He sent continuously with His Prophets [when we forget], He has promised us even more beauty, constant rest, such

---

[122] *Sunan* of Abū Dāwud, [Engl. Trans. vol.3 Kitāb As-Sunnah Chap. 1677 #4579] and declared *hasan sahīh* by *Shaykh* Al-Albani.

[123] *As-Salaf As-Sālih*; the pious predecessors who were the companions of the Prophet [ﷺ] and the next two generations after them.

good that we cannot even imagine. He also warned us if we disobey Him, worshipping His creation instead of or in addition to worshipping Him, the punishment awaiting us in this world and the next is absolute torment, WHY would any one throw away all His Mercy to them in useless rebellion to their one and only Creator? The time we spend on this earth compared to the eternity of the Hereafter will seem so little and useless [to one who lived as a unbeliever, disobedient to Allāh and the believer]. All the time and effort they tried to spend to get some petty worldly gain [for all the wealth, status, etc. amassed in this world will seem like nothing] instead of using it for good deeds for the Hereafter, will be far from their minds. But it will be to late, so use this time well, worship Allāh Alone in the manner He has ordered us to. Allāh, the Exalted, the Mighty said:

﴿ وَيَوْمَ تَقُومُ ٱلسَّاعَةُ يُقْسِمُ ٱلْمُجْرِمُونَ مَا لَبِثُواْ غَيْرَ سَاعَةٍ كَذَٰلِكَ كَانُواْ يُؤْفَكُونَ ﴾

﴿ And on that Day that the Hour will be established, the Mujrimūn [criminals, disbelievers, polytheists, sinners] will swear they stayed not but an hour - thus were they ever deluded [away from the truth [i.e., they used to tell lies and take false oaths, and turn away from the truth] in this life of the world].﴾ 30:55

Tawhīd is the belief in three things [i.e., three kinds only]:

1) _Tawhīd Ar-Rubūbiyyah._ توحيد الربوبية

This encompasses the belief in the [Oneness] Lordship of Allāh. That He Alone is the Lord of the entire Universe and He Alone creates, sustains, organizes, plans, etc. for it. Allāh the Almighty said:

﴿ إِنَّ رَبَّكُمُ ٱللَّهُ ٱلَّذِى خَلَقَ ٱلسَّمَٰوَٰتِ وَٱلْأَرْضَ فِى سِتَّةِ أَيَّامٍ ثُمَّ ٱسْتَوَىٰ عَلَى ٱلْعَرْشِ يُغْشِى ٱلَّيْلَ ٱلنَّهَارَ يَطْلُبُهُۥ حَثِيثًا وَٱلشَّمْسَ وَٱلْقَمَرَ وَٱلنُّجُومَ مُسَخَّرَٰتٍۭ بِأَمْرِهِۦٓ ۗ أَلَا لَهُ ٱلْخَلْقُ وَٱلْأَمْرُ ۗ تَبَارَكَ ٱللَّهُ رَبُّ ٱلْعَٰلَمِينَ ﴾

﴾ Indeed your Lord is Allāh, Who created the heavens and the earth in Six days, and then He rose over [Istawā] the Throne [in a manner befitting His Majesty]. He brings the night as a cover over the day, seeking it rapidly, and [He created] the sun, the moon, the stars subjected to His Command. Surely, His is the creation and the Commandment. Blessed is Allāh, the Lord of the Ālamīn [mankind , jinn and all that exists]. ﴿ *7:54.*

2) _Tawhīd Al-Ulūhiyyah._ توحيد الألوهية

The belief that all worship is for Allāh Alone i.e., prayer, slaughter, fasting, vowing etc. Allāh the Exalted said:

﴿ وَٱعْبُدُوا۟ ٱللَّهَ وَلَا تُشْرِكُوا۟ بِهِۦ شَيْـًٔا ﴾

﴾ Worship Allāh and join none with Him in worship,... ﴿ 4:36

﴿ وَإِلَٰهُكُمْ إِلَٰهٌ وَٰحِدٌ ۖ لَّآ إِلَٰهَ إِلَّا هُوَ ٱلرَّحْمَٰنُ ٱلرَّحِيمُ ﴾

﴾ And your Ilāh [God] is one Ilāh [God Allāh], La ilāha illa Huwa [there is none who has the right to be worshipped but He], the Most gracious, the Most Merciful. ﴿ 2:163.

3) _Tawhīd Al-Asmā` wa As-Sifāt._ توحيد الأسماء والصفات

Tawhīd Al-Asmā` wa As-Sifāt encompasses the belief in the uniqueness of the names and characteristics of Allāh. We affirm all of the names and characteristics that Allāh has affirmed for Himself as well as what His Messenger [ﷺ] has affirmed for Him. We must accept these names and characteristics in accordance with the Qur`ān and Authentic *Sunnah* with the understanding of the *Salaf* without changing them or disagreeing with them. Allāh the Most High said:

﴿ وَلِلَّهِ ٱلْأَسْمَآءُ ٱلْحُسْنَىٰ فَٱدْعُوهُ بِهَا ۖ وَذَرُوا۟ ٱلَّذِينَ يُلْحِدُونَ فِىٓ أَسْمَـٰٓئِهِۦ ۚ سَيُجْزَوْنَ مَا كَانُوا۟ يَعْمَلُونَ ﴿١٨٠﴾ ﴾

﴾And [all] the Most beautiful Names belong to Allāh so call on Him by them, and leave the company of those who belie or deny [or utter impious speech against]His names. They will be requited for what they used to do.﴿ 7:180.

[*Shaykh* Sālih Al-'Abūd, *shaykh* 'Ubayd Al-Jābirī [حفظهما الله], as well as others have said that the division of *Tawhīd* into 3 categories was first done by Abū Hanīfah the earliest of the four Imams, who died in the year 150H and was from the three preferred generations. He did not invent these categories but simply clarified what was left with us by the Prophet [ﷺ] to teach the people their religion.]

I make this extremely important chapter short as we shall cover the related matter in the following chapter, by the will of Allāh.

CHAPTER 4

SHIRK [POLYTHEISIM]

Let us clarify what *Shirk* is, lest one committing it feels free from it or one avoiding it falls into it unknowingly. And may Allāh the All-Aware, the Self-Subsisting, keep us far from it , Āmīn.

Shirk means polytheism in any form. Polytheism refers to the worship of any creation instead of or along with the only true Deity, Allāh, the Almighty. *Shirk* is a sin He will not forgive except with complete repentance and thereafter absolute abstention. Allāh said:

﴿ يَسْـَٔلُونَكَ عَنِ ٱلسَّاعَةِ أَيَّانَ مُرْسَىٰهَا ۖ قُلْ إِنَّمَا عِلْمُهَا عِندَ رَبِّى ۖ لَا يُجَلِّيهَا لِوَقْتِهَآ
إِلَّا هُوَ ۚ ثَقُلَتْ فِى ٱلسَّمَـٰوَٰتِ وَٱلْأَرْضِ ۚ لَا تَأْتِيكُمْ إِلَّا بَغْتَةً ۗ يَسْـَٔلُونَكَ كَأَنَّكَ حَفِىٌّ
عَنْهَا ۖ قُلْ إِنَّمَا عِلْمُهَا عِندَ ٱللَّهِ وَلَـٰكِنَّ أَكْثَرَ ٱلنَّاسِ لَا يَعْلَمُونَ ﴿١٨٧﴾ ﴾

﴾ Verily, Allāh forgives not that partners should be set up with Him in worship, but He forgives except that [anything else] to whom He pleases, and whoever sets up partners with Allāh in worship, he has indeed invented a tremendous sin.﴿ 4:48

﴿ ٱللَّهُ ٱلَّذِى خَلَقَكُمْ ثُمَّ رَزَقَكُمْ ثُمَّ يُمِيتُكُمْ ثُمَّ يُحْيِيكُمْ ۖ هَلْ مِن شُرَكَآئِكُم مَّن
يَفْعَلُ مِن ذَٰلِكُم مِّن شَىْءٍ ۚ سُبْحَـٰنَهُۥ وَتَعَـٰلَىٰ عَمَّا يُشْرِكُونَ ﴿٤٠﴾ ﴾

﴾ Allāh is He who created you, then provided food for you, then will cause you to die, then [again] He will give you life [on the Day of Resurrection]. Is there any of your [so-called] partners [of Allāh] that do anything of that? Glory is to Him! And Exalted is He above all that [evil] they associate [with Him].﴿ 30:40

﴿ وَأَلْقَوْا۟ إِلَى ٱللَّهِ يَوْمَئِذٍ ٱلسَّلَمَ ۖ وَضَلَّ عَنْهُم مَّا كَانُوا۟ يَفْتَرُونَ ﴿٨٧﴾ ﴾

﴾ And they will offer [their full] submission to Allāh [Alone] on that Day, and their false deities[all that they used to invoke besides Allāh, e.g. idols,

saints, priests, monks, angels, jinn, Jibrā'īl, Messengers] will vanish from them.﴿ 16:87

﴿ ۞ مُنِيبِينَ إِلَيْهِ وَاتَّقُوهُ وَأَقِيمُوا الصَّلَوٰةَ وَلَا تَكُونُوا مِنَ الْمُشْرِكِينَ (٣١) مِنَ
الَّذِينَ فَرَّقُوا دِينَهُمْ وَكَانُوا شِيَعًا كُلُّ حِزْبٍ بِمَا لَدَيْهِمْ فَرِحُونَ (٣٢) وَإِذَا
مَسَّ النَّاسَ ضُرٌّ دَعَوْا رَبَّهُم مُّنِيبِينَ إِلَيْهِ ثُمَّ إِذَا أَذَاقَهُم مِّنْهُ رَحْمَةً إِذَا فَرِيقٌ مِّنْهُم
بِرَبِّهِمْ يُشْرِكُونَ (٣٣) ﴾

﴾ ...and be not of the mushrikūn [the polytheists, idolaters, disbeliveers in the Oneness of Allāh]. Of those who split up their religion [i.e., who left the true Islāmic Monotheism], and became sects, [i.e., they invented new things in the religion [bida'], and followed their vain desires], each sect rejoicing in that which is with it. And when harm touches men, they cry sincerely only to their Lord [Allāh], turning to Him in repentance; but when He gives them a taste of His Mercy, behold, a party of them associates partners in worship with their Lord.﴿ 30:31-33

We were asked at the beginning of our creation to affirm the Oneness of Allāh and therefore have the fitrah that every human is born with, inclining us towards monotheism that only later in life is distorted.

Allāh, the Almighty, the Exalted, said:

﴿ وَإِذْ أَخَذَ رَبُّكَ مِنۢ بَنِىٓ ءَادَمَ مِن ظُهُورِهِمْ ذُرِّيَّتَهُمْ وَأَشْهَدَهُمْ عَلَىٰٓ أَنفُسِهِمْ
أَلَسْتُ بِرَبِّكُمْ قَالُوا بَلَىٰ شَهِدْنَآ أَن تَقُولُوا يَوْمَ الْقِيَـٰمَةِ إِنَّا كُنَّا عَنْ هَـٰذَا
غَـٰفِلِينَ (١٧٢) أَوْ تَقُولُوٓا إِنَّمَآ أَشْرَكَ ءَابَآؤُنَا مِن قَبْلُ وَكُنَّا ذُرِّيَّةً مِّنۢ بَعْدِهِمْ
أَفَتُهْلِكُنَا بِمَا فَعَلَ الْمُبْطِلُونَ (١٧٣) ﴾

﴾ And [remember] when your Lord brought forth from the children of Adam, from their loins, their seed [or from Adams loin his offspring] and made them testify as to themselves [saying] 'Am I not your Lord?' They said: ' Yes! We testify,' lest you should say on the Day of resurrection:

'Verily, we have been unaware of this. Or lest you should say, ' It was only our fathers aforetime who took others as partners in worship along with Allāh, and we were [merely their] descendents after them; will You then destroy us because of the deeds of men who practiced bātil [i.e., polytheism and committing crimes and sins, invoking and worshipping others besides Allāh]. **7:172-173**

" Allāh will say to that person of the [Hell] Fire who will receive the least punishment, ' If you had everything on earth would you give it as a ransom to free yourself [i.e., save yourself from this Fire]?' He will say, 'Yes'. Then Allāh will say, ' While you were in the backbone of Adam, I asked you much less than this, [i.e., not to worship others besides Me] but you insisted on worshipping others besides Me." [124]

To understand this verse and *hadīth* better we shall use the explanation of one of the companions. "Ubayy Ibn Ka'b [ﷺ], while interpreting the above verse [***"And [remember] when your Lord..."]*** said that Allāh gathered all the offspring of Adam at one place, formed them into groups, for instance, He separated the Prophets, saints, martyrs, pious people, obedient ones, disobedient ones into different groups. Similarly, He segregated the Jews, the Christians, the Polytheists and the followers of every religion. Then whatever facial features and shapes one had to be given in this world, Allāh made them appear exactly in the same manner there accordingly. Someone who was made to appear as good-looking. Someone was made to appear as bad-looking... Then all of them were given the faculty of speech and then asked, 'Am I not your *Rabb*.' All of them acknowledged the Lordship of Allāh and then Allāh took a pledge from all of them to the effect that they shall not take anyone as there ruler and master except Him Alone and shall not consider anyone worthy of being worshipped except Him Alone. Then Allāh made all of the seven strata of the heavens and the earth as a witness

[124] *Sahīh Al-Bukhārī*, [Eng. Trans. vol. 4 #551].

and said that the Prophets shall be sent unto you to remind you of this pledge of yours and they shall bring with them the heavenly Scriptures."[125]

An excerpt from Shah Ismail Shahīd's, *Taqwiyat-ul-Iman* is quite enlightening, by Allāh's will, to point out some of the obvious.

The excuse of forgetfulness shall not be accepted.

If someone thinks that after being in this world, we no longer remember the said pledge and in case we commit an act of *shirk* now, we shall not be punished there is no question of forgetfulness. The answer to this notion of theirs is that there are many things a man does not remember but once reminded by a credible and authentic person, it all comes back to his memory. For instance no one remembers his date of birth but once he hears about it from people, he has no qualms about saying it with certainty that I was born on such and such a date, in such and such a year at such and such an hour. He only recognizes his parents upon hearing from people. He does not consider anyone else his mother. In case one does not perform his obligations towards his mother and claims someone else as his mother, the people are bound to ridicule and censure him. In response to their chidings, if he postulates that as long as I do not remember my birth, why should I consider this woman as my mother? People have no reason to castigate me about it. Once this person blurts out such a statement, people shall definitely regard him to be a perfect moron and a rude person. It thus becomes known to us that since a man believes in many a thing to the extent of certitude on the basis of hearing them merely from people, how is it that he should disbelieve the teachings of the Prophets who are people of great status and magnificent caliber!

---

[125] Excerpt from *Taqwiyat-ul-Iman*, by Shah Ismail Shahīd. Origin in *Musnad* of Imām Ahmad.

There are two types of *Shirk*:

1] ***Shirk Al-Akbar*** [Major *Shirk*].

This is the worst of them; it involves the making of invocations, intention of worship or total obedience to other than Allāh. And Allāh said:

﴿ وَإِلَىٰ رَبِّكَ فَارْغَب ﴿٨﴾ ﴾

﴾***And to your Lord [Alone] turn [all your intentions and hopes and] your invocations.***﴿ ***94:8***

2] ***Shirk Al-Asghar*** [minor *shirk*, or *riyā`*, showing off.]

Any actions whose performance was meant for display. This includes legal forms of worship like prayer done in the appropriate manner, however it is done [perfectly] for the sake of fame. The Prophet [ﷺ] said:

"Shall I not tell you what I fear for you more than the false messiah? The companions said, ' Indeed O Messenger of Allāh.' He said:' Inconspicuous shirk, as when a person improves his rendering of the salāh when he knows that others are watching."[126]

"It is as inconspicuous as a black ant moving on a black stone in the darkness of night."[127]

*"Verily that which I fear for you most of all is **Minor Shirk** or showing of. actions Allāh will say on the Day of Judgment when He is rewarding the people for that which they used to do; 'Go to those whom you used to show off in the world and see if you find any reward with them!'"*[128]

It is hard to detect and easy to fall into.

---

[126] *Musnad* of Imām Ahmad as well as Ibn Mājah declared *hasan* by Al-Haythamī.

[127] *Kitāb At-Tawhīd*, by Muhammad Ibn 'Abd Al-Wahhāb, English translation pg.139. Origin of the *hadīth* found in *Musnad* of Imām Ahmad and authenticated by *Shaykh* Al-Albānī.

[128] *Musnad* of Imām Ahmad and declared *sahīh* by *Shaykh* Al-Albānī.

Other Things to Know about *Shirk*.

Rather than try to cover each kind in depth I think it would benefit you more to use particular instances and Allāh knows best. To achieve this end we shall use excerpts from *Shaykh Al-Islām* Mu<u>h</u>ammad Ibn Abd Al-Wahhāb's, *Kitāb At-Taw<u>h</u>īd* [129].

1] To wear a ring, twine or anything similar to them for prevention or lifting of harm or affliction is an act of *Shirk*.

Allāh, the Almighty, said:

﴿ وَلَئِن سَأَلْتَهُم مَّنْ خَلَقَ ٱلسَّمَٰوَٰتِ وَٱلْأَرْضَ لَيَقُولُنَّ ٱللَّهُ ۚ قُلْ أَفَرَءَيْتُم مَّا تَدْعُونَ مِن دُونِ ٱللَّهِ إِنْ أَرَادَنِىَ ٱللَّهُ بِضُرٍّ هَلْ هُنَّ كَٰشِفَٰتُ ضُرِّهِۦٓ أَوْ أَرَادَنِى بِرَحْمَةٍ هَلْ هُنَّ مُمْسِكَٰتُ رَحْمَتِهِۦ ۚ قُلْ حَسْبِىَ ٱللَّهُ ۖ عَلَيْهِ يَتَوَكَّلُ ٱلْمُتَوَكِّلُونَ ﴿٣٨﴾ ﴾

﴾ Say: Tell me then, the things that you invoke besides Allāh, - if Allāh intended some harm for me, could they remove His Harm, or if He [Allāh] intended some mercy for me, could they withhold His Mercy? Say: sufficient for me is Allāh: in Him those who trust [i.e., believers] must put their trust.﴿ 39:38

"The Prophet [ﷺ] once saw a man with a brass ring on his hand and asked him, '**What is this?**' The man replied, 'To overcome the weakness of old age.' He said, '**Remove it, for, it can only add to your weakness. Should death overtake you while you are wearing it, you would never succeed.**'"[130]

---

[129] Authors note: some information has its exact order changed, and notes, Qur`ān and *<u>h</u>adīth* added to fit the concise manner the chapter need be arranged in. However the authenticity and meaning is still intact, by the will of Allāh.

[130] *Kitāb At-Taw<u>h</u>īd*, by Mu<u>h</u>ammad Ibn 'Abd Al-Wahhāb, English translation pg. 43. Origin of the *<u>h</u>adīth* found in *Musnad* of Imām A<u>h</u>mad .

2] On taking orders from others.

Allāh, the Almighty said:

﴿ أُو۟لَٰٓئِكَ ٱلَّذِينَ يَدْعُونَ يَبْتَغُونَ إِلَىٰ رَبِّهِمُ ٱلْوَسِيلَةَ أَيُّهُمْ أَقْرَبُ
وَيَرْجُونَ رَحْمَتَهُۥ وَيَخَافُونَ عَذَابَهُۥٓ ۚ إِنَّ عَذَابَ رَبِّكَ كَانَ مَحْذُورًا ﴿٥٧﴾ ﴾

﴾ Those whom they call upon [like Jesus- the son of Mary, Ezra, angels and others] desire [for themselves] means of access to their Lord [Allāh] as to which of them should be nearest and they [Jesus, Ezra, angels, etc.] hope for His Mercy and fear His Torment. Verily the Torment of your Lord is something to be afraid of.﴿ 17:57

﴿ ٱتَّخَذُوٓا۟ أَحْبَارَهُمْ وَرُهْبَٰنَهُمْ أَرْبَابًا مِّن دُونِ ٱللَّهِ وَٱلْمَسِيحَ ٱبْنَ مَرْيَمَ
وَمَآ أُمِرُوٓا۟ إِلَّا لِيَعْبُدُوٓا۟ إِلَٰهًا وَٰحِدًا ۖ لَّآ إِلَٰهَ إِلَّا هُوَ ۚ سُبْحَٰنَهُۥ عَمَّا يُشْرِكُونَ ﴿٣١﴾ ﴾

﴾ They [Jews and Christians] took their rabbis and their monks to be their lords besides Allāh [by obeying them in things which they made lawful or unlawful according to their own desires without being ordered by Allāh], and [they also took as their Lord] Messiah, son of Mary, while they [Jews and Christians] were commanded [in the Tawrāt [Torah] and the Injīl [Gospel]] to worship none but One Ilāh [god- Allāh] La ilāha illa Huwa [none has the right to be worshipped but He].﴿ 9:31

﴿ وَمِنَ ٱلنَّاسِ مَن يَتَّخِذُ مِن دُونِ ٱللَّهِ أَندَادًا يُحِبُّونَهُمْ كَحُبِّ ٱللَّهِ ۖ وَٱلَّذِينَ
ءَامَنُوٓا۟ أَشَدُّ حُبًّا لِّلَّهِ ۗ وَلَوْ يَرَى ٱلَّذِينَ ظَلَمُوٓا۟ إِذْ يَرَوْنَ ٱلْعَذَابَ أَنَّ ٱلْقُوَّةَ لِلَّهِ
جَمِيعًا وَأَنَّ ٱللَّهَ شَدِيدُ ٱلْعَذَابِ ﴿١٦٥﴾ ﴾

﴾ And of mankind are some who take [for worship] others besides Allāh as rivals [to Allāh]. They love them as they love Allāh but those who believe love Allāh more [than anything else].﴿ 2:165

Allāh warns us in the following verses then says:

﴿ وَمَا هُم بِخَٰرِجِينَ مِنَ ٱلنَّارِ ﴿١٦٧﴾ ﴾

﴾ And they will never get out of the Fire.﴿ 2:167

3] Slaughtering for other than Allāh.

Allāh, the Almighty, said:

﴿ فَصَلِّ لِرَبِّكَ وَٱنْحَرْ ﴿٢﴾ ﴾

﴿ *Therefore turn in prayer to your Lord and sacrifice [to Him only].* ﴾ [108:2]

"A man entered Paradise because of a fly and a man entered Hell-Fire because of a fly.' They [the companions] asked, ' How was that possible O Messenger of Allāh?' He said, ' Two men passed by people who had an idol by which they would not allow anyone to pass without making a sacrifice to it. They ordered one man to make a sacrifice. He said, 'I have nothing to present as an offering.' The people told him, ' Sacrifice something, even if it be a fly! So he presented a fly [to their idol]. They opened the way for him, and thus he entered the Hell Fire. They said to the other man, ' Sacrifice something!' He said, ' I will never sacrifice anything to other than Allāh, Most Majestic and Glorious.' So they struck his throat and killed him; and he therefore entered Paradise."[131]

The man who went to Hell Fire was a Muslim. If he would have been a [*Kāfir*] disbeliever, the Prophet [ﷺ] would not have said, **"He went to Hell merely for a fly."**

4] To seek help from other than Allāh [*Istighāthah*] or to invoke other than Him is an act of *Shirk*.

Allāh, the Most Exalted, said:

﴿ وَلَا تَدْعُ مِن دُونِ ٱللَّهِ مَا لَا يَنفَعُكَ وَلَا يَضُرُّكَ فَإِن فَعَلْتَ فَإِنَّكَ إِذًا مِّنَ ٱلظَّٰلِمِينَ ﴿١٠٦﴾ وَإِن يَمْسَسْكَ ٱللَّهُ بِضُرٍّ فَلَا كَاشِفَ لَهُۥٓ إِلَّا هُوَ وَإِن يُرِدْكَ بِخَيْرٍ فَلَا رَآدَّ لِفَضْلِهِۦ يُصِيبُ بِهِۦ مَن يَشَآءُ مِنْ عِبَادِهِۦ وَهُوَ ٱلْغَفُورُ ٱلرَّحِيمُ ﴿١٠٧﴾ ﴾

---

[131] *Kitāb At-Tawhīd*, by Muhammad Ibn 'Abd Al-Wahhāb, English translation pg. 53. Origin of the *hadīth* found in *Masnad* of Imām Ahmad .

﴾ *And invoke not other than Allāh any that will neither profit you nor hurt you, but [in case] you did so, you shall certainly be of the dhālimūn [wrong doers]. And if Allāh touches you with hurt, there is none who can remove it but He; and if He intends any good for you, there is none who can repel His Favour which He causes to reach whomsoever of His slaves He will. And He is the Oft-Forgiving, Most Merciful.* ﴿ *10:106-107*

﴿ وَمَنْ أَضَلُّ مِمَّن يَدْعُواْ مِن دُونِ ٱللَّهِ مَن لَّا يَسْتَجِيبُ لَهُۥٓ إِلَىٰ يَوْمِ ٱلْقِيَٰمَةِ وَهُمْ عَن دُعَآئِهِمْ غَٰفِلُونَ ۝ وَإِذَا حُشِرَ ٱلنَّاسُ كَانُواْ لَهُمْ أَعْدَآءً وَكَانُواْ بِعِبَادَتِهِمْ كَٰفِرِينَ ۝ ﴾

﴾ *And who is more astray than one who calls [invokes] besides Allāh, such as will not answer him till the Day of Resurrection; and who are [even] unaware of their calls [invocations] to them? And when Mankind are gathered [on the Day of Resurrection] they [false deities] will become enemies for them and will deny their worshipping.* ﴿ *46:5-6*

This is a major form of *Shirk*. Religious sects like the Catholics and even some Muslim sects worship dead saints in the guise of intercession. As Allāh is the All-Aware, He doesn't need intercessors to hear or present your needs, this argument is void. We shall deal with the type of intercession that Allāh will permit on the Day of Standing. Since the pious people they seek intercession from are dead, they are unaware, as Allāh said, of all the speech directed towards them, and will disown them on that Day. These people have gone so far as to build places of worship over their graves, they then kiss their graves, leave gifts and make sacrifices earnestly supplicating to these dead people. This is the work of the cursed *Shayṯān*, making them believe these futile and sinful acts are of benefiṯ to them. Sisters, beware and warn your families, this can only lead to the Hell-Fire forever! " Umm Salamah mentioned to Allāh's Messenger [ﷺ] that in Abyssinia she saw a church full of pictures and statues. He [ﷺ] said:

"When a righteous man or a pious worshipper among them dies, they build a place of worship over his grave and set up all kinds of pictures and statues. They are the worst of all creatures before Allāh. They combine two evils; worshipping at the graves and making graven images and statues." [132]

5] On Sorcery [*Sihr*] and Soothsayers.

Allāh, the Mighty, said:

﴿ وَلَمَّا جَآءَهُمْ رَسُولٌ مِّنْ عِندِ ٱللَّهِ مُصَدِّقٌ لِّمَا مَعَهُمْ نَبَذَ فَرِيقٌ مِّنَ ٱلَّذِينَ أُوتُوا۟ ٱلْكِتَـٰبَ كِتَـٰبَ ٱللَّهِ وَرَآءَ ظُهُورِهِمْ كَأَنَّهُمْ لَا يَعْلَمُونَ ﴿١٠١﴾ وَٱتَّبَعُوا۟ مَا تَتْلُوا۟ ٱلشَّيَـٰطِينُ عَلَىٰ مُلْكِ سُلَيْمَـٰنَ ۖ وَمَا كَفَرَ سُلَيْمَـٰنُ وَلَـٰكِنَّ ٱلشَّيَـٰطِينَ كَفَرُوا۟ يُعَلِّمُونَ ٱلنَّاسَ ٱلسِّحْرَ وَمَآ أُنزِلَ عَلَى ٱلْمَلَكَيْنِ بِبَابِلَ هَـٰرُوتَ وَمَـٰرُوتَ ۚ وَمَا يُعَلِّمَانِ مِنْ أَحَدٍ حَتَّىٰ يَقُولَآ إِنَّمَا نَحْنُ فِتْنَةٌ فَلَا تَكْفُرْ ۖ فَيَتَعَلَّمُونَ مِنْهُمَا مَا يُفَرِّقُونَ بِهِۦ بَيْنَ ٱلْمَرْءِ وَزَوْجِهِۦ ۚ وَمَا هُم بِضَآرِّينَ بِهِۦ مِنْ أَحَدٍ إِلَّا بِإِذْنِ ٱللَّهِ ۚ وَيَتَعَلَّمُونَ مَا يَضُرُّهُمْ وَلَا يَنفَعُهُمْ ۚ وَلَقَدْ عَلِمُوا۟ لَمَنِ ٱشْتَرَىٰهُ مَا لَهُۥ فِى ٱلْـَٔاخِرَةِ مِنْ خَلَـٰقٍ ۚ وَلَبِئْسَ مَا شَرَوْا۟ بِهِۦٓ أَنفُسَهُمْ ۚ لَوْ كَانُوا۟ يَعْلَمُونَ ﴿١٠٢﴾ ﴾

﴿ And when there came to them a Messenger from Allāh [Muhammad ﷺ] confirming what was with them, a party of those who were given the Scripture threw away the Book of Allāh behind their backs as if they did not know! They followed what the Shayātīn [devils] gave out [falsely of the magic] in the lifetime of Sulaymān [Solomon]. Sulaymān did not disbelieve, but the Shayātīn disbelieved, teaching men magic and such things that came down at Babylon to the two angels, Hārūt and Mārūt, but neither of these two [angels] taught anyone [such things] till they had said, ' We are only for trial, so disbelieve not [by learning this magic from us].' And from these [angels] people learn that by which they cause separation of between man and a wife, but they could not thus harm

[132] *Sahīh Al-Bukhārī*, [Eng. Trans. vol. 2 #425].

anyone except by Allāh's Leave. And they learn that which harms them and profits them not And indeed they knew that the buyers of it [magic] would have no share in the Hereafter.﴿ 2:101-102

"Save yourselves from the seven destroyers.' The companions [ﷺ] asked: 'O Messenger of Allāh, what are those?' He said, 'To associate anything with Allāh, sorcery [magic], without any just cause killing a life Allāh has forbidden, taking interest [usury], usurping the wealth of orphans, turning back from the battlefield, and making a false charge [accusation] against the chaste but unmindful women [i.e., they never even think of anything touching their chastity]." [133]

" When Allāh decrees some order in the heaven, the angels flutter their wings indicating complete surrender to His saying, which sounds like chains being dragged on rock. And when the [state of] fear is banished from them their hearts, they say, 'What is it that your Lord has said?' They say: 'The truth.' And He is the Most High, the Most Great.' Then the stealthy listeners [devils] hear this order, and these stealth listeners are like this, one over the other [Sufyān, a sub-narrator demonstrated that by holding his hand upright and separating the fingers]. A stealthy listener hears a word, which he will convey to that which is below him and the second will convey it to the wizard or foreteller. Sometimes a flame [fire] may strike the devil before he can convey it sometimes he may convey it before that flame [fire] strikes him, whereupon the wizard adds to that word a hundred lies. Then the people will say, 'Didn't he [the magician] tell such and such a thing on such and such a date?' So that magician is said to have told the truth because of the statement which has been heard from the heavens." [134]

---

[133] *Kitāb At-Tawhīd*, by Muhammad Ibn 'Abd Al-Wahhāb, [Eng. Trans. Pg. 96. origin in *Al-Bukhārī* and *Muslim*].

[134] *Sahīh Al-Bukhārī*, [Eng. Trans. Vol.6 # 223].

6] Clarification on types of Sorcery.

The Messenger of Allāh [ﷺ] said:

"Verily, Al-'Iyāfah [letting birds fly to foretell events] and At-Tarq [drawing lines on earth to predict events] and At-Tiyarah [taking sight on some object as a bad omen] are Al-Jibt [sorceries/ magic]." [135]

"Whoever learns a part of astrology [taking knowledge from the stars] has learned a part of sorcery [magic]. Those who learn more are getting that much more [sin to their credit]." [136]

" Whoever tied a knot and blew on it, has committed sorcery and whoever has committed sorcery has committed shirk. Whoever wears an amulet or talisman will be subject to its control." [137]

"Shall I not tell ***you*** *what Al-'Adh [literally lying, sorcery etc.] is? It is* ***conveying false*** *rumors for the purpose of causing disputes between people."* [138]

"Some eloquent speech is as effective as magic. [So beautiful that it constitutes sorcery]" [139]

[I am sure most people have attended a gathering where a person speaks with such eloquence that they transform lies or half truths into what seems to be so realistic and truthful. They stir up their audience, captivating their minds and hearts to a point that they change their opinions. However the

---

[135] *Kitāb At-Tawhīd*, by Muhammad Ibn 'Abd Al-Wahhāb, [Eng. Trans. Pg. 99.Origin in *Musnad* of Imām Ahmad. #15350].

[136] *Kitāb At-Tawhīd*, by Muhammad Ibn 'Abd Al-Wahhāb, [Eng. Trans. Pg, 99. Sunan of Abū Dāwud. Eng. Trans. Vol.3. #3896].

[137] *Kitāb At-Tawhīd*, by Muhammad Ibn 'Abd Al-Wahhāb, [Eng. Trans. pg. 100. Origin in *Sunan* of Nasā'ī].

[138] *Kitāb At-Tawhīd*, by Muhammad Ibn 'Abd Al-Wahhāb, [Eng. Trans. *Sahīh Muslim*, Vol. 4, #4718].

[139] *Kitāb At-Tawhīd*, by Muhammad Ibn 'Abd Al-Wahhāb, [Eng. Trans. Pg. 100. Origin in *Sahīh Al-Bukhārī* Eng. Trans. Vol. 7. #662].

same audience later on when it is repeated back to them, they might feel foolish at being so gullible while the people with weaker personalities might still hang on to it even if the truth is pointed out to them with proofs.]

"Whoever visited a fortuneteller or a soothsayer and believes in his words, has disbelieved in what was revealed to Muhammad [ﷺ][i.e., the Qur`ān]." [140]

"Whoever goes to a fortune teller and asks him something and believes in his words will have his prayer rejected for forty days." [141]

7] Curing through magic spells.

Allāh's Messenger[ﷺ] was asked about *An-Nushrah* [the act of seeking cure from magical spells/incantation], he said:

"It is one of the deeds of Satan." [142]

Ibn Al-Qayyim wrote, '*An-Nushrah* is removing effects of sorcery/spell from the affected one, and is of two types. [one permissible one not]

1) The use of magic [sorcery] to remove the effects of another magic and it is an act of the Satan to which the comment of Imam Al-Hasan Al-Basrī applies i.e., that one who performs it and the patient, both get closer to the Satan by that which he loves. Satan then removes the effects of magic from the afflicted.
2) The effects of magic can be removed by using recitation of Qur`ānic verses, by offering legitimate prayers [*ruqyah*] also by using pharmaceutical preparations. This is the permissible method.

---

[140] *Kitāb At-Tawhīd*, by Muhammad Ibn 'Abd Al-Wahhāb, Pg. 101. [Origin in *Sunan* of Abū Dāwud. Eng. Trans. Vol.3. #3895].

[141] *Kitāb At-Tawhīd*, by Muhammad Ibn 'Abd Al-Wahhāb. Pg. 101. [Origin in *Sahīh Muslim* Vol.4 #5540].

[142] *Kitāb At-Tawhīd*, by Muhammad Ibn 'Abd Al-Wahhāb, Pg. 104. [Origin in *Musnad* of Imām Ahmad. #13621].

8] Bad omens.

The Prophet [ﷺ] said:

"Whoever is turned back by At-Tiyarah[bad omens] has committed shirk.' They asked, 'What is the atonement for such a sin?' The Prophet [ﷺ] answered, 'To say: O Lord there is no good except the good which You bestow. There is no evil except the evil, which You decree. And there is no true God except You.'" [143]

9] Seeking judgment from other than Allāh and His Messenger is hypocrisy [and *shirk*].

Allāh, the Almighty said:

﴿ أَفَحُكْمَ ٱلْجَٰهِلِيَّةِ يَبْغُونَ ۚ وَمَنْ أَحْسَنُ مِنَ ٱللَّهِ حُكْمًا لِّقَوْمٍ يُوقِنُونَ ﴿٥٠﴾ ﴾

﴾ Do they seek the judgment of [the days] of ignorance? And who is better in judgment than Allāh for a People who have firm Faith.﴿ 5:50

"There was a dispute between two men. One of them said:' Let us take the dispute to the Prophet [ﷺ] for his judgment' but the other said' Take it to Ka'b Ibn Ashraf ' [one was a Jew the other was a Muslim hypocrite the hypocrite suggested Ka'b]. Thereafter both of them came to 'Umar [ؓ] [after the Messenger of Allāh sent them to him to repeat what had occurred]. One of them told him the story so he asked the other who was not content to take the case to the Prophet [ﷺ]. ' Is it so?' He said 'Yes'. 'Umar then struck him with his sword and killed him."[144]

10] What is said about the one whom is not satisfied with an oath taken by Allāh's name.

---

[143] *Kitāb At-Tawhīd*, by Muhammad Ibn 'Abd Al-Wahhāb, Pg. 108. [*Musnad* of Imām Ahmad].

[144] *Kitāb At-Tawhīd*, by Muhammad Ibn 'Abd Al-Wahhāb, Pg. 135.

Should be satisfied with it, and whoever is not satisfied with it is not from the slaves of Allāh." [145]

11] Whoever makes fun of anything where mention is made of Allāh or the Qur`ān or the Messenger [ﷺ] commits disbelief.

﴿ وَلَئِن سَأَلْتَهُمْ لَيَقُولُنَّ إِنَّمَا كُنَّا نَخُوضُ وَنَلْعَبُ قُلْ أَبِاللَّهِ وَءَايَٰتِهِۦ وَرَسُولِهِۦ كُنتُمْ تَسْتَهْزِءُونَ ۝ لَا تَعْتَذِرُوا۟ قَدْ كَفَرْتُم بَعْدَ إِيمَٰنِكُمْ إِن نَّعْفُ عَن طَآئِفَةٍ مِّنكُمْ نُعَذِّبْ طَآئِفَةًۢ بِأَنَّهُمْ كَانُوا۟ مُجْرِمِينَ ۝ ﴾

﴾ If you ask them [about this], they declare: ' We were only talking idly and joking', say: ' Was it at Allāh, and His Āyāt [proofs, evidences, signs, verses, revelations, etc.] and His Messenger [ﷺ] that you were mocking, make no excuse, you have disbelieved after you had believed. ﴿ 9:65-66

This means that the magnitude of such a sin is that it makes you a disbeliever [*Kāfir*][146], may Allāh, the Majestic, keep us far from such *kufr*, Āmīn.

---

[145] *Kitāb At-Tawhīd*, by Muhammad Ibn 'Abd Al-Wahhāb, Pg. 141. [Original *hadīth* collected by Ibn Mājah with good *isnād*]

[146] It is important to note that *takfīr* [i.e., declaring a *Muslim* to be a *kāfir*] is a very serious issue that should always be left in the hands of the scholars and should never be left in the hands of ordinary people even if they have some knowledge of religion. There are some important pre-conditions that the scholar or scholars must investigate thoroughly before the declaration can made:

i] The person must have reached the legal age of maturity.
ii] The person must not be retarded, insane or otherwise mentally incapacitated.
iii]The person must know that they are contradicting the laws and fundamental principles of Islām.
iv]The person must have willingly decided to do or say the act in question and must not have been forced or unwilling to do so.
v]The person must not have been in a state of forgetfulness.
vi]The person must not have been a *mujtahid* who was exerting himself seeking the truth.

Only after the scholars have thoroughly investigated all of these pre-conditions can the declaration be made, and then it is the responsibility of the appropriate government

12] To swear and take an oath [binding] upon Allāh.

"A man said: By Allāh! Allāh would not forgive such and such a [person]. Whereupon Allāh, the Exalted and Glorious said! ' Who is he who swears by Me that I would not grant pardon to so and so? I have granted pardon to so and so and blotted out your [the swearer's] deeds." [147]

In another ***hadīth*** it is said that the swearer was a faithful worshipper. Abū Hurayrah [ﷺ] said: "His one statement destroyed his life in this world and the Hereafter." I would like to remind the sister again about the *hadīth*, "**Hell is closer to us than our shoe laces**", this is an excellent example of how it is so.

Clarification of Intercession [as it is to be understood by all the children of Ādam].

First of all, one should never seek intercession from anyone in this worldly life as it amounts to *shirk*. Secondly, intercession will only be done on the Day of Resurrection and it will only be for the people of *Tawhīd*, whom Allāh is pleased with. And intercession can only be done by one also upon *Tawhīd* with whom Allāh is pleased. In other words, intercession will be done only on the Day of Judgment by the prophets, angels, martyrs and other such pious people for Muslims, who worshipped none but Allāh Alone. What may be done on earth is the intercession for each other with each other e.g. in courts of law.

To clarify this further, we shall use excerpts from *'Taqwiyat-ul-Iman'*

Only after the scholars have thoroughly investigated all of these pre-conditions can the declaration be made, and then it is the responsibility of the appropriate government authorities to impose the punishment and it should never be left up to ordinary individuals to impose the punishment.

[147] *Kitāb At-Tawhīd*, by Muhammad Ibn 'Abd Al-Wahhāb, Pg. 182. [Origin in *Sahīh Muslim*, Vol.4 #6350]

1) Intercession due to ones high-ranking status

[This includes the idea that]" the one who is near and dear to Allāh" or who enjoys high status in this world can intercede for you with Allāh, ". This is utterly impossible. A person who recognizes a creation to be such a mediator, is a polytheist and undoubtedly an ignorant person. He [or she] has not understood the meaning of Ilāh [Deity] and has not appreciated the status of The King of Kings at all.

...Everything comes into existence merely by His Will and He does not require matter and substance to create things...No one can either harm Him or benefit Him."

Allāh said:

﴿ قُلْ هُوَ ٱللَّهُ أَحَدٌ ۝١ ٱللَّهُ ٱلصَّمَدُ ۝٢ لَمْ يَلِدْ وَلَمْ يُولَدْ ۝٣ وَلَمْ يَكُن لَّهُۥ كُفُوًا أَحَدٌۢ ۝٤ ﴾

﴿ Say:' He is Allāh, [the] One. 'Allāh As-Samad [Allāh the Self-Sufficient Master, Whom all creatures need,[He neither eats nor drinks]]. 'He begets not nor was He begotten. ' And there is none co-equal or comparable unto Him.﴾ 112:1-4

2) Acceptance of ones intercession out of love.

"The king driven by love of the concerned person, takes into account the fact that invoking a beloved's displeasure shall in fact inflict pain on himself and hence he concedes to the request of his beloved. This kind of occurrence in the court of Allāh, the Almighty is impossible. If someone reckons a prophet or a saint to be this kind of intercessor, he is also a pure polytheist and an utterly ignorant person."

The third kind of intercession the esteemed author puts forth, is the one recognized by the *Salaf*.

3]Interceding with permission.

To bring a better understanding to the sister we shall use the author's most descriptive example.

" The third kind of intercession implies the situation wherein a thief indeed is found guilty of theft but he has not committed it by way of profession but has unfortunately slipped into it [being victim of circumstances]. Out of a feeling of guilt, this person now feels extremely remorseful, his head lowered downward constantly being gnawed by the fear of punishment. Paying due respect to the law of the land, he considers himself to be vice-ridden a perpetrator of sin and thus eligible for punishment. He does not flee the king and does not request a courtier or minister to intercede with the king for his amnesty. He seeks no support other than the king himself... The king, taking pity on his deplorable condition intends to connive at his delinquency but also wants to uphold the law of the country lest it should be looked down on by the people. Now a governor or minister after getting a nod from the king comes forward to intercede on his behalf. So the king grants pardon the thief apparently on the plea that so long as the governor has himself interceded for him he has to honor it."

REMEMBER dear sister, *Shirk* is inconspicuous.

" It is as inconspicuous as a black ant moving [crawling] on a black stone in the darkness of night."

It is to it is to swear: 'by Allāh and by your life' and 'by my life.' It is also to say, 'Had there not been this little dog or the duck in the house, the thief would not have entered,' Or like the statement of a man his companion, 'By Allāh's Will and your will...' or 'Had it not been Allāh's and so-and-so's will...' etc. Do not mention anybody with Allāh because all of it is *Shirk.*[148]

Finally to help you remember your place in creation so that you do not transgress your bounds, the Prophet [ﷺ] informed us:

[148] End of excerpt.

"Do you know how much the distance between the earth and Heaven is?' We said, 'Allāh and His Messenger know better.' Then he [ﷺ] said, 'The distance between them is 500 years, and the distance between one heaven and the next is 500 years, and the dimension of each heaven will take 500 years to travel, and there is a sea between the Throne which has between its lowest and highest ends the distance like that between the heavens and the earth [i.e., 500 years]. And Allāh, the Most Exalted is above that and nothing is secret from Him of the deeds of the children of Ādam [humans]." [149] *In another hadīth by Ibn Mas'ūd the addition, "and the distance between the seventh heaven to the Kursī [foot stool of Allāh] is also 500 years, and the distance between the Kursī and the water is again 500 years. And the Throne is above the water, and Allāh, the Almighty is above the Throne..."[in a manner befitting His Majesty].*

[149] Sunan of Abū Dāwud, [Eng. Trans. Vol. Pg.]. Declared sahīh by Ibn Al-Qayyim.

CHAPTER 5

THE DRESS OF A BELIEVING LADY

Allāh, the Mighty, the Majestic, said in His Book:

﴿ وَمَا كَانَ لِمُؤْمِنٍ وَلَا مُؤْمِنَةٍ إِذَا قَضَى ٱللَّهُ وَرَسُولُهُۥٓ أَمْرًا أَن يَكُونَ لَهُمُ ٱلْخِيَرَةُ مِنْ أَمْرِهِمْ ۗ وَمَن يَعْصِ ٱللَّهَ وَرَسُولَهُۥ فَقَدْ ضَلَّ ضَلَٰلًا مُّبِينًا ﴿٣٦﴾ ﴾

« It is not fitting for a believer, man or woman, when a matter has been decided by Allāh and His Messenger to have any opinion about their decision. And whoever disobeys Allāh and His Messenger [ﷺ], he has indeed strayed into plain error. » 33:36

He further commands us:

﴿ أُو۟لَٰٓئِكَ ٱلَّذِينَ لَعَنَهُمُ ٱللَّهُ ۖ وَمَن يَلْعَنِ ٱللَّهُ فَلَن تَجِدَ لَهُۥ نَصِيرًا ﴿٥٢﴾ أَمْ لَهُمْ نَصِيبٌ مِّنَ ٱلْمُلْكِ فَإِذًا لَّا يُؤْتُونَ ٱلنَّاسَ نَقِيرًا ﴿٥٣﴾ ﴾

«O you who believe! Obey Allāh and obey the Messenger [Muhammad ﷺ [and those of you [Muslims] who are in authority. [And] if you differ in any thing amongst yourselves, refer it to Allāh and His Messenger [ﷺ], if you believe in Allāh and in the Last Day. That is better and more suitable for final destination. » 4:59

﴿ يَٰبَنِىٓ ءَادَمَ قَدْ أَنزَلْنَا عَلَيْكُمْ لِبَاسًا يُوَٰرِى سَوْءَٰتِكُمْ وَرِيشًا ۖ وَلِبَاسُ ٱلتَّقْوَىٰ ذَٰلِكَ خَيْرٌ ﴿٢٦﴾ ﴾

« O children of Adam! We have bestowed raiment upon you to cover yourselves [screen your private parts etc.] and as a adornment, and the raiment of righteousness, that is better. » 7:26

﴿ يَٰبَنِيٓ ءَادَمَ لَا يَفۡتِنَنَّكُمُ ٱلشَّيۡطَٰنُ كَمَآ أَخۡرَجَ أَبَوَيۡكُم مِّنَ ٱلۡجَنَّةِ يَنزِعُ عَنۡهُمَا
لِبَاسَهُمَا لِيُرِيَهُمَا سَوۡءَٰتِهِمَآۚ إِنَّهُۥ يَرَىٰكُمۡ هُوَ وَقَبِيلُهُۥ مِنۡ حَيۡثُ لَا تَرَوۡنَهُمۡۗ إِنَّا
جَعَلۡنَا ٱلشَّيَٰطِينَ أَوۡلِيَآءَ لِلَّذِينَ لَا يُؤۡمِنُونَ ﴿٢٧﴾ ﴾

﴿ O children of Adam! Let not Shayṯān [Satan] deceive you as he got your parents [Adam and Hawwā [Eve]] out of Paradise, stripping them of their raiment's to show them their private parts. Verily, he and his sort [his soldiers from the Jinn or his tribe] see you from where you cannot see them. Verily, We made the Shayāṯīn [devils] Awliyā` [protectors and helpers] for those who believe not.﴾ 7:27

Allāh, the All-Knowing, then informs us what exactly He means by this ['*cover yourselves*'].

﴿ وَقُل لِّلۡمُؤۡمِنَٰتِ يَغۡضُضۡنَ مِنۡ أَبۡصَٰرِهِنَّ وَيَحۡفَظۡنَ فُرُوجَهُنَّ وَلَا يُبۡدِينَ زِينَتَهُنَّ
إِلَّا مَا ظَهَرَ مِنۡهَاۖ وَلۡيَضۡرِبۡنَ بِخُمُرِهِنَّ عَلَىٰ جُيُوبِهِنَّۖ وَلَا يُبۡدِينَ زِينَتَهُنَّ إِلَّا
لِبُعُولَتِهِنَّ أَوۡ ءَابَآئِهِنَّ أَوۡ ءَابَآءِ بُعُولَتِهِنَّ أَوۡ أَبۡنَآئِهِنَّ أَوۡ أَبۡنَآءِ
بُعُولَتِهِنَّ أَوۡ إِخۡوَٰنِهِنَّ أَوۡ بَنِيٓ إِخۡوَٰنِهِنَّ أَوۡ بَنِيٓ أَخَوَٰتِهِنَّ أَوۡ نِسَآئِهِنَّ أَوۡ مَا مَلَكَتۡ
أَيۡمَٰنُهُنَّ أَوِ ٱلتَّٰبِعِينَ غَيۡرِ أُوْلِي ٱلۡإِرۡبَةِ مِنَ ٱلرِّجَالِ أَوِ ٱلطِّفۡلِ ٱلَّذِينَ لَمۡ
يَظۡهَرُواْ عَلَىٰ عَوۡرَٰتِ ٱلنِّسَآءِۖ وَلَا يَضۡرِبۡنَ بِأَرۡجُلِهِنَّ لِيُعۡلَمَ مَا يُخۡفِينَ مِن زِينَتِهِنَّۚ
وَتُوبُوٓاْ إِلَى ٱللَّهِ جَمِيعًا أَيُّهَ ٱلۡمُؤۡمِنُونَ لَعَلَّكُمۡ تُفۡلِحُونَ ﴿٣١﴾ ﴾

﴿ And tell the believing women to cover their gaze[from looking at forbidden things] and protect their private parts [from illegal sexual acts etc.] and not to show off their adornment except only that which is apparent [like palms of hands or one eye or both eyes for necessity to see the way or outer dress like veil, gloves, apron etc.] and draw their veils all over their juyūb [i.e., bodies, faces, necks, bosoms etc.] and not to reveal their adornment except to their husbands, their fathers, their husbands fathers, their sons, their husbands sons, their brothers or their brothers

sons or their sisters sons or their [Muslim] women [i.e., sisters in Islām] or the [female] slaves whom their right hand possesses or old male servants who lack vigor, or small children who have no sense of sex. And let them not stamp their feet so as to reveal what they hide of their adornment. And all of you beg Allāh to forgive you all, O believers that you may be successful. ﴾ ***24:31***

I do not think anyone who enters Islām is looking for anything except success in this world and the next, so heed the commands of your Lord and stop looking to anything or anyone in this world to tell you how to 'modernize' your religion to fit in with them in their lust for this world.

Allāh, the Exalted, the Mighty, then says:

﴿ يَـٰٓأَيُّهَا ٱلنَّبِىُّ قُل لِّأَزْوَٰجِكَ وَبَنَاتِكَ وَنِسَآءِ ٱلْمُؤْمِنِينَ يُدْنِينَ عَلَيْهِنَّ مِن جَلَـٰبِيبِهِنَّ ۚ ذَٰلِكَ أَدْنَىٰٓ أَن يُعْرَفْنَ فَلَا يُؤْذَيْنَ ۗ وَكَانَ ٱللَّهُ غَفُورًا رَّحِيمًا ﴿٥٩﴾ ﴾

﴿ ***O Prophet! Tell your wives and your daughters and the women of the believers to draw their cloaks [veils] all over their bodies [i.e., screen themselves completely except one eye or both to see the way]. That will be better, that they should be known [as free respectable women] so as not to be annoyed.*** ﴾ ***33:59***

Therefore, the woman in entirety [i.e., her person] is her Aura [private part or part that must be covered] and this includes her voice [i.e., talking in an attractive tone or normally, unnecessarily, in the presence of non-*mahram* men, if it is necessary to speak in such a position she should make herself sound as businesslike as possible]. The Prophet [ﷺ] said:

"[All of] the woman is 'Awrah, whenever she goes out the Shaytān beautifies her [in the sight of men]."[150]

[150] Narrated by At-Tirmidhī who said that the *hadīth* is *hasan sahīh gharīb*. Also, *Shaykh* Al-Albānī declared the *hadīth* to be *sahīh* in his checking of *Mishkāt Al-Masābīh*.

The only way to Worship Allāh is to follow His Commands. As for those that poke fun at or ridicule the commands of Allāh, which obviously includes the matter of *hijāb* for the lady, is a disbeliever. This is in accordance with the statement of Allāh [when a man ridiculed the companions of the Prophet [ﷺ] and then came to the Prophet [ﷺ] claiming he didn't intend it except as a joke]:

﴿وَلَئِن سَأَلْتَهُمْ لَيَقُولُنَّ إِنَّمَا كُنَّا نَخُوضُ وَنَلْعَبُ قُلْ أَبِاللَّهِ وَآيَاتِهِ
وَرَسُولِهِ كُنتُمْ تَسْتَهْزِئُونَ ﴿٦٥﴾ لَا تَعْتَذِرُوا قَدْ كَفَرْتُم بَعْدَ إِيمَانِكُمْ إِن
نَّعْفُ عَن طَائِفَةٍ مِّنكُمْ نُعَذِّبْ طَائِفَةً بِأَنَّهُمْ كَانُوا مُجْرِمِينَ ﴿٦٦﴾﴾

﴾ If you ask them, they declare:' We were only talking idly and joking.' Say: Was it at Allāh and His Āyāt [proofs and evidences, verses, lessons, signs and revelations] and His Messenger you were mocking? Make no excuse, you have disbelieved after you had believed.﴿ 9:65-66

And because of this the scholars of the *Salaf* say, to make fun of a believer [for following the commands of Allāh] is to make fun of Allāh, may He protect us from such folly, Āmīn.

At-*Tabarruj*.

Any woman that does not cover herself as ordered by Allāh and His Messenger [ﷺ] has committed **At-*Tabarruj***, which is the display of a woman's charms.

Muhammad Ibn Ismail said in his book entitled *'The Hijab, Why?'* translated into English by Dr. Saleh as-Saleh: "*Tabarruj*: linguistically it means the display of beauty by a woman, showing her face, her body features, and using all means to attract men other than her husband. In Islāmic terms it means the display of beauty by women; also it is said:' to walk and/or move her body in a 'show off way'. Some said it is every form of beautification displayed by a woman in order to 'look good' in the eyes of strangers: even if the head veil of the woman is chosen to have bright colors and attractive features and it is intended as a mean to capture the sight of people then it is also considered to be the *tabarruj* of *jāhiliyyah* [days of ignorance].

***Tabarruj* is an Attribute of the people of the Hell.**

The Messenger of Allāh [ﷺ] said:

"Of the people of Hell there are two types whom I have never seen, they are the ones possessing whips like the tail of an ox and they flog people with them. The second one, women who would be naked in spite of their being dressed, who are seduced [to wrong paths] and seduce others with their hair like humps. These women would not get into Paradise and they would not perceive the odor of Paradise although it's fragrance can be perceived from such and such distance."[151]

Allāh, the Exalted, said:

﴿ وَقَرْنَ فِي بُيُوتِكُنَّ وَلَا تَبَرَّجْنَ تَبَرُّجَ الْجَاهِلِيَّةِ الْأُولَىٰ ﴾

﴿And stay in your houses quietly and do not display yourselves like that of the times of ignorance.﴾ 33:33

Therefore it is better to not leave one's house except for a real need, to cut down on any chance of *tabarruj*. And whenever leaving home one should be dressed in appropriate *hijāb* anyway. With the large groups of new converts that have no Muslim family to protect her and her Islām, and the economy etc., I am aware of the fact that a lot of the sisters need to go out to address their various needs. However, she should remember her Lord at all times and obey His commands. She need not discard all or part of her *hijāb* simply on the fear of being one who sticks out because she is supposed to be different from the unbelievers! The rule stands fear Allāh as much as you can then do what is necessary i.e., if you are forced to leave your hands and face out for example, and Allāh is the All-Seer of what you do. The sister should say:

﴿ سَمِعْنَا وَأَطَعْنَا ﴾

﴿We hear and we obey.﴾ 24:51

The Prophet [ﷺ] already warned us all:

[151] *Sahīh Muslim*. [Eng. Trans. Vol.3 # 5310]

"You would tread the same path as was trodden by those before you inch by inch and step by step so that if they had entered into the hole of a desert lizard, you would follow them in this also. We said: ' Allāh's Messenger, do you mean the Jews and Christians [by your words], 'those before you'? He said: ' Who else [than these two religious groups]?" [152]

So differ from them, their idea of fashion is not to cover the body claiming that beautification is to uncover as much as possible while enhancing the uncovered parts, may Allāh, the Almighty, the Wise keep us far from such repugnant forms of intentional and flagrant disobedience to Him, Āmīn. Also, the sad presence of these so called 'modern' [Muslim] women have gone so far as to belittle the orders of Allāh [calling for *hijāb*] by insinuating *hijāb* means the wearer is lacking in intellect or otherwise deficient. And to be a scholar, business woman, doctor or a housewife who is capable of keeping up with her children's affairs and her husband's affairs in this computerized high tech world she must remove her *hijāb* to let her intellect burst through! Well those poor misguided souls need to sit down and relearn their religion.

Additionally, *Tabarruj*, facilitates the sin of *zinā* [fornication]. First, by the obvious display the actual act is encouraged and second, the *zinā* of the eye as it makes it difficult to obey the command of Allāh:

﴿ قُل لِّلْمُؤْمِنِينَ يَغُضُّوا مِنْ أَبْصَارِهِمْ وَيَحْفَظُوا ﴾

﴾ Tell the believing men to lower their gaze [from looking at forbidden things]...﴿ 24:30

﴿ وَقُل لِّلْمُؤْمِنَاتِ يَغْضُضْنَ مِنْ أَبْصَارِهِنَّ وَيَحْفَظْنَ ﴾

﴾ Tell the believing women to lower their gaze and not to show off their adornment except to...﴿ 24:31

The Prophet [ﷺ] said:

"The adultery of the eye is the lustful look..." [153]

---

[152] *Sahīh Al-Bukhārī*,[Eng. Trans. Vol. 9 #422].

[153] *Sahīh Muslim*, [Eng. Trans. Vol. 4 #6422].

'Ā`ishah [ﷺ] the wife of the Prophet [ﷺ] said to some women of Banī Tamīm who came to visit her dressed in light clothing [i.e., not thick enough]: "If indeed you are believing women, then truly this is not the dress of the believing woman, and if you are not believing women then enjoy."[154]

[She said this as non-believers enjoy in this world only as they have torture only in the next world, because they transgressed bounds not worshipping Allāh at all or in the manner He ordered, being disobedient and finding enjoyment in the unlawful.]

All believers should have a sense of *ghīrah*.

The Prophet of Allāh, Muhammad [ﷺ], said about *ghīrah*:

"O followers of Muhammad! There is none, who has a greater sense of ghīrah [self-respect] than Allāh, so He has forbidden that his slave commits illegal sexual intercourse or that His slave girl commit illegal sexual intercourse. O followers of Muhammad! If you but knew what I know you would laugh less and weep more."[155]

Ali [ﷺ] the fourth rightly guided Caliph of the believers said:

"It was related to me that you women used to crowed the *kuffār* [disbelieving men] from the non-Arabs in the markets; don't you have *ghīrah*? Islām considers *ghīrah* an integral part of faith."[156]

Ghīrah may be described as the natural jealousy a man has for the women in his family i.e., mother, wife sister, daughter; and the natural jealousy a woman has for the men in her family; regarding protection of their morals, integrity etc. it is a kind of self-respect.

---

[154] *'The Hijab, ... Why?'* [Origin in *Sunan* of An-Nasā`ī].

[155] *Sahīh Al-Bukhārī*, [Eng. Trans. vol. 7 pg. 110]

[156] *'The Hijab,... Why?* [Origin in *Sahīh Muslim*]

Requirements for the believing ladies *hijāb*.

The exact nature is up to the sister provided that the following requirements are met in accordance with the commands of Allāh and His Messenger [ﷺ]. I might point out here that this means in addition to her regular clothing [over them].Also, the clothing she wears underneath her *hijāb* should be appropriate to wear in the presence of her Muslim sisters which according to some of the scholars of the *Salaf*, must cover her body from neck to feet including her arms. However, what may be displayed are the parts that can be [normally] adorned i.e., up to her elbows or ankles or the portion of her neck a necklace is worn on, and Allāh knows best. Not all scholars feel it is *wājib* to veil one's face however, there is a *hadīth* widely used by those trying to convince the sisters of the permissibility of leaving off some of her *hijāb*. This *hadīth* is *da'īf* [weak] according to some of our respected scholars of the *Salaf* and cannot be used for the following three reasons according to shaykh bin Bāz[157]:

1] One of the narrators, Khālid Ibn Durayk, narrated upon 'Ā`ishah [ﷺ] but he had never even met her. Thus the chain is disrupted [*mursal*].

2] Also in the chain of narrators is Sa'īd Ibn Bashīr he is considered *da'īf* by the scholars of *hadīth* sciences, therefore his *hadīth* is not proof for anything.

3] And in it [the chain] is Qatādah who used a word meaning he heard it directly or indirectly, and it is not known which as he didn't specify thus it is a kind of deception regardless of the intention.

I purposely detailed it to crush the persistent doubts raised in the heads of our new sisters from this *hadīth*. The *hadīth* in question is narrated upon 'Ā`ishah [ﷺ]:

"Asmā [ﷺ] daughter of Abū Bakr [ﷺ][her sister], entered upon the Prophet of Allāh [ﷺ] wearing thin clothes. The Prophet of Allāh [ﷺ] turned his attention from her. He said: ' **O Asmā, when a woman reaches the age of**

[157] In his essay, " The legal ruling concerning not covering and *hijāb*", found in the book entitled, *A Collection Of Essays Concerning Hijab And Not Covering* [pg. 57-58].

menstruation, it does not suit her that she displays her parts of her body except this and this, and he pointed to her hands and face."[158]

Since a woman may not unveil herself in front of her brother-in-law as Asmā [ﷺ] was the sister-in-law of the Prophet [ﷺ], they [those who are of this opinion] say it is proof she may leave her house with her face and hands unveiled. However since it is *da'īf*, this leaves naught but the truth , "**[All of] the woman is *'Awrah.*"** I point out to the sister that the *hijāb*'s effectiveness to serve its purpose must go hand in hand with her manner or behavior. That is to say she should not swagger, pull it tightly around her nor be so lax as to let it fall of or open, and Allāh is the All-Aware.

The following are excerpts from the book, *'The Hijab...Why?'*, by Muhammad Ismail.

1) It should cover the entire body.

The author is in agreement with the position that the face and hands of the woman must be covered as detailed in the book: 'The Return of the *Hijāb* - Part 3."[However] some scholars say it is permissible to uncover the face and hands of the woman as long as there is no *fitnah* [infatuation] caused by her or inflicted on her. If:

a) She is beautiful and beautifies her face or hands with external substances,
b) The society around her is corrupt where men do not lower their gaze, then it is prohibited for her to uncover her face and hands.

[Note: in this day and time almost all countries in the world fall into the category whereby she is forbidden to uncover her face]

2] The *hijāb* should not be a display.

Allāh ordained it [the *hijāb*] so as to cover the beauty of women. Allāh said:

---

[158] Sunan of Abū Dāwud, [Eng. Trans. Vol.3 # 4092 pg. 1144-1145] Declared *da'īf* by Shaykh Ibn Bāz.

﴿ وَلَا يُبْدِينَ زِينَتَهُنَّ إِلَّا مَا ظَهَرَ مِنْهَا ﴾

﴾ And not to show their beauty except that which is apparent ﴿ 24:31

﴿ وَلَا تَبَرَّجْنَ تَبَرُّجَ ٱلْجَٰهِلِيَّةِ ﴾

﴾ And do not display yourself like that of the times of ignorance. ﴿ 33:33

It is also not logical that the *hijāb* be a source of display.[in other words no brilliant colors and attractive designs on it]

3] The *hijāb* must be thick and not transparent.

The purpose must be achieved. In order for the *hijāb* to cover, it must not be made of transparent material making the woman covered only by name! While in reality she is naked. The Prophet [ﷺ] said:

"In the latest part of my ummah [nation of Muslims] there shall be women who would be naked in spite of being dressed; their hair like the humps of the Bukht camel, curse them for they are indeed cursed."

In another *hadīth* he [ﷺ] added:

"They would not enter Paradise and would not perceive its odor, although it's odor can be perceived at such and such a distance."

This indicates that a woman could cause herself a grave and destructive sin if she puts on a garment that is thin and transparent which clearly shows or reveals her body's features.

4] *Hijāb* must be roomy, flowing and not tight.

The *hijāb* is a safeguard against *fitnah*. If tight the *hijāb* will be descriptive of the woman's body and this violates the purpose of *hijāb*. Usāmah Ibn Zayd [رضي الله عنه] said:

"The Messenger of Allāh [ﷺ] dressed me with a thick Qubtiyyah [cotton dress from Egypt] which was a gift from Dahyā Al-Kalbī. So I gave it to my wife to wear. He [ﷺ] said: 'What made you not wear the Qubtiyyah?' I said: 'I dressed my wife with it.' He [ﷺ] said: 'Order her to put an undergarment [or gown] under it, because I am afraid it may describe the size of her bones.' "

5] The *h̲ijāb* should not be perfumed with incense [or any other perfume].

The Messenger of Allāh [ﷺ] said:

"Any woman who perfumes herself and passes some people that they smell her scent, then she is a zāniyah [one who commits zinā]."

6] The *h̲ijāb* should not resemble men's dress.

The Messenger of Allāh [ﷺ] said:

"Women who assume manners of men are not from us and also those men who assume the manners of women."

"The Prophet [ﷺ] cursed the man who wears the dress of a woman and the woman who wears the dress of a man."

"Three would not enter Paradise and Allāh would not look at them on The Day of Resurrection]The one who is undutiful to his parents ii]the woman who assumes the manners and behavior of men and takes their similitude iii]and the one who knowingly condones and facilitates zinā for his wife."

[E.g. a sister using the Muslim man's cap as a head dress]

7] The *h̲ijāb* should not resemble the garments of the *kuffār* women.

The Messenger of Allāh [ﷺ] said:

"The one who takes the similitude [manner] of a certain people becomes one of them."

Abdullah Ibn 'Umar [رضي الله عنه] said:

"The Prophet [ﷺ] saw me wearing two clothes dyed in saffron, whereupon he said: 'These clothes are [usually worn] by the kuffār, so do not wear them'."

8] The *h̲ijāb* is not for fame.

The Messenger of Allāh [ﷺ] said:

"The one who wears a garment designed for worldly fame. Allāh will make him wear a garment of humility on The Day of Resurrection then he will be set ablaze."

The garment of fame is any garment a person wears to make him or her famous. This applies whether the garment is highly precious and shows admiration to the life of this world or if it is chosen of low quality to show lack of interest in worldly life. The person may put on clothes with distinct colors so as to draw attention, act proudly and [or] arrogantly.

9] Watch for 'concealed' ways of display.

Examining the various conditions about the *hijāb*, one would clearly recognize that many of the young Muslim women are not fulfilling these conditions. They consider what they put on now wrongly as '*hijāb*'. Allāh, defeated the plots of the enemies of the Islāmic revival, and held the believing men and women steadfast in obedience of Allāh. So they realized that they should deal with the Islāmic revival in a wicked way in order to sway this revival away from its course toward Allāh. They started to spread innovated forms of '*hijāb*' as a midway solution for the woman to 'please' her Lord [they claim so!] and at the same time accommodate her society to preserve her beauty and glamour.

The modern 'boutique' stores were declining in their trade due to the widespread use of the Islāmic *hijāb*. Suddenly the markets were flooded with altered forms of *tabarruj* under the name 'modern/contemporary *hijāb*'. In the beginning this was protested and the women were cautious.

A group of 'displaying women' who were embarrassed with the Islāmic *hijāb* rushed toward the 'contemporary *hijāb*' to 'relieve' themselves from the pressing social realities caused by the spread of *hijāb*. With time, the phenomenon of concealed display became widespread and known as 'contemporary *hijāb*'. Women friendly to this course think they are the best of girls and the best of wives yet they are as one poet said:

If they relate to the *hijāb*
It is the relation of an intruder.

So! O women of this kind, be mindful of Allāh and His Messenger [ﷺ], and do not be deceived by those who may 'bless' this action of yours and conceal their true intentions. So it is proper to follow your sisters who truly adhere to the Islāmic *hijāb* and its conditions. Allāh, the Almighty said:

﴿ إِنَّ ٱلَّذِينَ قَالُواْ رَبُّنَا ٱللَّهُ ثُمَّ ٱسْتَقَـٰمُواْ تَتَنَزَّلُ عَلَيْهِمُ ٱلْمَلَـٰٓئِكَةُ أَلَّا تَخَافُواْ وَلَا تَحْزَنُواْ وَأَبْشِرُواْ بِٱلْجَنَّةِ ٱلَّتِى كُنتُمْ تُوعَدُونَ ﴾

﴾ Verily those who say, ' Our Lord is Allāh [Alone]' and then they stood straight and obeyed Him, on them the angels shall descend [at the time of their death] [saying]: ' Fear not nor grieve! But receive the glad tidings of Paradise, which you have been promised! ﴿ 30:30

'Umar Ibn Al-Khattāb [ﷺ] commenting on the verse said:
"They by Allāh, followed the straight path of Allāh by obeying Him and did not dodge it like wolves." [End of excerpt]

Other things the sister should watch for related to her dress.

1] The believing woman should not resemble or imitate the *Kuffār*.
"The one who takes on a similitude [manner] of a certain people becomes of them"[159]

a) Long nails:
These are against the fitrah [nature of the human being that we were created with] as well as the fitrah of the prophets of Allāh.
" The five acts of fitrah are; circumcision [for the male], shaving the pubes, clipping the mustache, cutting the nails, plucking [or shaving] the hair under the arms" [160]

"Anas[ﷺ] reported the time limit has been prescribed for us... that it should not be neglected for more than forty nights."[161]

b) Nail varnish:
Except that the sister faithfully removes the varnish five times a day whenever she needs to make *Wudū`*, she should not wear it as it prevents

---

[159] *Sunan* of Abū Dāwud, [Eng. Trans. Vol. 3, pg.1127] Declared hasan sahīh by *Shaykh* Al-Albānī.
[160] Sahīh *Muslim*, [Eng. Trans. Vol. 1, pg.159].
[161] Sahīh *Muslim*, [Eng. Trans. vol. 1, pg. 159].

the water from reaching her nails as it must. Henna [skin dye] on the other hand may be used as the water can pass through it to her nails and skin by the will of Allāh. Besides, nail varnish is not a necessity like a bandage over a wound for example,, this can be wiped over, if removing it and letting the water touch it would harm or prolong its healing.

"Perform ablution perfectiy and thoroughly for Abū Al-Qāsim [the Prophet [ﷺ]] said, 'Save your heels from the fire.'" [by washing them not leaving any dry spot][162]

"Whenever Ibn Sīrīn performed ablution he used to wash the place that was under the ring."[163]

"On the Day of Resurrection my followers will be called, Al-Ghurr Al-Muhajjalūn, from the traces of ablution and whoever can increase the area of his radiance should do so [i.e., by performing ablution regularly and completely]." [164]

I will again point out to the sister that all parts included in the area of ablution must not be left dry this means removing jewelry for the *Wudū`* then replacing it after completion if desired.

c) High heeled shoes:

It is a definite imitation of the *Kuffār* for a believing lady to try to walk down the street in such shoes! It goes against the principle of hijāb whose aim is to cover her beauty. There is no way for any woman to walk in these shoes except that it makes her walk in an alluring fashion appealing to men, not to mention the sound they make when they touch the ground! Especially those women living in the land of the non-believers, they must avoid such ways of inviting that sort of attention as the men may put the evil thoughts that Satan incites in them, into action. Beware! However, in my humble opinion if she must wear them it is best done in the midst of other women for special occasions or in her husband's presence, and Allāh knows best.

---

[162] *Sahīh Al-Bukhārī*, [Eng. Trans. vol.1 pg. 116]

[163] *Sahīh Al-Bukhārī*, [Eng. Trans. vol. pg. 116 chapter].

[164] *Sahīh Al-Bukhārī*, [Eng. Trans. vol. 1 pg. 102].

d) Make-Up:
It is acceptable by the will of Allāh, if she is wearing a face veil upon leaving the house. If she does not veil herself she must refrain from using make-up when she must leave the house. Like everything else in Islām, if she decides to use make-up she should do it in moderation, not completely changing her features nor should she resemble a clown. If her veil leaves her eyes out she should not beautify her eyes on leaving the house. [see point 1. Requirements of *hijāb*]

2) How to dress in front of...?
In front of her husband alone, whatever he finds pleasing, by the will of Allāh. It is up to the couple. However when they are blessed with children and they grow up enough to understand, she needs to modify her attire to cover sufficiently. By this I mean the same as she would wear in front of other grown family members or other believing women [indoors]. This, according to the scholars of the *Salaf*, covers everything from her neck to feet and shoulders to hands. The parts in the aforesaid places that may be uncovered in front of the above mentioned people are; places that can normally be adorned e.g. Her arms up to the elbow and a little above that [she probably needs to expose this for work at home anyway], or her ankles and a little above that, and Allāh knows best. Tight clothing again, is not allowed unless none but her husband is present, the same goes for fashions that include very short clothing like mini skirts. **HOWEVER**, family members that may see her in such attire does not include In-laws [brother In-laws etc.]. Rather in front of them [Brother In-laws] she should be in full *hijāb*! The Prophet of Allāh [ﷺ] said:

> "**Beware of entering upon the ladies.**" A man from the Ansār said: 'Allāh's Messenger, what about *Al-Hamuw* [mainly brothers of the husband i.e., those who could have married the woman], the in-laws of the wife,[the brothers of her husband or his nephews etc.].' The Prophet [ﷺ] replied, '**The in-laws of the wife are death itself.**'" [165]

---

[165] *Sahīh Al-Bukhārī*, [Eng. Trans. vol. 7 pg. 117].

This being so as *zinā* [adultery] may occur between them. From her husband's family the only males Allāh has permitted her to reveal herself to are only TWO: her husband's father and her husband's sons; and the rest are from her family or those slave/servants who are incapable of sexual intercourse and very small children. Allāh, the Exalted said she may reveal her self to:

﴿إِلَّا لِبُعُولَتِهِنَّ أَوْ ءَابَآئِهِنَّ أَوْ ءَابَآءِ بُعُولَتِهِنَّ أَوْ أَبْنَآئِهِنَّ أَوْ أَبْنَآءِ بُعُولَتِهِنَّ أَوْ إِخْوَٰنِهِنَّ أَوْ بَنِىٓ إِخْوَٰنِهِنَّ أَوْ بَنِىٓ أَخَوَٰتِهِنَّ أَوْ نِسَآئِهِنَّ أَوْ مَا مَلَكَتْ أَيْمَٰنُهُنَّ أَوِ ٱلتَّٰبِعِينَ غَيْرِ أُو۟لِى ٱلْإِرْبَةِ مِنَ ٱلرِّجَالِ أَوِ ٱلطِّفْلِ ٱلَّذِينَ لَمْ يَظْهَرُوا۟ عَلَىٰ عَوْرَٰتِ ٱلنِّسَآءِ﴾

﴾...their husbands, or their fathers, or their husbands' fathers, or their sons, or their husbands' sons, or their brothers or their brothers' sons, or their sisters' sons... or old male servants who lack vigor, or small children who have no sense of feminine sex.﴿ 24:31

Thus, male cousins [hers and her husband's], husband's nephews, husband's brothers, the fathers of her brothers' or sisters' spouses, basically anyone who cannot travel alone with her i.e., is not *mahram* for her, cannot see her. She should always be on guard regardless of customs etc. If in doubt, she should pick up a copy of the translation of the Noble Qur`ān [if she cannot read Arabic] and read chapter 24:31. She may also read chapter 4:23 for those forbidden in marriage as it applies to women also i.e., *forbidden in marriage for the woman, her father, her son her brother, her father's brothers, her mother's brothers, her brother's daughters, her foster father[i.e., his wife suckled her], her foster milk-suckling brothers [i.e., any man suckled by that same woman], her husband's father, her step-sons from her husband who has gone into her, if he has not gone into her she can marry him and her daughter's husband [i.e., the daughter she gave birth to]*. Those forbidden in marriage are *mahram* to her and she may uncover in front of them and Allāh knows best. Therefore, the sister should be careful with whom she may appear to without *hijāb*.

3) **Those she may uncover in front of must be also one who will not describe her**.

Allāh has informed us of whom we can appear to without *hijāb*. However, if these people are known to describe or disclose whatever they see of her to non-*mahram* males then she should cover herself in their presence also. And a Muslim woman should never describe another sister to any male! The Prophet of Allāh [ﷺ] said:

"A woman should not look at or touch another woman to describe her to her husband in such a way as if he was looking at her." [166]

4] The non-believers who knew you before you were blessed with Islām .

I feel it is of grave importance to mention that in front of the *kuffār*, male or female, who knew and saw you in your *jāhiliyyah* you may not uncover yourself even if it was the day before that they saw you out of *hijāb* and still remember what you look like! First and foremost, Allāh, the Exalted, the Wise, has informed you who may see you, secondly, they are non-believers and except for real necessity you should not befriend them nor seek their help. Allāh, the Almighty said:

﴿ لَّا تَجِدُ قَوْمًا يُؤْمِنُونَ بِٱللَّهِ وَٱلْيَوْمِ ٱلْءَاخِرِ يُوَآدُّونَ مَنْ حَآدَّ ٱللَّهَ وَرَسُولَهُۥ
وَلَوْ كَانُوٓا۟ ءَابَآءَهُمْ أَوْ أَبْنَآءَهُمْ أَوْ إِخْوَٰنَهُمْ أَوْ عَشِيرَتَهُمْ ۚ أُو۟لَٰٓئِكَ كَتَبَ فِى
قُلُوبِهِمُ ٱلْإِيمَٰنَ وَأَيَّدَهُم بِرُوحٍ مِّنْهُ ۖ وَيُدْخِلُهُمْ جَنَّٰتٍ تَجْرِى مِن تَحْتِهَا ٱلْأَنْهَٰرُ
خَٰلِدِينَ فِيهَا ۚ رَضِىَ ٱللَّهُ عَنْهُمْ وَرَضُوا۟ عَنْهُ ۚ أُو۟لَٰٓئِكَ حِزْبُ ٱللَّهِ ۚ أَلَآ إِنَّ حِزْبَ ٱللَّهِ
هُمُ ٱلْمُفْلِحُونَ ﴿٢٢﴾ ﴾

﴾ You [O Muhammad ﷺ] will not find any people who believe in Allāh and the Last Day, making friendship with those who oppose Allāh and His

[166] *Sahīh Al-Bukhārī*, [Eng. Trans. Vol.7 pg.122].

Messenger, even though they were their fathers or their sons or their brothers or their kindred [people]. For such He has written Faith in their hearts, and strengthened them with a rūh [proofs, light and guidance] from Himself. And He will admit them to Gardens [Paradise] under which rivers flow to dwell therein [forever]. Allāh is pleased with them, and they with Him. They are the Party of Allāh. Verily it is the party of Allāh that will be successful. ﴾ ***58:22***

Would you not want to be of the Party of Allāh instead of being satisfied with a sense of belonging amongst those who refuse to acknowledge and worship Him? Surely it is hard to give up all you knew to embark alone on what you have little knowledge about except that you believe it to be the only truth, that it [Islām] is knowing that the day will come when you have no choice but to be alone in front of your Lord and their Lord with only Allāh, your Lord and theirs, as the Judge and Enforcer. And this decision of yours as a deciding factor, Allāh will bring you by the will of Allāh, better companions who wish good in this world and the hereafter. The *hijāb* in full must be worn in their presence.

5] *Hijāb* is a cover for the sister when she must be out but it doesn't serve much purpose if she doesn't modify her behavior e.g. 'hanging out'.

This is because the *hijāb* is to physically cover you and give a sense of dignity and respect to the woman and all that see her that she is not disturbed by the will of Allāh. Allāh, the Almighty said:

﴿ لَّا جُنَاحَ عَلَيْهِنَّ فِىٓ ءَابَآئِهِنَّ وَلَآ أَبْنَآئِهِنَّ وَلَآ إِخْوَٰنِهِنَّ وَلَآ أَبْنَآءِ إِخْوَٰنِهِنَّ
وَلَآ أَبْنَآءِ أَخَوَٰتِهِنَّ وَلَا نِسَآئِهِنَّ وَلَا مَا مَلَكَتْ أَيْمَٰنُهُنَّ ۗ وَٱتَّقِينَ ٱللَّهَ ۚ إِنَّ ٱللَّهَ
كَانَ عَلَىٰ كُلِّ شَىْءٍ شَهِيدًا ﴿٥٥﴾ ﴾

﴾ ***O Prophet! Tell your wives and your daughters and the women of the believers to draw their cloaks [veils] all over their bodies. That will be better, that they should be known [as free respectable women] so as not to be annoyed.*** ﴿ ***33:59***

Therefore the 'Hanging out' of our young men and women has no place in Islām. The disheartening reports of our young women loitering around the *masjid* or stores frequented by men in inadequate *hijāb* at that ‹to be seen and to see is from *jāhiliyyah* [ignorance] and needs to be stopped. I seek refuge with Allāh from the accursed Satan who makes these deeds seem pleasing to them. They should know they will be held accountable to Allāh for all the *fitnah* [trouble] they cause or are involved in and should sincerely repent to Allāh, the Most Merciful and ask for His forgiveness. Our life in this world is a preparation for our lives in the next and eternal life of the Hereafter, even though one may feel it is distant it is closer to you than your shoe straps[167]. Pride, in any form like showing-off one's clothing, is a trait of the people of the Hell Fire.

"Whenever Allāh's Messenger [ﷺ] completed the prayer with *taslīm*, the women used to get up immediately and Allāh's Messenger[ﷺ] would remain at his place for a while before getting up. [the sub narrator, Az-Zuhrī said, 'We think and Allāh knows better, that[it was so] that the women might leave before the men get in touch with them]."[168]

'May I not inform you about the inmates of Paradise? Every meek person who is considered to be humble and if they were to adjure in the name of Allāh, Allāh would certainly fulfill it. May I not inform you about the inmates of Hell-Fire? They are all proud, mean and haughty." [169]

---

[167] The full *hadīth* is in *Sahīh Al-Bukhārī* [Eng. Trans. vol. 8, #495]. The wording is" Heaven and Hell are closer to you than your shoe straps". The point to be made here is that there are only two abodes in the Hereafter and they are closer to you...

[168] *Sahīh Al-Bukhārī*, [Eng. Trans. vol.1 pg. 458].

[169] *Sahīh Muslim* [Eng. Trans. vol.4 pg. 1485].

The use of Gold.

I would like to clarify this for the sister by the will of Allāh. Its use for the Muslim female is permissible but is <u>*harām*</u> for the Muslim male.

"The Prophet [ﷺ] got some ornaments presented by Negus as a gift to him. They contained a gold ring with an Abyssinian stone. The Prophet [ﷺ] took it by means of a stick or his finger, called Umāmah, the daughter of his daughter Zaynab, and said: '*Wear it, my daughter*'."[170]

And 'Ā`ishah [ﷺ] wife of the Prophet [ﷺ] wore gold rings. As for the <u>*hadīth*</u> where the Prophet [ﷺ] said:

"If anyone wants to put a ring of fire on one he loves, let him put a gold ring on him; if anyone wants to put a necklace of fire on one he loves, let him put a necklace of gold on him, and if anyone wants to put a bracelet of fire on one he loves let him put a gold bracelet on him. Keep silver and amuse yourselves with it."[171]

This is for the male Muslim. The female may wear it but, the scholars of the *Salaf* point out she should not go overboard in her love and collection of it, moderation is the way of Islām.

Silk.

It is permissible for the female and <u>*harām*</u> for the male:

"The Prophet [ﷺ] took silk and held it in his right hand, and took gold and held it in his left hand and said: '*Both of these are prohibited to the males of my community*'."[172]

---

[170] Sunan of Abū Dāwud, [Eng. Trans. vol.3 pg. 1175]. And *Shaykh* Al-Albānī said that this <u>*hadīth*</u> has a good chain of narration.

[171] Sunan of Abū Dāwud [Eng. Trans. vol.3 pg.1175]. And *Shaykh* Al-Albānī declared this <u>*hadīth*</u> to be <u>*hasan*</u>.

[172] Sunan of Abū Dāwud, [Eng. Trans. vol. 3 #4046]. And *Shaykh* Al-Albānī declared this <u>*hadīth*</u> to be *Sahīh*.

CHAPTER 6

THE IGNORANCE WE BRING IN WITH US

Allāh the Most High, the Exalted said:

﴿ يَـٰٓأَيُّهَا ٱلَّذِينَ ءَامَنُواْ لَا تَتَّخِذُواْ ٱلَّذِينَ ٱتَّخَذُواْ دِينَكُمْ هُزُوًا وَلَعِبًا مِّنَ ٱلَّذِينَ أُوتُواْ ٱلْكِتَـٰبَ مِن قَبْلِكُمْ وَٱلْكُفَّارَ أَوْلِيَآءَ ۚ وَٱتَّقُواْ ٱللَّهَ إِن كُنتُم مُّؤْمِنِينَ ﴿٥٧﴾ ﴾

﴾ O you who believe do not take as friends and protectors those who take your religion as mockery and fun from amongst those who received the scripture before you nor from the Idolaters; and fear Allāh concerning this if you are truly Believers.﴿ 5:57

In this chapter I shall attempt to point out some of the major issues that plague our sisters [from the characteristics of *jāhiliyyah*, ignorance] in Islām, both new and old alike.

1) Obedience.

This is of paramount importance as it is the basic foundation we build on in Islām. Since obedience to Allāh will bring you to *Tawhīd*, and as such you will obey all His laws sent through His Prophet Muhammad [ﷺ] by the will of Allāh leading to success in this world and the next. However, for some lamentable reasons, the sisters do not see it as such and listen to their own desires coupled with pressures from societies they are in. therefore, buckling under pressure. In any country there are people and laws to be obeyed most of which do not even come close to what Allāh has sent to His creation as guidance. In spite of this, they are obeyed and held in high esteem and few are flagrantly thrown aside. However, the supreme laws sent to us by Allāh the Almighty, the Majestic, the Creator of all you see and cannot see, are ridiculed or just thrown to the side. Verily, He is the Patient, for He could destroy them as easily as He created them. Obedience is undoubtedly the path any Believing woman chooses.

a) First and foremost every Muslim, male or female must obey Allāh and His Messenger [Muhammad ﷺ] and the Muslim leader over them, as stated in the following verses from the Qur`ān.

﴿ يَـٰٓأَيُّهَا ٱلَّذِينَ ءَامَنُوٓاْ أَطِيعُواْ ٱللَّهَ وَأَطِيعُواْ ٱلرَّسُولَ وَأُوْلِى ٱلْأَمْرِ مِنكُمْ ﴾

﴾ O you who believe! Obey Allāh and obey the Messenger [Muhammad ﷺ] and those of you [Muslims] who are in authority. ﴿ 4:59

﴿ مَّن يُطِعِ ٱلرَّسُولَ فَقَدْ أَطَاعَ ٱللَّهَ وَمَن تَوَلَّىٰ فَمَآ أَرْسَلْنَـٰكَ عَلَيْهِمْ حَفِيظًا ۝٨٠ ﴾

﴾ He who obeys the Messenger [Muhammad ﷺ] has indeed obeyed Allāh, but he who turns away, then We have not sent you [O Muhammad [ﷺ]] as a watcher over them. ﴿ 4:80

We also have the statements of the Prophet [ﷺ]:

"If somebody sees his Muslim ruler doing something he disapproves of, he should be patient, for whoever becomes separate from the Muslim group even for a span and then dies, he will die as those who died in the Pre-Islāmic period of ignorance [as rebellious sinners]."[173]

"Whoever obeys me, obeys Allāh, and whoever disobeys me, disobeys Allāh, and whoever obeys the ruler I appoint, obeys me, and whoever disobeys him disobeys me."[174]

b) Both must also obey their parents as stated by Allāh:

﴿ وَوَصَّيْنَا ٱلْإِنسَـٰنَ بِوَٰلِدَيْهِ حُسْنًا وَإِن جَـٰهَدَاكَ لِتُشْرِكَ بِى مَا لَيْسَ لَكَ بِهِۦ عِلْمٌ
فَلَا تُطِعْهُمَآ إِلَىَّ مَرْجِعُكُمْ فَأُنَبِّئُكُم بِمَا كُنتُمْ تَعْمَلُونَ ۝٨ ﴾

﴾ And We have enjoined upon man to be good and dutiful to his parents; but if they strive to make you join with Me [in worship] anything [as a partner [of which you have no knowledge, then obey them not. Unto Me is your return and I shall tell you what you used to do. ﴿ 29:8

---

173 *Sahīh Al-Bukhārī*, [Eng. Trans. Vol. 9. Pg. 193. #257].

174 *Sahīh Al-Bukhārī*, [Eng. Trans. Vol. 9. Pg. 189. #251].

﴿ وَقَضَىٰ رَبُّكَ أَلَّا تَعْبُدُوٓاْ إِلَّآ إِيَّاهُ وَبِٱلْوَٰلِدَيْنِ إِحْسَٰنًا ۚ إِمَّا يَبْلُغَنَّ عِندَكَ ٱلْكِبَرَ أَحَدُهُمَآ أَوْ كِلَاهُمَا فَلَا تَقُل لَّهُمَآ أُفٍّ وَلَا تَنْهَرْهُمَا وَقُل لَّهُمَا قَوْلًا كَرِيمًا ﴿٢٣﴾ وَٱخْفِضْ لَهُمَا جَنَاحَ ٱلذُّلِّ مِنَ ٱلرَّحْمَةِ وَقُل رَّبِّ ٱرْحَمْهُمَا كَمَا رَبَّيَانِى صَغِيرًا ﴾

﴿ And your Lord has decreed that you worship none but Him. And that you be dutiful to your parents. If one of them or both of them attain old age in your life, say not to them a word of disrespect, nor shout at them but address them in terms of honor .And lower unto them the wing of mercy, and say:' My Lord! Bestow on them your Mercy as they did bring me up when I was young.' ﴾ 17:23-24

The Prophet [ﷺ] said:

"There are three for whom Allāh has forbidden paradise. The alcoholics, the one who is disobedient to his parents, the cuckold who allows his wife to behave wickedly [lewdly]."[175]

c] In addition to this, we [sisters] are also commanded to obey our husbands. Allāh said:

﴿ ٱلرِّجَالُ قَوَّٰمُونَ عَلَى ٱلنِّسَآءِ بِمَا فَضَّلَ ٱللَّهُ بَعْضَهُمْ عَلَىٰ بَعْضٍ وَبِمَآ أَنفَقُواْ مِنْ أَمْوَٰلِهِمْ ۚ فَٱلصَّٰلِحَٰتُ قَٰنِتَٰتٌ حَٰفِظَٰتٌ لِّلْغَيْبِ بِمَا حَفِظَ ٱللَّهُ ۚ وَٱلَّٰتِى تَخَافُونَ نُشُوزَهُنَّ فَعِظُوهُنَّ وَٱهْجُرُوهُنَّ فِى ٱلْمَضَاجِعِ وَٱضْرِبُوهُنَّ ۖ فَإِنْ أَطَعْنَكُمْ فَلَا تَبْغُواْ عَلَيْهِنَّ سَبِيلًا ۗ إِنَّ ٱللَّهَ كَانَ عَلِيًّا كَبِيرًا ﴿٣٤﴾ ﴾

﴿ Men are the protectors and maintainers of women, because Allāh has made one of them to excel the other, and because they spend [to support them] from their means. Therefore righteous women are devoutly obedient [to Allāh and to their husbands], and guard in their husbands'

---

[175] *Musnad* of Imām Ahmad, and declared sahīh by *Shaykh* Al-Albānī.

absence what Allāh orders them to guard [e.g. their chastity, their husbands property]. ***4:34***

The Prophet [ﷺ] said:

"All of you are guardians and are responsible for your wards. The ruler is a guardian, the man is a guardian of his family: the lady is a guardian and responsible for her husbands house and his offspring and so all of you are guardians and are responsible for your wards." [176]

Therefore the response to a request or order is not 'no' or ' go do it yourself', with an afterthought of who does he think he is. But rather it is the remembrance of Allāh's Word's:

...because Allāh has made one excel the other.

...because they spend [to support them] from their means.

She need not bother about his intention as that is for Allāh to deal with. Her husband is not just a man, he is by the will of Allāh, a Muslim, a creation of Allāh, created to serve a purpose, just as the woman is not just that, but a creation of Allāh, brought into being to serve a purpose, for both it is to Worship Allāh. In order to worship Allāh, you must obey Him and part of that is to obey your husband. Moreover, Allāh placed His creation 'man' over His creation 'woman'. Accepting this fact, she should try to gain Paradise by Allāh's abundant Mercy, through obedience to her husband as well doing other acts of worship. We have been informed by the Prophet [ﷺ] that a believing lady can enter Paradise from any door she wishes if she does four things:

a) observes her prayer, dutifully, five times a day in the way we have been commanded.
b) observes her fasts in accordance to the *Sunnah*, every *Ramadān*.
c) Protects her private parts from all except her husband.

---

[176] *Sahīh Al-Bukhārī* [Eng. Trans. vol. 7 pg. 98].

d) Obeys her husband to the best of her ability, except if he orders her to do what is against the laws of Allāh.[177]

2) Racism.

The second largest piece of baggage carried along from *jāhiliyyah*, is racism. Unfortunately this is not even confined to new converts but to those born in Islām. Allāh the Originator, the Fashioner, says in His Book:

﴿ يَـٰٓأَيُّهَا ٱلنَّاسُ إِنَّا خَلَقْنَـٰكُم مِّن ذَكَرٍ وَأُنثَىٰ وَجَعَلْنَـٰكُمْ شُعُوبًا وَقَبَآئِلَ لِتَعَارَفُوٓا۟ ۚ إِنَّ أَكْرَمَكُمْ عِندَ ٱللَّهِ أَتْقَىٰكُمْ ۚ إِنَّ ٱللَّهَ عَلِيمٌ خَبِيرٌ ﴾

﴾ O mankind! We have created you from a male and a female, and made you nations and tribes, that you may know one another. Verily the most honorable of you with Allāh is that [believer] who has taqwā [i.e., one of the Muttaqūn [pious]]. Verily Allāh is All-Knowing, All-Aware. ﴿ 49:13

Allāh created us with the same mother and father [Adam and Huwa [Eve]] then gave such diverse appearance in His creation of mankind "***that you might know one another***" and no person of any race or tribe is better than another except, "***that [believer] who has taqwā***". Allāh reminds us after giving us this criterion that elevates one over another, that regardless of our opinion, He is the All-Knowing; All-Aware, so He knows what we do not. How presumptuous it is of a person to think their color or tribe is worth any recognition as a criterion for honor! Only the Prophet [ﷺ] would have right to do so as he was the best of Allāh's creation yet he was not arrogant on account of it. What is appalling is that its origin is from Satan, may the curse of Allāh be upon him. Allāh tells us:

---

[177] Narrated by Ibn Hibbān in his *Sahīh* and Imām Ahmad in his *Musnad* and declared *sahīh* by *Shaykh* Al-Albānī.

﴿ وَلَقَدْ خَلَقْنَـٰكُمْ ثُمَّ صَوَّرْنَـٰكُمْ ثُمَّ قُلْنَا لِلْمَلَـٰٓئِكَةِ ٱسْجُدُوا۟ لِـَٔادَمَ فَسَجَدُوٓا۟ إِلَّآ
إِبْلِيسَ لَمْ يَكُن مِّنَ ٱلسَّـٰجِدِينَ ۝١١ قَالَ مَا مَنَعَكَ أَلَّا تَسْجُدَ إِذْ أَمَرْتُكَ ۖ قَالَ
أَنَا۠ خَيْرٌ مِّنْهُ خَلَقْتَنِى مِن نَّارٍ وَخَلَقْتَهُۥ مِن طِينٍ ۝١٢ قَالَ فَٱهْبِطْ مِنْهَا فَمَا يَكُونُ
لَكَ أَن تَتَكَبَّرَ فِيهَا فَٱخْرُجْ إِنَّكَ مِنَ ٱلصَّـٰغِرِينَ ۝١٣ قَالَ أَنظِرْنِىٓ إِلَىٰ يَوْمِ
يُبْعَثُونَ ۝١٤ قَالَ إِنَّكَ مِنَ ٱلْمُنظَرِينَ ۝١٥ قَالَ مَا مَنَعَكَ أَلَّا تَسْجُدَ إِذْ أَمَرْتُكَ ۖ
قَالَ أَنَا۠ خَيْرٌ مِّنْهُ خَلَقْتَنِى مِن نَّارٍ وَخَلَقْتَهُۥ مِن طِينٍ ۝١٢ قَالَ فَٱهْبِطْ مِنْهَا فَمَا
يَكُونُ لَكَ أَن تَتَكَبَّرَ فِيهَا فَٱخْرُجْ إِنَّكَ مِنَ ٱلصَّـٰغِرِينَ ۝١٣ قَالَ أَنظِرْنِىٓ إِلَىٰ يَوْمِ
يُبْعَثُونَ ۝١٤ ﴾

﴾ And surely, We created you [your father Adam] and then gave you shape [the noble shape of a human being], then We told the angels, ' Prostrate to Adam,' and they prostrated, except Iblīs [Satan], he refused to be of those who prostrate.[Allāh] said: 'What prevented you [O Iblīs] that you did not prostrate, when I commanded you? Iblīs said,' I am better than he [Adam] is, You created me from fire, and him You created from clay. [Allāh] said: '[O Iblīs] get down from this [Paradise]; it is not for you to be arrogant here. Get out, for you are of the humiliated and disgraced.' [Iblīs] said: 'Allow me respite till the Day they are raised up [i.e., the Day of Resurrection]. [Allāh] said, 'You are of those allowed respite. [Iblīs] said;' Because You have sent me astray, surely I will sit in wait against them [humans] on your straight path. Then I will come to them from before them and behind them from their right and from their left, and you will not find most of them as thankful ones [i.e., they will not be dutiful to Allāh].' [Allāh] said [to Iblīs]; ' Get out from this [Paradise] disgraced and expelled. Whoever of them [mankind] will follow you, then surely I will fill Hell with you all.﴿ 7:11-18

Racism is one of the plots of Satan to lead mankind into Hell with him, so beware sisters, steer clear of his schemes and Allāh Alone is our helper. Here are a couple of *hadīths* to ponder over, the Prophet [ﷺ] said:

"Indeed Allāh has removed from you the blind loyalties of jāhiliyyah and the pride for ancestry. Either be a pious believer, or a miserable insolent. [All of] you are the children of Adam and Adam is from dust. Let some men cease to take pride in others who are nothing but burning coal for the Hell Fire, it will be easier for Allāh to handle them than a dung beetle driving his nose into filth."[178]

Abū Mūsā Al-Ash'arī reported that the Prophet [ﷺ] said:

"Allāh created Adam from a handful [of soil] which He took from the whole earth: so the children of Adam are in accordance with the earth; some red, some white, some black and some a mixture, also smooth and rough, bad and good."[179]

Part of a longer hadīth reads, *"... whoever invites to tribalism, or aids in tribalism and is killed he dies the death of jāhiliyyah... he is not of me and I am not of him."*[180]

3] Constant close association and love for the disbelievers.

Yet another problem from the period of ignorance is the close association and thereby love for those disobedient to Allāh. Allāh said:

﴿ يَـٰٓأَيُّهَا ٱلَّذِينَ ءَامَنُواْ لَا تَتَّخِذُواْ ٱلَّذِينَ ٱتَّخَذُواْ دِينَكُمْ هُزُوًا وَلَعِبًا مِّنَ ٱلَّذِينَ أُوتُواْ ٱلْكِتَـٰبَ مِن قَبْلِكُمْ وَٱلْكُفَّارَ أَوْلِيَآءَ ۚ وَٱتَّقُواْ ٱللَّهَ إِن كُنتُم مُّؤْمِنِينَ ﴿٥٧﴾ ﴾

﴾ O you who believe do not take as Awliyā` [friends and protectors] those who take your religion as mockery and fun from amongst those who

---

[178] *Sunan* of Abū Dāwud, [Eng. Trans. Vol. 3 Pg. 1418 #5097]. Declared to be *hasan* by *Shaykh* Al-Albānī.

[179] *Sunan* of Abū Dāwud, [Eng. Trans. Vol.3 pg.1314 #4678]. Declared *sahīh* by Shaykh Al-Albānī.

[180] *Sahīh Muslim*, [Engl. Trans. Vol.3 #4555].

***received the Scripture before you nor from the Idolaters; and fear Allāh concerning this if you are truly Believers.*﴾ 5:57**

﴿ يَـٰٓأَيُّهَا ٱلَّذِينَ ءَامَنُوا۟ لَا تَتَّخِذُوٓا۟ ءَابَآءَكُمْ وَإِخْوَٰنَكُمْ أَوْلِيَآءَ إِنِ ٱسْتَحَبُّوا۟
ٱلْكُفْرَ عَلَى ٱلْإِيمَـٰنِ ۚ وَمَن يَتَوَلَّهُم مِّنكُمْ فَأُو۟لَـٰٓئِكَ هُمُ ٱلظَّـٰلِمُونَ ﴿٢٣﴾ قُلْ إِن
كَانَ ءَابَآؤُكُمْ وَأَبْنَآؤُكُمْ وَإِخْوَٰنُكُمْ وَأَزْوَٰجُكُمْ وَعَشِيرَتُكُمْ وَأَمْوَٰلٌ
ٱقْتَرَفْتُمُوهَا وَتِجَـٰرَةٌ تَخْشَوْنَ كَسَادَهَا وَمَسَـٰكِنُ تَرْضَوْنَهَآ أَحَبَّ إِلَيْكُم مِّنَ ٱللَّهِ
وَرَسُولِهِۦ وَجِهَادٍ فِى سَبِيلِهِۦ فَتَرَبَّصُوا۟ حَتَّىٰ يَأْتِىَ ٱللَّهُ بِأَمْرِهِۦ ۗ وَٱللَّهُ لَا يَهْدِى ٱلْقَوْمَ
ٱلْفَـٰسِقِينَ ﴿٢٤﴾ ﴾

﴿ *O you who believe! Take not as Awliyā` [supporters and helpers] your fathers and your brothers if they prefer disbelief to Belief. And whoever of you does so, then he is one of the dhālimūn [wrong-doers]. Say;' If your fathers, your sons, your wealth you have gained, the commerce in which you fear a decline, and the dwellings in which you delight are dearer to you than Allāh and His Messenger, and striving hard and fighting in His Cause, then wait until Allāh brings about His Decision [torment]. And Allāh guides not the people who are the fāsiqūn [rebellious, disobedient to Allāh.*﴾ 9:23-24

Allāh has forbidden us to take disbelievers as friends or helpers. Therefore, unless they are family, there is no reason to be around them except if it is absolutely necessary e.g. at school or the work place. However, a Muslim never chooses a disbeliever over a Muslim, family or not. I should explain that your family still has rights upon you and this will be covered in a separate subtitle later by the will of Allāh. Contact should be minimal and inviting them to Islām should be on matters you have knowledge about. We should never compromise our religion nor treat the Muslims with harshness to please the *kuffār* because they 'embarrass' you by *kuffār* standards, perhaps because they [Muslims] are covered adequately or they point out that they won't be around alcohol etc. This is not an archaic religion, rather it is for all people and for the rest of time, it is the only religion accepted by Allāh. Allāh said:

﴿ وَمَن يَبْتَغِ غَيْرَ ٱلْإِسْلَٰمِ دِينًا فَلَن يُقْبَلَ مِنْهُ وَهُوَ فِى ٱلْءَاخِرَةِ مِنَ ٱلْخَٰسِرِينَ ﴾

***﴾ And who ever seeks a religion other than Islām, it will never be accepted of him and in the Hereafter he will be one of the losers. ﴿* 3:85**

I should point out, Allāh chose this religion for us gave it a name 'Islām' and perfected it, every aspect of our lives is covered and every question is answered. If any human being is not following it, *he or she* is at a loss and in darkness. A Believer never apologizes for any part of Islām. Few are really on it [the true path] and if you are, you should thank Allāh and beg Him to keep you on it. Allāh said:

﴿ ٱلْيَوْمَ أَكْمَلْتُ لَكُمْ دِينَكُمْ وَأَتْمَمْتُ عَلَيْكُمْ نِعْمَتِى وَرَضِيتُ لَكُمُ ٱلْإِسْلَٰمَ دِينًا ﴾

***﴾ This day, I have perfected your religion for you, completed My Favor upon you, and have chosen Islām as your religion. ﴿* 5:3**

When this verse was revealed the Jews at the time said to 'Umar Ibn Al-Khattāb [ﷺ], "You [Muslims] recite a verse, and had it been revealed to us, we would have taken the day of its revelation as a day of celebration."[1] This is because they knew just how beautiful and important this verse is.[2] And so Allāh warns us:

﴿ وَدَّ كَثِيرٌ مِّنْ أَهْلِ ٱلْكِتَٰبِ لَوْ يَرُدُّونَكُم مِّنۢ بَعْدِ إِيمَٰنِكُمْ كُفَّارًا حَسَدًا مِّنْ عِندِ أَنفُسِهِم مِّنۢ بَعْدِ مَا تَبَيَّنَ لَهُمُ ٱلْحَقُّ ۖ فَٱعْفُوا۟ وَٱصْفَحُوا۟ حَتَّىٰ يَأْتِىَ ٱللَّهُ بِأَمْرِهِۦٓ ۗ إِنَّ ٱللَّهَ عَلَىٰ كُلِّ شَىْءٍ قَدِيرٌ ﴿١٠٩﴾ ﴾

***﴾ Many of the people of the scripture [Jews and Christians] wish that if they could turn you away as disbelievers after you have believed, out of envy from their own selves, even after the truth [that Muhammad ﷺ is Allāh's Messenger] has become manifest unto them. ﴿* 2:109**

﴿ وَمَآ أَكْثَرُ ٱلنَّاسِ وَلَوْ حَرَصْتَ بِمُؤْمِنِينَ ﴿١٠٣﴾ ﴾

***﴾ And most of mankind will not believe even if you desire it eagerly. ﴿* 12:103**

---

1 *Sahīh Al-Bukhārī*, [Eng. Trans. vol. 6 pg.103].

2 Note: *Muslims* do not make up holidays without proof from authentic *Sunnah*.

Therefore, the excuse of getting close to the point of sin under the guise of *da'wah* [propagating the religion] is not acceptable, they will try to influence you to their misguided ways till you forget right from wrong! If they don't accept it as it is in its perfection that is upon them. So do not fall into sin along with them thereby putting yourself in the path of the wrath of Allāh such as celebrating their holidays, consuming alcohol or pork, listening to evil talk etc. in thinking you can convert them. Conversion of family or former companions[183] is to be done in permissible circumstances that is without breaking the laws of Allāh, may Allāh facilitate us all, Āmīn. You should surround yourself with Muslims upon the Qur`ān and authentic *Sunnah* of the Prophet [ﷺ] with the understanding of the companions [ﷺ]. That is proper and fitting of a believing lady.

4] Our Cultures.

We all by the will of Allāh have some sort of culture from whatever part of the world we are from as far as foods, dress, speech or occasions is concerned. However, Islāmic culture is what is first and thereafter whatever from your culture that does not go against the laws of Allāh and His Messenger [ﷺ] we keep, whatever is *harām* [unlawful in Islām] we leave out. Allāh the Almighty said:

﴿ وَإِذَا قِيلَ لَهُمُ ٱتَّبِعُوا۟ مَآ أَنزَلَ ٱللَّهُ قَالُوا۟ بَلْ نَتَّبِعُ مَآ أَلْفَيْنَا عَلَيْهِ ءَابَآءَنَآ ۗ أَوَلَوْ كَانَ ءَابَآؤُهُمْ لَا يَعْقِلُونَ شَيْـًٔا وَلَا يَهْتَدُونَ ١٧٠ ﴾

﴿ When it is said to them, ' follow what Allāh has revealed, ' they say, ' No! We shall follow the way of our fathers. ' What! Even though their fathers were devoid of wisdom and guidance? ﴾ 2:170.

3 Female friends only, the men should be led to the *masjid* that they may talk to other men, it is not acceptable for a believing lady to be alone with or talk to non *mahram* [see glossary] men.

His Prophet [ﷺ] warned us,

"Whoever does an action that we have not commanded then that action shall be rejected." [184]

Therefore, if after knowing what we have been ordered to do in Islām there are things from our culture that is *halāl* we may keep it then leave the rest. For example certain foods are enjoyed by a people which is *halāl*, then enjoy, or giving certain gifts on the marriage of their child, or in the case of a mother living with her daughter for a while after the birth of a child, then continue as it is acceptable by the will of Allāh. Others however, are tantamount to sin, some of which, we shall cover by the will of Allāh.

a] Traditional dress.

Most traditional dress, not all, can be worn in the presence of permitted family or other Muslim sisters as it generally covers the parts she should cover in the presence of the aforementioned people [see chapter on dress]. However, outdoors or in the presence of non-*mahram* men she must still put on a cloak and full *hijāb*. Even sisters whose traditional dress includes a headdress of any sort, need *hijāb* in addition. This is because a loose headscarf or a head-wrap leaves her ears, neck, hair, bosom and face out not to mention the rest of her body. Unless the traditional dress includes *hijāb* which covers the parts Allāh has ordered her to cover[185], the traditional dress is to be worn under her *hijāb*.

b] Mahr [Dowry/Bridal Money].

Allāh the Exalted the Mighty said,

﴿ وَءَاتُواْ ٱلنِّسَآءَ صَدُقَـٰتِهِنَّ نِحۡلَةٗۚ فَإِن طِبۡنَ لَكُمۡ عَن شَيۡءٖ مِّنۡهُ نَفۡسٗا فَكُلُوهُ هَنِيٓـٔٗا مَّرِيٓـٔٗا ﴾

﴿ And give to the women [whom you marry] their Mahr [obligatory bridal-money given by the husband to the wife at the time of marriage] with a good heart; but if they, out of their own good pleasure, remit any part of it to you, take it, and enjoy it without fear of any harm [as Allāh has made it lawful]. ﴾ 4:4.

---

[184] *Sahīh Muslim*, [Eng. Trans. Vol.3 pg. 1025-1026].

[185] See chapter on 'Dress of a believing lady'.

Therefore [contrary to some cultures], Allāh has commanded the man to give the lady dowry. Neither the lady nor her family is supposed to give dowry to the man. The man may not force her to return the dowry as it is hers to do with as she wills. However if she by her own sweet will, not through pressure or fear, decides after receiving it [the *Mahr*] to return some of it to her husband then that is legal as Allāh stated in the previous verse. For more details on the *Mahr*, it is covered in the chapter on *nikāh* [marriage].

c] Speech.

i] Included in this are the oaths and swearing by other than Allāh, which is tantamount to *Shirk*. For example, 'I swear by my dead mother' or ' by George' or any other creation, all of this is to be left behind. The Prophet [ﷺ] said:

"Lo! Allāh forbids you to swear by your fathers, so whoever has to take an oath, he should swear by Allāh or keep quiet." [186]

The Prophet [ﷺ] also said,

"Whoever swears saying his oath, ' By Al-Lāt and Al-'Uzza,'[187] *should say, 'None has the right to be worshipped but Allāh'; and whoever says to his friend, 'Come let me gamble with you', should give something in charity."* [188]

Therefore if one forgets and swears any such oath [i.e., by any created thing] then they should say the above statement of *Tawhīd*. Also, one should note that certain types of speech from *jāhiliyyah* calls for expiation as mentioned above. Further, if one swears by Allāh they should tell the truth.

ii] Also, foul language, backbiting, cursing others and constant gossiping is to be avoided at all costs. The references in the Qur`ān and *hadīths* on these topics are numerous. Allāh said:

---

[186] *Sahīh Al-Bukhārī*, [Eng. Trans. vol. 8 #642].

[187] Idols which used to be worshipped in the time of pre-Islāmic ignorance.

[188] *Sahīh Al-Bukhārī*, [Eng. Trans. vol.8 #645].

﴿ يَـٰٓأَيُّهَا ٱلَّذِينَ ءَامَنُوا۟ ٱجْتَنِبُوا۟ كَثِيرًا مِّنَ ٱلظَّنِّ إِنَّ بَعْضَ ٱلظَّنِّ إِثْمٌ ۖ وَلَا تَجَسَّسُوا۟ وَلَا يَغْتَب بَّعْضُكُم بَعْضًا ۚ أَيُحِبُّ أَحَدُكُمْ أَن يَأْكُلَ لَحْمَ أَخِيهِ مَيْتًا فَكَرِهْتُمُوهُ ۚ وَٱتَّقُوا۟ ٱللَّهَ ۚ إِنَّ ٱللَّهَ تَوَّابٌ رَّحِيمٌ ﴾

﴾ O you who believe! Avoid much suspicion; indeed some suspicions are sins. And spy not, neither backbite one another. Would one of you like to eat the flesh of his dead brother? You would hate it [so hate backbiting]. And fear Allāh.﴿ 49:12

﴿ وَيْلٌ لِّكُلِّ هُمَزَةٍ لُّمَزَةٍ ﴾

﴾ Woe to every slanderer and backbiter.﴿ 104:1

The Prophet [ﷺ] said:

"A qattāt[189] *will not enter Paradise."* [190]

"The worst people in the sight of Allāh on the Day of Resurrection will be the double faced people who appear to some people with one face and to other people with another face."[191]

"Do you know what is backbiting?' they said 'Allāh and his Messenger know best', He [ﷺ] said, *'It is saying something about your brother which he dislikes.'* Someone asked, 'Supposing what I said about my brother is true was true?', and he [ﷺ] replied, *' If what you say about him is true you have backbitten him, and if it is not true you have slandered him."*[192]

"If somebody curses a believer, then his sin will be as if he murdered him."[193]

"Men accustomed to cursing will not be intercessors or witnesses on the Day of Resurrection." [see chapter on *Shirk* for clarification of intercession][194]

---

[189] A person who conveys information from one person to another with the intention of causing harm and enmity between them.

[190] *Sahīh Al-Bukhārī*, [Eng. Trans. vol.8 #82].

[191] *Sahīh Al-Bukhārī*, [Eng. Trans. vol.8 #84].

[192] *Sahīh Muslim*, [Eng. Trans. Vol.4 #6265].

[193] *Sahīh Al-Bukhārī*, [Engl. Trans. vol.8 # 73].

[194] *Sahīh Muslim*, [Engl. Trans. Vol.4 #6283].

" The strong man is not the good wrestler but the strong man is he who controls himself when he is angry." [for the sake of Allāh][195]

"The most despicable amongst the people to Allāh is the ruthless argumentative person." [196]

"If anyone conceals the faults of a Muslim Allāh will conceal his faults in this world and in the next. Allāh helps His slave as long as he helps his brother."[197]

"Do you know who the bankrupt one is? The bankrupt one from my Ummah is one who comes one the Day of Judgment having performed Prayer, Fasting and giving the Zakāh . However, Along with all this, he had abused this person, slandered that person, eaten the wealth of that person and unlawfully spilt the blood of that person. These people will take from his good deeds. If, however, his good deeds are exhausted, then their sins will be put upon him and then he will be thrown into the Fire."[198]

Consequently, the tongue of a Muslim is to be controlled and she should have the best of character and speech especially towards the Muslims. She should not let the fact that other Muslims sin in this aspect, to allow her to lapse but should advise them and think about her own soul. As a final reminder the Prophet [ﷺ] said:

" The worst people are those whom the people desert or leave in order to save themselves from their dirty language or from their transgression."[199]

d] Special occasions.

These are present within Islām and outside Islām, however upon accepting Islām, one is obligated to leave all those celebrations and holidays that are not permissible in Islām. Examples of those against Islāmic practices are many ranging from birthdays of regular people, saints or prophets to weird

---

[195] *Sahīh Muslim*, [Engl. Trans. Vol.4 #6313].

[196] *Sahīh Muslim*, [Eng. Trans. Vol. 4 #6447 pg. 1403].

[197] *Sahīh Muslim*, [Engl. Trans. Vol. 4 #6518].

[198] *Sahīh Muslim*, [Eng. Trans. vol. 4 #6251].

[199] *Sahīh Al-Bukhārī*, [Eng. Trans. vol. 8. #80].

or absurd devilish ones like Halloween, as celebrated in the West. If one examines the origins of some of these holidays especially ones considered *religious*, they stem from pagan practices of peoples of old destroyed by Allāh! We should be careful of imitating the *kuffār* in what they consider 'harmless' practices and be aware of trying to please them at the expense of your religion. We neither celebrate such nor do we congratulate them on such occasions. Allāh said:

﴿ يَـٰٓأَيُّهَا ٱلَّذِينَ ءَامَنُوا۟ لَا تَتَّخِذُوا۟ بِطَانَةً مِّن دُونِكُمْ لَا يَأْلُونَكُمْ خَبَالًا وَدُّوا۟ مَا عَنِتُّمْ قَدْ بَدَتِ ٱلْبَغْضَآءُ مِنْ أَفْوَٰهِهِمْ وَمَا تُخْفِى صُدُورُهُمْ أَكْبَرُ ۚ قَدْ بَيَّنَّا لَكُمُ ٱلْـَٔايَـٰتِ ۖ إِن كُنتُمْ تَعْقِلُونَ ﴿١١٨﴾ ﴾

﴾ O you who believe! Take not as [your] bitānah [advisors, consultants, protectors, helpers, friends] those outside your religion [pagans, Jews, Christians, and Hypocrites] since they will not fail to do their best to corrupt you. Their desire is to harm you severely. Hatred has already appeared from their mouths, but what their breasts conceal is far worse. Indeed We have made plain to you the Āyāt [proofs, evidences, verses] if you understand.﴿ 3:118

The occasions celebrated in Islām are :

a] *'Īd Al-Fitr*.

This is the celebration [or festival] at the end of the month of *Ramadān*. On the sighting of the moon indicating the change of the month we stop the fast and the next day is the *'Īd* [i.e., the first day of Shawwāl], which is celebrated for three days. The celebration is of course according to the acceptable practices, which are:

Sadaqah Al-Fitr [compulsory charity to be paid upon the end of *Ramadān*]

"The Prophet [ﷺ] ordered the people to pay *Zakāh Al-Fitr* before going to the *'Īd* prayer."[200]

It is due from every Muslim.

" Allāh's Messenger [ﷺ] made it incumbent on all the slave or free Muslims, male or female, to pay one *sā`* of dates or barley as *Zakāh Al-Fitr*."[201]

---

[200] *Sahīh Al-Bukhārī*, [Eng. Trans. vol. 2 # 585].

This includes the very old and the very young i.e., as long the child is born when it is due.

'*Īd* Prayer.

It is *Sunnah* to eat a little after Fajr prayer and before going to the *'Īd* prayer which is held after sunrise.

"The Prophet of Allāh [ﷺ] never proceeded [for the prayer] on the Day of *'Īd Al-Fiṯr* unless he had eaten some dates."

Anas also narrated:

"The Prophet [ﷺ] used to eat an odd number of dates."[202]

There is no *adhān* or *Iqāmah* for the *'Īd* prayer. Also, the prayer is offered before the *khuṯbah* [sermon]. All Muslims must come out for the prayer even the menstruating sisters except that they [Those on their menses] do not enter the *muṣallā* [prayer area]. Narrated Umm 'Aṯiyyah [ﷺ]:

" We were ordered to go out [for *'Īd*] and also to take along with us the menstruating women, mature girls and virgins staying in seclusion. The menstruating women could present themselves at the religious gathering and keep invocation of Muslims but should keep away from their *muṣallā*."[203]

This prayer is of course in addition to the five daily-prescribed prayers.

Permissible entertainment.

Singing [permissible lyrics] and playing a tambourine with no bells attached. Narrated 'Ā`ishah [ﷺ]:

"Allāh's Messenger [ﷺ] came to my house while two girls were singing beside me the songs of Bu'āth [a story about the war between the two tribes of the Anṣār before Islām]. The Prophet [ﷺ] lay down and turned his face to

---

[201] *Ṣaḥīḥ Al-Bukhārī*, [Eng. Trans. vol. 2 # 580]. One *ṣā'* is approximately 3 kg.

[202] *Ṣaḥīḥ Al-Bukhārī*, [Eng. Trans. vol. 2 # 73].

[203] *Ṣaḥīḥ Al-Bukhārī*, [Eng. Trans. vol. 2 # 97].

the other side. Then Abū Bakr came and spoke harshly to me saying, 'Musical instruments of the Satan near the Prophet [ﷺ]? Allāh's Messenger [ﷺ] turned his face toward him and said, '**Leave them.**' [204] In another narration it continues, "It happened on the *'Īd* day and Allāh's Messenger [ﷺ] said, '**O Abū Bakr! There is an *'Īd* for every nation and this is our *'Īd*.**" In part of the first narration continues that the people of Banī Arfidah where playing with shields and spears [as display] 'Ā`ishah [رضي الله عنها] continued: "either I requested the Prophet [ﷺ] or he asked me whether I would like to see the display. I replied in the affirmative. Then the Prophet [ﷺ] made me stand behind him and my cheek was touching his cheek and he was saying, '**Carry on! O Banī Arfidah,**' till I got tired. The Prophet [ﷺ] asked me, '**Are you satisfied [Is that sufficient for you]?**' I replied in the affirmative and he told me to leave."[205] In another narration of the same *hadīth* in Muslim is, "some Abyssinians came and gave a demonstration of armed fight on the *'Īd* day in the mosque."[206]

Narrated Ar-Rabī', the daughter of Mu'awwadh Ibn 'Afrā`:
"After the consummation of my marriage, the Prophet [ﷺ] came and sat on my bed as you are sitting now, and our little girls started beating the tambourines and reciting elegiac, verses mourning my father who had been killed in the battle of Badr. One of them said, 'Among us is a Prophet who knows what will happen tomorrow.' On that the Prophet [ﷺ] said, '*Leave this [saying] and keep on saying the verses which you had been saying before'.*"[207]

Food and drink.

Whatever you chose so long as it is not from among the *harām*. In Islām, all food and drink is permissible except that which is pointed out in the Qur`ān

---

[204] *Sahīh Al-Bukhārī*, [Eng. Trans. vol. 2 #70].

[205] *Sahīh Al-Bukhārī*, [Eng. Trans. vol. 2 # 70].

[206] *Sahīh Muslim*, [Eng. Trans. vol. 2 #1943]. Also in *Muslim* is the addition "I remember the Messenger of Allāh [ﷺ] standing at the door of my apartment screening me with his mantle." #1941

[207] *Sahīh Al-Bukhārī*, [Eng. Trans. vol.7 #77]. Note the tambourine here is a simple drum [daff] with no tinkling plates round it.

and *Sunnah* as forbidden [pork, dead meat [or not slaughtered with the exception of fish], meat which is slaughtered and the name of other than Allāh is mentioned [e.g. an idol], blood and alcohol]. To find out more see the chapter on foods. Also, Muslims do not over-eat but as in all the practices in Islām we adopt moderation. Narrated Ibn 'Umar [ﷺ]:

"Allāh's Messenger [ﷺ] said, ' **A believer eats in one intestine [is satisfied with little food], and a *kāfir* [unbeliever] or a hypocrite eats in seven intestines [eats too much].**" [208]

As a reminder, always mention the name of Allāh over your food before you eat, [i.e., بسم الله *'Bismillāh'*]

ii] *'Īd Al-Adhā* [sacrifice]

This celebration is on the 10th day of *Dhul-Hijjah.* It continues for four days. The celebration in all aspects is the same as *'Īd Al-Fitr* with the exception of sacrifice[209] after the prayer. Allāh said:

﴿ وَلِكُلِّ أُمَّةٍ جَعَلْنَا مَنسَكًا لِّيَذْكُرُوا ٱسْمَ ٱللَّهِ عَلَىٰ مَا رَزَقَهُم مِّنۢ بَهِيمَةِ ٱلْأَنْعَـٰمِ ﴾

﴾ And for every nation We have appointed religious ceremonies, that they may mention the Name of Allāh over the beast of cattle that He has given them for food. ﴿ 22:34

[208] *Sahīh Al-Bukhārī*, [Eng. Trans. vol. 7. # 306].

[209] Sacrifice in Islām - It is the slaughter of an animal [cattle: ox; cow, sheep, camel, goat.] on certain specified occasions like *Hajj*, *'Īd* or *'Aqīqah* of a child. It is done by uttering the name of Allāh over it before it is killed, then its meat is given away in charity and eaten by the persons involved. Allāh said;

﴿ فَكُلُوا مِنْهَا وَأَطْعِمُوا ٱلْبَآئِسَ ٱلْفَقِيرَ ﴾

﴾ Then eat thereof and feed therewith the poor who have a very hard time. ﴿ 22:28

﴿ لَن يَنَالَ ٱللَّهَ لُحُومُهَا وَلَا دِمَآؤُهَا وَلَـٰكِن يَنَالُهُ ٱلتَّقْوَىٰ مِنكُمْ ﴾

﴾ It is neither their meat nor their blood that reaches Allāh, but it is piety from you that reaches Him. ﴿ 22:37

His Prophet [ﷺ] said,

"The first thing to be done on this day [first day of 'Īd Al-Adhā] is to pray; and after returning from the prayer we slaughter our sacrifices [in the name of Allāh] and whoever does so, he has acted according to our Sunnah." [210]

The permissible food and entertainment is as above.

iii] *'Aqīqah* [it is the sacrifice of sheep on the occasion of the birth of a child as a token of gratitude to Allāh.].

When a child is born whoever can afford to, should sacrifice one sheep for a girl and two for a boy. A child can be named the day it is born, if no *'Aqīqah* will be held for it. It is also from the *Sunnah* to perform *tahnīk*, which is the chewing a sweet food e.g. dates and rubbing it in the mouth of the new baby. The purpose of which is to train it to eat. In an authentic *hadīth* narrated upon the authority of Abū Mūsā who said:

"A son was born to me and I took him to the Prophet [ﷺ] who named him Ibrāhīm, did *tahnīk* for him with a date, invoked Allāh to bless him and returned him to me." [211]

The *Adhān* should be called in its right ear immediately after its birth. Abū Rāfi' reported:

"I saw the messenger of Allāh [ﷺ] uttering the adhān in the ear of Al-Hasan Ibn 'Alī when Fātimah gave birth to him."[212]

iv] The *Nikāh* [marriage ceremony]**and the *Walīmah*** [wedding banquet]

It is considered obligatory to give a banquet upon marriage, the Prophet [ﷺ] said:

"Give a banquet, even with one sheep." [213]

This celebration is similar to the *'Īd* as far as food, drinks and entertainment are concerned.

---

[210] *Sahīh Al-Bukhārī*, [Eng. Trans. vol. 2 #71].

[211] *Sahīh Al-Bukhārī*, [Eng. Trans. vol. 7 #376].

[212] Sunan of Abū Dāwud, [Eng. Trans. Vol. 3 #5086]. Declared *hasan* by *Shaykh* Al-Albānī.

[213] *Sahīh Al-Bukhārī*, [Eng. Trans. Vol. 7].

5] Music.

Allāh, the Almighty, the Reckoner, said:

﴿ وَمِنَ ٱلنَّاسِ مَن يَشْتَرِى لَهْوَ ٱلْحَدِيثِ لِيُضِلَّ عَن سَبِيلِ ٱللَّهِ بِغَيْرِ عِلْمٍ وَيَتَّخِذَهَا
هُزُوًا ۚ أُو۟لَـٰٓئِكَ لَهُمْ عَذَابٌ مُّهِينٌ ﴿٦﴾ ﴾

***{ And of Mankind is he who purchases idle talks [i.e., music, singing etc.] to mislead [men] from the Path of Allāh without knowledge, and takes it [the Path of Allāh or the Verses of the Qur`ān] by way of mockery. For such there will be a humiliating torment [in the Hell-Fire].}* 31:6**

﴿ وَإِذْ قُلْنَا لِلْمَلَـٰٓئِكَةِ ٱسْجُدُوا۟ لِـَٔادَمَ فَسَجَدُوٓا۟ إِلَّآ إِبْلِيسَ كَانَ مِنَ ٱلْجِنِّ فَفَسَقَ عَنْ
أَمْرِ رَبِّهِۦٓ ۗ أَفَتَتَّخِذُونَهُۥ وَذُرِّيَّتَهُۥٓ أَوْلِيَآءَ مِن دُونِى وَهُمْ لَكُمْ عَدُوٌّۢ ۚ بِئْسَ لِلظَّـٰلِمِينَ بَدَلًا ﴾

***{ And [remember] when We said to the angels: 'Prostrate yourselves unto Adam.' So they prostrated themselves except Iblīs [Satan]. He was one of the jinn; he disobeyed the Command of his Lord. Will you then take him [Iblīs] and his offspring as protectors and helpers rather than Me while they are enemies to you? What an evil exchange for the <u>dh</u>ālimūn [polytheists, and wrong-doers].}* 18:50**

﴿ وَإِذْ قُلْنَا لِلْمَلَـٰٓئِكَةِ ٱسْجُدُوا۟ لِـَٔادَمَ فَسَجَدُوٓا۟ إِلَّآ إِبْلِيسَ قَالَ ءَأَسْجُدُ لِمَنْ خَلَقْتَ
طِينًا ﴿٦١﴾ قَالَ أَرَءَيْتَكَ هَـٰذَا ٱلَّذِى كَرَّمْتَ عَلَىَّ لَئِنْ أَخَّرْتَنِ إِلَىٰ يَوْمِ ٱلْقِيَـٰمَةِ
لَأَحْتَنِكَنَّ ذُرِّيَّتَهُۥٓ إِلَّا قَلِيلًا ﴿٦٢﴾ قَالَ ٱذْهَبْ فَمَن تَبِعَكَ مِنْهُمْ فَإِنَّ جَهَنَّمَ
جَزَآؤُكُمْ جَزَآءً مَّوْفُورًا ﴿٦٣﴾ وَٱسْتَفْزِزْ مَنِ ٱسْتَطَعْتَ مِنْهُم بِصَوْتِكَ وَأَجْلِبْ
عَلَيْهِم بِخَيْلِكَ وَرَجِلِكَ وَشَارِكْهُمْ فِى ٱلْأَمْوَٰلِ وَٱلْأَوْلَـٰدِ وَعِدْهُمْ ۚ وَمَا يَعِدُهُمُ
ٱلشَّيْطَـٰنُ إِلَّا غُرُورًا ﴿٦٤﴾ إِنَّ عِبَادِى لَيْسَ لَكَ عَلَيْهِمْ سُلْطَـٰنٌ ۚ وَكَفَىٰ بِرَبِّكَ وَكِيلًا ﴾

{ And [remember] when We said to the angels: 'Prostrate yourselves unto Adam.' So they prostrated themselves except Iblīs [Satan]. He[Satan] said: 'Shall I prostrate myself to one whom You created from clay?' [Iblīs [Satan]] said: 'See this one whom You have honored above me, if You give me respite [keep me alive] to the Day of Resurrection, I will surely

seize and mislead his offspring [by sending them astray] all but a few! Allāh said, 'Go, and whosoever of them follows you, surely Hell will be the recompense of you [all] - an ample recompense. And befool them gradually those whom you can among them with your voice [i.e., songs, music, and any other call for Allāh's disobedience], make assaults on them with your Calvary and your infantry, share with them wealth and children [by tempting them to earn money by illegal ways -usury, or by committing illegal sexual intercourse], and make promises to them.' But the Satan promises nothing but deceit. Verily My slaves [i.e., the true believers of Islāmic monotheism] -- you have no authority over them. And All-Sufficient is your Lord as a Guardian. ﴾ *17:61-65*

The Prophet [ﷺ] said:

"From among my followers there will be some people who will consider illegal sexual intercourse, the wearing of silk, the drinking of alcoholic drinks, and the use of musical instruments, as lawful."[214]

The wearing of silk referred to here is the prohibition of silk for men, women are permitted to wear it.[215] He [ﷺ] also said:

"The [Hell] Fire is surrounded by all kinds of desires and passions, while Paradise is surrounded by all kinds of disliked undesirable things." [216]

Unchecked desires and animalistic passions lead to the Fire while self control, perseverance, and chastity and all other virtues and the obedience to Allāh and His Messenger [ﷺ] lead to Paradise. What leads to Hell is easy to do while what leads to Paradise is difficult to do. It may seem difficult when one first accepts Islām to give up certain passions one had before, like music when most of the world is trying to tell you how harmless and even beneficial it is. However it is quite easy when weighed against the Hell- Fire as a reward! Allāh and His Messenger [ﷺ] have informed us that music is

---

[214] Sahīh *Al-Bukhārī*, [Eng. Trans. vol. 7 #494b].

[215] Sahīh *Al-Bukhārī*, [Eng. Trans. vol. 7 #731 and #733].

[216] Sahīh *Al-Bukhārī*, [Eng. Trans. vol. 8 #494]. Commentary following from *Fath Al-Bār`i*. Al-'Asqalānī's explanation of Sahīh *Al-Bukhārī*. Will be found in the Eng. Translation of *Al-Bukhārī*.

the instrument of Satan and is forbidden in Islām. It distracts one from the worship and remembrance of Allāh, it spreads corruption [through lewd lyrics etc.] and is a root and instrument of evil spread by *Shayṯān*. Those in the music industry are aware of how deeply it is so. In Islām, the only instrument allowed [on occasions like weddings and *'Īd*] is the *daff*, a kind of drum which looks like a tambourine with no bells attached.[217]

Males or females may do the permissible singing or poetry on occasions with the following rules;

1] The Lyrics are religious or related e.g. battles or they are educational e.g. for children or grammar [no obscenity involved] and such. The Prophet [ﷺ] used to recite the following poetry during the digging of the trench during that battle:

"O Allāh had it not been for You,
We would not have been guided,
Nor would we have given in charity,
Nor prayed.
So, bestow on us calmness, and when we meet the enemy.
Make our feet firm..." [218]

2] Musical instruments do not accompany it [except the daff].

3] Women may not 'perform' for men. Their voice is their *'Awrah* [private part in this case an attractive feature of a woman to a man].

4] It is not a profession to take up.

And may Allāh make us of the rightly guided, Āmīn.

Remember that although it is permissible to recite poetry according to the previous guidelines, it should not be so much as to distract from the remembrance of Allāh. The Prophet [ﷺ] said,

"It is better for a man to fill the inside of his body with pus than poetry." [219]

---

[217] See *hadīth* on prohibition of musical instruments under music. The *daff* is the only instrument that is permissible. All other wind /air, stringed instrument or drum is forbidden.

[218] *Sahīh Al-Bukhārī*, [Eng. Trans. vol.4 #272].

[219] *Sahīh Al-Bukhārī*, [Eng. Trans. vol. 7 #175].

And the scholars disapprove or reject the numerous 'Islāmic' songs emerging in this day and time one of the reasons being it is likening our religion to the *kuffār* to include songs in it [the *kuffār* use hymns and the like].

6] Changing Allāh's creation [our bodies].

a] Tattooing, making space in ones teeth, cutting ones body or face [scarring], burning marks into your body [for beautification], plucking or shaving your eyebrows, artificially lengthening hair etc.

"Allāh has cursed those women who practice tattooing and those who get themselves tattooed, and those who remove their face hairs, and those who create space between their teeth artificially to look beautiful, and such women as change the features created by Allāh." [220]

The Prophet [ﷺ] also said:

"Allāh has cursed the lady who artificially lengthens [her or someone else's] hair, and the one who gets her hair lengthened." [221]

According to the scholars of the *Salaf*, facial hair that is unusual for a woman to have such as a beard or mustache due to medication or some other reason, may be removed, and Allāh knows best.

b] Hair.

- As seen in the preceding *hadīth* we may not lengthen our hair artificially. This includes the use of attachments and wigs.
- Ladies may not shave their heads bald nor may they imitate the strange hairstyles of the *kuffār* or wear men's hairstyles. The Prophet [ﷺ] said: *"One who takes on the similitude [manner] of a certain people becomes of them."* [222]

---

[220] *Sahīh Al-Bukhārī*, [Eng. Trans. vol. 7 #815].

[221] *Sahīh Al-Bukhārī*, [Eng. Trans. vol. 7 # 816].

And, *"The Prophet [ﷺ] cursed those men who are in similitude [assume the manners] of women and those women who are in similitude [assume the manners] of men."*[223]

Also, during *'Umrah* and *Hajj*, only the Men are ordered to shave their heads. Women only trim an inch of hair, the scholars of the *Salaf* say the hair of a woman is an honor for her just as a man's beard is an honor for him. According to the scholars of *Ahl As-Sunnah wa Al-Jamā'ah* like *Shaykh* 'Abdul Al-Muhsin Al-'Abbād, the *hadīth* on not cutting ones hair in different lengths is pertinent to males, the females may do so for beautification [excluding strange *kuffār* haircuts].

- We may dye our hair so long as we avoid the color black. Henna and *kattam* are favored for it. The Prophet [ﷺ] said:

"Jews and Christians do not dye their hair so you should do the opposite of what they do."[224]

"The best things which gray hair are changed with are henna and kattam."[225]

"At the end of time there will be a people who will use this black dye like the crops of doves who will not experience the fragrance of Paradise."[226]

The use of the color black is usually used to try to keep the observer under the impression the person is younger than they really are and hence it is considered a kind of deception.

---

222 Sunan of Abū Dāwud, [Eng. Trans. Vol.3 Pg.1127]. Declared *hasan sahīh* by *Shaykh* Al-Albānī.

223 *Sahīh Al-Bukhārī*, [Eng. Trans. vol. 7 #773].

224 *Sahīh Al-Bukhārī*, [Eng. Trans. vol. 7 #786].

225 Sunan of Abū Dāwud, [Eng. Trans. vol. 3 #4193]. Kattam are leaves of a kind of tree growing in Yemen its dye is applied with henna to the hair. Henna is a skin dye. Declared *sahīh* by *Shaykh* Al-Albānī.

226 Sunan of Abū Dāwud, [Eng. Trans. vol. 3 #4200]. Declared *sahīh* by Al-Albānī.

CHAPTER 7

OUR MENSES IN ISLĀM

Allāh, the Exalted said:

﴿ وَيَسْـَٔلُونَكَ عَنِ ٱلْمَحِيضِ ۖ قُلْ هُوَ أَذًى فَٱعْتَزِلُوا۟ ٱلنِّسَآءَ فِى ٱلْمَحِيضِ ۖ وَلَا تَقْرَبُوهُنَّ حَتَّىٰ يَطْهُرْنَ ۖ فَإِذَا تَطَهَّرْنَ فَأْتُوهُنَّ ﴾

﴿ They ask you concerning menstruation. Say: that is a harm [a harmful thing for a husband to have sexual intercourse with his wife while she is having her menses], therefore keep away from women during menses and go not unto them till they are purified [from menses and have a bath].﴾ 2:222

The Prophet [ﷺ] said:

"This is a thing ordained for the daughters of Adam."[227]

This topic is a large one because of the different circumstances ladies undergo. I shall therefore endeavor to cover it under the prohibited and permissible acts in her daily life. By the will of Allāh, it will answer most common questions. A Muslim lives their life in between *salāh* waiting for the next *salāh* to come in. And in so doing by the will of Allāh one keeps away from evil as they are constantly remembering Allāh and waiting to worship Allāh [in *salāh*]. Therefore the first stop is *salāh*.

1) *Salāh*.

At the onset of her menses one cannot pray. However if the *Adhān* has been called for whatever *salāh* is due when she notices her period, that prayer is due upon her when she is purified. The Prophet [ﷺ] said:

"Whoever could get one Rak'ah of prayer [in its proper time] he has got the prayer."[228]

[227] *Sahīh Al-Bukhārī*, [Engl. Trans. Vol.1].

And in a *hadīth* narrated upon 'Ā`ishah [ﷺ] :

" The Prophet [ﷺ] said to me: ' Give up your prayer when your menses begin and when it has finished wash the blood off your body [take a bath] and start praying. " [229]

It is of paramount importance for the sister to keep a close track of her prayers, I have come up with a simple method that will help the sister, by the will of Allāh.

If your period starts anytime in the day or night and you have not made the *salāh* of that time yet [*fard salāh*] it is probably due on you, with three exceptions:

- The adhān has been called and you have already made your *salāh*.

Example: The adhān is called for *'Asr salāh*, you are already in *wudū`* or make it soon after the adhān. You make your *salāh* and a half-hour after that you notice the onset of your menses, it is obviously not due on you and you do not need to make it up.

- The time between sunrise and *Dhuhr salāh*. If you made *Fajr salāh* on time then there is no *salāh* due.
- The time between *'Ishā` salāh* and *Fajr salāh* at night. If you made *'Ishā`* on time. In this case there is no *fard salāh* due from you, so there is none to make up.

I should point out that the same is true for the end of her menses even if she has not yet bathed. If the period ends and she sees her sign of purity and she had enough time to have made one Rak'ah before the next adhān [if she had otherwise been clean], she needs to take a bath and make it up after her bath. It should also be noted that for the woman in labor who is not bleeding yet, *salāh* is still due on her as the pain is looked at the same way as a sick persons' pain.

---

[228] *Sahīh Al-Bukhārī*, [Eng. Trans. vol. 1 #554].

[229] *Sahīh Al-Bukhārī*, [Eng. Trans. vol.1 #327].

2) Fasting.

Fasting is also prohibited during menses. In part of a long narration, the Prophet [ﷺ] said:

"Is it not true that a woman can neither pray nor fast during her menses?"[230]

And just like her prayers, if her menses start on a day that she is fasting, she breaks her fast. And if it is the fast from the month of *Ramadān* or any obligatory fast like for an oath or *fidyah* [compensation], she makes it up when she is purified. This is true even if she notices it one minute before sunset. Supererogatory [voluntary] fasts need not be made up.

3) Clothing.

It is good to have a separate garment for use during menses as the Mothers of the Believers [the wives of the Prophet [ﷺ]] and the female Believers of that time used to do so. However, It is not obligatory. Umm Salamah [رضي الله عنها] narrates:

"While I was lying with the Prophet [ﷺ] under a woolen sheet, I got my menses. I slipped away and put on the *clothes* for menses. The Prophet [ﷺ] said, '**Have you got your menses?**' I replied, 'Yes'. He called me and I slept with him under the woolen sheet." [231]

4) Her spouse.

Allāh, the Almighty, the Wise, has prohibited sexual relations while on ones menses.

﴿ وَيَسْـَٔلُونَكَ عَنِ ٱلْمَحِيضِ ۖ قُلْ هُوَ أَذًى فَٱعْتَزِلُوا۟ ٱلنِّسَآءَ فِى ٱلْمَحِيضِ ۖ وَلَا تَقْرَبُوهُنَّ حَتَّىٰ يَطْهُرْنَ ۖ فَإِذَا تَطَهَّرْنَ فَأْتُوهُنَّ ﴾

[230] *Sahīh Al-Bukhārī*, [Eng. Trans. vol. 1 #301].

[231] *Sahīh Al-Bukhārī*, [Eng. Trans. vol. 1 #297].

﴾ They ask you concerning menstruation say: ' that it is a harm [a harmful thing for a husband to have a sexual intercourse with his wife while she is having her menses], there fore keep away from women during their menses and do not go unto them till they have purified [from menses and taken a bath].﴿ 2:222

When Allāh orders us to do anything our reply is 'we hear and obey', whether we understand or not. However the wisdom as to why sexual intercourse with a menstruating woman is prohibited, can be appreciated from a medical and hygienic standpoint and Allāh knows best. "According to a well-known authority, severe Menorrhagia, parametric irritation and parametric inflammations have been observed to follow such indiscretions [coition]."[232] We shall now obtain more detail from the *hadīth* of His Prophet [ﷺ]. Her spouse may do all other regular activities with her, eat, talk, he may recite Qur`ān while reclining in her lap, sleep in the same bed etc.

"Do everything except intercourse." [233]

And in another *hadīth* narrated by 'Ā`ishah [ؓ]

"During my menses he used to order me to put an *izār* [dress worn below the waist] and he used to fondle me "[234] and in another narration of the same *hadīth* she added: "None of you could control his sexual desire as the Prophet [ﷺ] could."[235]

Also: "While in menses I used to comb the hair of the Prophet [ﷺ]"[236]

"The Prophet [ﷺ] used to lean on my lap and recite Qur`ān while I was in my menses."[237]

---

[232] Footnotes in Sahīh Muslim, taken from Kisch, *Sexual Life of Women*; pg. 173.

[233] *Sahīh Muslim*, [Eng. Trans. vol. 1 #592].

[234] *Sahīh Al-Bukhārī*, [Eng. Trans. vol. 1 #298].

[235] *Sahīh Al-Bukhārī*,[Eng. Trans. vol. 1 #299].

[236] *Sahīh Al-Bukhārī*, [Eng. Trans. vol. 1 #294].

[237] *Sahīh Al-Bukhārī*, [Eng. Trans. vol. 1 #296].

And Umm Salamah [ﷺ] narrated another *hadīth* that the Prophet [ﷺ] said: "... **'Have you got *nifās* [menses]?'** I replied, 'Yes'. He then called me and made me lie under the same sheet."[238]

5) Reading Qur`ān and *Hadīth*.

- Touching the Qur`ān is prohibited by many of the scholars of the *Salaf*.
- Touching and reading a copy of the translation of the Qur`ān is permitted as it is not considered to be the actual Qur`ān even if the Arabic text appears alongside the translation, this opinion is held by the well known scholars upon the way of the *Salaf*. " The prohibition of touching the Qur`ān does not cover such translations. There is no prohibition on a ***muhdith*** touching commentaries of the Qur`ān which explain its meanings. The same holds true for books of *Hadīth*."[239]
- Reading books of ***Hadīth*** and books where verses of the Qur`ān are included is permissible.
- Listening to someone else recite Qur`ān is permitted as seen in the previous *hadīth*.
- Touching the Qur`ān by a woman who is a teacher or a student of Qur`ān is allowed provided that a cloth or pencil is used to turn the pages and Allāh knows best. "Abū Wā`il used to send his menstruating maidservant to bring the Qur`ān from Abū Razīn by carrying it from the Hanger."[240]
- Reciting the Qur`ān from memory. " The majority of scholars are of the opinion that it is not prohibited for her to recite the Qur`ān. Imam *Al-Bukhārī*, Ibn Jarīr, At-Tabarī and Ibn Al-Mundhir, Imam Mālik and Imam Ash-Shāfi'ī are of the opinion that it is permissible for her to recite an Ayah [verse of the Qur`ān]. *Shaykh Al-Islām* Ibn Taymiyyah said: 'Basically, there is no *Sunnah* to prevent her from reciting the Qur`ān. The *hadīth* that a menstruating woman and the one who is in *janābah*

---

[238] *Sahīh Al-Bukhārī*, [Eng. Trans. vol. 1 #297].

[239] A fatwā by Sheik Abdullah Ibn Jibrīn.

[240] *Sahīh Al-Bukhārī*,[Eng. Trans. vol.1 Chapter 5].

should not recite anything of the Qur`ān is a weak *hadīth* as agreed upon by knowledgeable scholars. In fact women at the time of the Prophet [ﷺ] used to have their monthly cycles and had the recitation of the Qur`ān been prohibited [as is the case with *salāh*] then the Prophet [ﷺ] would have made it clear to his Ummah [Islāmic community] and his wives would have known."[241]

6) *Hajj* and *'Umrah*.

She may assume Ihram as usual and perform all the ritual acts except the *Tawāf* around the Ka'bah and the two *rak'ahs* of prayer afterwards. 'Ā`ishah [ﷺ] narrated:

"We set out with the Prophet [ﷺ] for *Hajj* and when we reached Sarif I got my menses. When the Prophet [ﷺ] came to me, I was weeping. He asked, *'Why are you weeping?'* I said, 'I wish if I had not performed *Hajj* this year.' He asked, *'May be that you got your menses?'* I replied, 'Yes'. He then said, *'This is a thing which Allāh has ordained for all daughters of Adam. So do what all the pilgrims do except that you do not perform the Tawāf round the Ka'bah till you are clean.'"*[242]

The sister should not leave Makkah before she completes this [*Tawāf*]. If circumstances force her to, for example she will have no one to stay with or travel arrangements cannot be changed and she may be left stranded, then she may perform the *Tawāf* in an unclean state according to *Shaykh Al-Islām* Ibn Taymiyyah[243], and Allāh knows best.

7) Divorce.

It is prohibited to divorce ones wife while she is on her menses. When Ibn 'Umar [ﷺ] divorced his wife while she was on her period, his father,

---

[241] *The Natural Blood of Women, Shaykh* Al-'Uthaymīn. Pg.14.

[242] *Sahīh Al-Bukhārī*, [Eng. Trans. vol. 1 #302].

[243] *Hajj, Umrah and Ziyara*. By Dr. V. Abdurahim.pg.65.

'Umar Ibn Al-Khaṯṯāb [ﷺ] went to the Prophet [ﷺ] to inform him to check on the permissibility of this. The Prophet [ﷺ] said to him:

"Order him to take her back and keep her until she is clean then wait till she gets her next period and becomes clean whereupon if he wishes to keep her he can do so, and if he wishes to divorce her he can divorce her before having sexual intercourse with her; and that is the prescribed period which Allāh has fixed for the women meant to be divorced."[244]

8) Entering the *muṯallā* of the *masjid*.

She is forbidden to sit or stay in the *muṯallā* of a *masjid*. She may however pass through or collect something from it. The Prophet [ﷺ] said:

"...but the menstruating women should keep away from the muṯallā." [245]

Narrated 'Ā'ishah [ﷺ]:

"The Messenger of Allāh [ﷺ] said to me: *'Get the mat from the mosque.'* I said: 'I am menstruating!' Upon this he remarked: *'Your menstruation is not in your hand'.*"[246]

9) *Nifās* [the bleeding after the birth of a baby].

- The bleeding referred to here is regardless of whether the child is born alive or dead. As long as the features are distinguishable as being human [limbs or facial features] the blood is considered *nifās* and the same rules that apply to *hayḏ* [menses] apply to this type of blood as well. That is to say, *ṯalāh* and fasting is not due on her as well as the impermissibility of having relations with the spouse etc.

However the resulting blood from a miscarriage before three months or before human features are noticed, is considered spoilt blood and she is to

---

[244] *Saḫīḫ Al-Bukhārī* [Eng. Trans. vol. 7 #178].

[245] *Saḫīḫ Al-Bukhārī*, [Eng. Trans. vol. 1 #132].

[246] *Saḫīḫ Muslim*, [Eng. Trans. vol. 1 #587].

continue prayer and fasting etc. However, she uses the same rule as that of *istiḫāḏah* [which will follow shortly].

- As for a full term pregnancy or the birth of a child with distinguishable [human] features, "*Shaykh Al-Islām* Ibn Taymiyyah said: ' The blood seen when the woman starts her contractions is *nifās* and is not limited to 2 or 3 days. These contractions are followed by delivery or otherwise the released blood is not *nifās*. *Nifās* has no limit on the duration of its shorter or longer periods. Assuming the woman sees a flowing blood for more than forty, sixty or seventy days then the blood flow stops. This kind of bleeding is *nifās*. Suppose however that the bleeding continues then a limit of forty days is set as *nifās* because this period is the common period encountered by most women.' *Shaykh* Al-'Uthaymīn says: 'based upon the above if the bleeding of a woman continues beyond forty days and if there are signs that indicate that it will come to a stop [based on previous pregnancies or some other signs] then she should wait until the blood flow stops. If the *nifās* bleeding stops before the forty day- reference period and she becomes clean then she should take a bath, pray, fast and she can engage in sexual intercourse with her husband. The stopping of the flow of blood for less than a day does not qualify her to be clean. [i.e., a day or more is needed for her to be considered clean as mentioned in *Al-Mughnī*]"[247]

A quick summary:

Birth of a child without human features: the resulting blood is considered spoilt blood and she continues her worship as usual. She follows the rules for *istiḫāḏah* [continuous bleeding, see following topic]. The same goes for any blood during her pregnancy if there are no contractions or any other signs of the onset of labor involved then she follows the rules of *istiḫāḏah*. [few women actually continue menses in pregnancy if she is sure she is of them, *ḫayḏ* rules apply]

[247] *Shaykh* Al-'Uthaymīn's *Natural Blood of Women*, pg. 26

Normal birth of live child or dead child but with human features: then it is *nifās* and same rules of *hayd* [menses] apply. If the time period of blood flow is known to stop [from previous pregnancy etc.] then wait till it ends. If it is continuous then a period of forty days is set and she should bathe and worship as usual after that, with rules on *istihādah* applied.
If the blood flow stops before the forty-day period, she may take a bath and worship as usual and may indulge in relations with her spouse. If however the blood flow stops for less than a day then she is not counted as clean, the stoppage must be for a full day or more.

Al- Istihādah.

The woman who has continuous blood flow throughout the month is called a *mustahādah*, the condition is called *Al-Istihādah*. Fātimah bint Abī Hubaysh said to the Prophet [ﷺ] :

"I do not become clean [from bleeding]. Shall I give up my prayers?' Allāh's Messenger [ﷺ] replied: *'No, because it is from a blood vessel and not the menses. So when the real menses begins give up your prayers and when it [the period] has finished wash the blood off your body [take a bath] and offer prayers'.*"[248] In another narration, "My menstruation was too much and severe. So I came to the Prophet [ﷺ] to ask for his opinion. He said, '*This is the stroke of the devil, so observe your menses for six or seven days, then take a bath and when you see that you are purified and quite clean, pray for twenty-three or twenty-four days, and fast and pray for that will suffice you. And do so every month just as the other women menstruate [and are purified]. But if you are strong enough to delay the Dhuhr prayer and advance the 'Asr prayer, then take a bath and combine the Dhuhr and the 'Asr prayer; then delay the Maghrib prayer and advance the 'Ishā` prayer then take a bath and combine the two prayers, do so; and take a bath at Fajr.*' Allāh's Messenger [ﷺ] said of these two types actions: *'This one appeals more to my liking [i.e., taking a bath for every prayer].*" [249]

---

[248] *Sahīh Al-Bukhārī*, [Eng. Trans. vol.1 #303].

[249] Sunan of Abū Dāwud. [Eng. Trans. Vol. 1 #287]. Declared *hasan* by *Shaykh* Al-Albānī.

The sister can tell, either by previous normal periods or by the look and smell of the blood if it is from menses or not. When she is not on her menses she should keep herself clean from the blood with a pad or liner and make ablution for each prayer.[250] She may also [after her bath to purify herself from menses] engage in sexual intercourse with her husband. I should point out that 'continuous bleeding' does not only refer to heavy bleeding throughout the month. It also includes light bleeding or blood spots or streaks in clear or yellow discharge. Narrated 'Ā`ishah [ﷺ]:

"One of the wives of Allāh's Messenger[ﷺ] joined him in *I'tikāf* and she noticed blood and yellowish discharge [from her private parts] and put a dish under her when she prayed."[251]

10] The sign of purification from bleeding.

At the end of her menses, a lady sees a sign that her menses are over. She should not consider herself purified from bleeding as soon as she observes dryness, rather she should wait till she sees discharge and check the color. Yellowish or white discharge means she is clear, while brown or red indicate her period is still present. Umm 'Atiyyah [ﷺ] narrates:

"We never considered yellowish discharge as a thing of importance [i.e., as menses]."[252]

And 'Ā`ishah [ﷺ] would say:

"Do not hurry till you see the cotton pad is white [meaning the perfect disappearance of the menses]."[253]

---

[250] *Sahīh Al-Bukhārī*, [Eng. Trans. vol.1 #324].

[251] *Sahīh Al-Bukhārī*, [Eng. Trans. vol. 1 #307].

[252] *Sahīh Al-Bukhārī*, [Eng. Trans. vol.1 #323].

[253] *Sahīh Al-Bukhārī*, [Eng. Trans. vol.1 chapter 21].

The daughter of Zayd Ibn Thābit [ﷺ] was told that some women used to ask for candles at midnight to see whether the menses had stopped or not. On that the daughter of Zayd said that the ladies [the wives of the Prophet's companions] had never done so, and she blamed them [the former women].[254]

11] The Purification. [Bath]

Once the sign of purity is observed it becomes incumbent on the lady to take a bath as soon as possible. Such a bath is called a *Ghusl*, it is the way to purify oneself from the major impurities [menses and the state of Junub].

The Ghusl [or complete bath].

Narrated 'Ā`ishah [ﷺ] wife of the Prophet [ﷺ],

"Whenever Allāh's Messenger [ﷺ] took a bath of janābah he would begin by washing his hands, then pour water with his right hand on his left hand and wash his sexual organ. He would then perform ablution like that for prayer, then he would put his fingers in the water and run his fingers through the roots of his hair with them, then pour 3 handfuls of water over his head then pour water all over his body. Then wash his feet."[255] And in another narration: *"I placed water for the bath of the Prophet [ﷺ] and he poured water with his right hand on his left hand and washed them. Then he washed his private parts and rubbed his hands on the ground [for soap] washed them with water, rinsed his mouth and washed his nose by putting water in it and blowing it out, washed his face and poured water on his head. He withdrew from that place and washed his feet. A piece of cloth was given to him but he did not use it."*[256]

Today with soap and showers, this is even easier by the will of Allāh. As for the sisters' purification from menses there are two other things to add to this. Instead of pouring water over her head thrice which she may

---

[254] *Sahīh Al-Bukhārī*, [Eng. Trans. Vol. 1 chapter.21].

[255] *Sahīh Muslim*, [Eng. Trans. vol. 1 #616].

[256] *Sahīh Al-Bukhārī*, [Eng. Trans. vol.1 #259]

"Allāh has bestowed indulgence on a traveler to delay the observing of the fast and the shortening of prayer by half: but has given leave to an expecting mother or nursing woman to delay the observing of fast."[263]

However, as for the method of compensation, there are two opinions. The first is that she should make up the missed days as said above and the second is that she may feed a person for each day missed instead of the fast. We shall cover these in detail by the will of Allāh.

i] She must make up the fast [i.e., it is not optional].
Allāh the Exalted, said:

﴿ يُرِيدُ ٱللَّهُ بِكُمُ ٱلْيُسْرَ وَلَا يُرِيدُ بِكُمُ ٱلْعُسْرَ وَلِتُكْمِلُوا۟ ٱلْعِدَّةَ ﴾

﴾ Allāh intends for you ease, and He does not want to make things difficult for you. [He wants that you] must complete the same number [of days.] ﴿ *2:185*

It is this verse that is used as proof it must be made up by an equivalent number of days, by those who say that the pregnant or nursing mother only has the choice to postpone it and not to feed [the poor] instead.

ii] She may feed a poor person for each day instead.
Allāh, the Exalted the Mighty, said:

﴿ وَعَلَى ٱلَّذِينَ يُطِيقُونَهُۥ فِدْيَةٌ طَعَامُ مِسْكِينٍ ﴾

﴾ And as for those who can fast with difficulty, they have [a choice either to fast or] to feed a miskīn [poor person] [for every day]. ﴿ *2:184*

"***those who can fast with difficulty***" refers to the old and infirm according to many of the scholars and those who favor this opinion. In the very early dawn of Islām the healthy people who could fast were given a choice to fast or feed. Later on as Islām grew and the Muslims became firmer in their

---

[263] Sunan of Abū Dāwud. [Eng. Trans. Vol.2 #2402]. Declared *hasan sahīh* by *Shaykh* Al-Albānī.

Faith, Allāh abrogated the ruling in this verse concerning the healthy and replaced it with the ruling found in the next verse:

﴿فَمَن شَهِدَ مِنكُمُ ٱلشَّهْرَ فَلْيَصُمْهُ وَمَن كَانَ مَرِيضًا أَوْ عَلَىٰ سَفَرٍ فَعِدَّةٌ مِّنْ أَيَّامٍ أُخَرَ﴾

﴾ So whoever of you sights [the crescent on the first night of] the month [of Ramadān i.e., is present at home], he must observe sawm [fasts] that month, and whoever is ill or on a journey, the same number [of days which one did not observe fast must be made up] from other days.﴿ 2:185

Some of the scholars of the *Salaf*, say the verse allows the sick and the old and infirm to feed instead. They say that the previous verse still holds only for the old and ill who would fast with great difficulty or not at all. Whereas the other group feels the pregnant and nursing mothers have been included in the 'ill', and therefore they say that they may feed a poor person instead. They all agree that all healthy people must now fast. Some scholars like Imam Ahmad Ibn Hanbal, say she may do either. Others like Al-Hasan Al-Basrī, elaborate and state that if she is pregnant and worried only for herself she should make up the fast and if she is nursing and worried only for the child then she may feed a poor person for each day. Among the companions, Ibn 'Umar [ﷺ] was of those who felt that the verse [2:184] was abrogated and the women must fast. Whereas Ibn 'Abbās [ﷺ] used to advise his pregnant wives to feed poor people. Other scholars who felt she might feed include Abū Dāwud, Imam An-Nasā`ī and At-Tirmidhī, while those who felt she must make up the fast were Imām Al-Awzā'ī, the people of Al-Kūfah and Ibrāhīm An-Nakha'ī, Imam *Al-Bukhārī* also held this opinion.[264]

a) Those who wish to fast, then it is better to complete making up as soon as possible however, some scholars like *Shaykh* 'Uthaymīn did not find fault if she spent two years trying to make up if she has a strong reason.

[264] *Fath Al-Bāri`*, vol. 4 pg.222 and vol.8 pg. 26-29.

Making up may be done every day, every other day or however she can. Ibn 'Abbās [ﷺ] points out one may fast intermittently as Allāh said:

﴿ فَعِدَّةٌ مِّنْ أَيَّامٍ أُخَرَ ﴾

﴾ [The prescribed period should be made up for] by fasting some other days ﴿ 2:185 [265]

b) If she is going to feed a poor person she should do it during *Ramadān* however she could do it outside the month if she had to and Allāh knows best. It is one meal for one poor person for each day missed.

[265] *Sahīh Al-Bukhārī*, [Eng. Trans. vol. 3 The Book of Fasting. Chapter 40].

CHAPTER 9

THE BELIEVING LADY AND HER FAMILY

The sister should know that her family has rights upon her, whether they are Muslim or not, and she has rights on them.

And Allāh the Exalted, Most High, said:

﴿ وَٱعْبُدُوا۟ ٱللَّهَ وَلَا تُشْرِكُوا۟ بِهِۦ شَيْـًٔا ۖ وَبِٱلْوَٰلِدَيْنِ إِحْسَٰنًا وَبِذِى ٱلْقُرْبَىٰ ﴾

﴿ Worship Allāh and join none with Him in worship, and do good to parents and kinsfolk...﴾ 4:36

Parents [father and mother].

Obedience:

Whether her parents are Muslim or non-Muslim she must obey them except if they ask her to do something in disobedience to Allāh for there is no obedience of created things in disobedience to Allāh. Allāh the Mighty, the Majestic said:

﴿ وَوَصَّيْنَا ٱلْإِنسَٰنَ بِوَٰلِدَيْهِ حُسْنًا ۖ وَإِن جَٰهَدَاكَ لِتُشْرِكَ بِى مَا لَيْسَ لَكَ بِهِۦ عِلْمٌ فَلَا تُطِعْهُمَآ ۚ إِلَىَّ مَرْجِعُكُمْ فَأُنَبِّئُكُم بِمَا كُنتُمْ تَعْمَلُونَ ﴿٨﴾ ﴾

﴿ And we have enjoined on man to be good and dutiful to his parents; but if they strive to make you join with Me [in worship] anything [as a partner] of which you have no knowledge, then obey them not. Unto Me is your return and I shall tell you what you used to do.﴾ 29:8

Kindness, Mercy and Respect:

Allāh has also ordered us to be kind and respectful to them as they looked after us and brought us up. Note that Allāh mentions our duties to parents right after His orders to worship Him a number of times in the Qur`ān, this brings to light just how important our duties to them are.

﴿ وَقَضَىٰ رَبُّكَ أَلَّا تَعْبُدُوٓا۟ إِلَّآ إِيَّاهُ وَبِٱلْوَٰلِدَيْنِ إِحْسَـٰنًا ۚ إِمَّا يَبْلُغَنَّ عِندَكَ ٱلْكِبَرَ
أَحَدُهُمَآ أَوْ كِلَاهُمَا فَلَا تَقُل لَّهُمَآ أُفٍّ وَلَا تَنْهَرْهُمَا وَقُل لَّهُمَا قَوْلًا كَرِيمًا ﴿٢٣﴾
وَٱخْفِضْ لَهُمَا جَنَاحَ ٱلذُّلِّ مِنَ ٱلرَّحْمَةِ وَقُل رَّبِّ ٱرْحَمْهُمَا كَمَا رَبَّيَانِى صَغِيرًا ﴾

﴿ And you Lord has decreed that you worship none but Him. And that you be dutiful to your parents. If one or both of them attain old age in your life, say not to them a word of disrespect, nor shout at them but address them in terms of honor. And lower unto them the wing of submission and humility through mercy, and say, 'My Lord! Bestow on them Your Mercy as they did bring me up when I was small.'﴾ 17:23-24

﴿ وَصَاحِبْهُمَا فِى ٱلدُّنْيَا مَعْرُوفًا ﴾

﴿...but behave with them in this world kindly﴾ 31:15

Your Mother.
Allāh, the Almighty said:

﴿ وَوَصَّيْنَا ٱلْإِنسَـٰنَ بِوَٰلِدَيْهِ حَمَلَتْهُ أُمُّهُۥ وَهْنًا عَلَىٰ وَهْنٍ وَفِصَـٰلُهُۥ فِى عَامَيْنِ أَنِ
ٱشْكُرْ لِى وَلِوَٰلِدَيْكَ إِلَىَّ ٱلْمَصِيرُ ﴿١٤﴾ ﴾

﴿ And We have enjoined on man[to be dutiful and good] to his parents. His mother bore him in weakness and hardship upon weakness and hardship, and his weaning is in two years - give thanks to Me and to you parents. Unto Me is the final destination.﴾ 31:14

"A man came to Allāh's Messenger[ﷺ] and said, 'O Allāh's Messenger! Who is more entitled to be treated with the best companionship by me?' The Prophet [ﷺ] said, **'Your mother.'** The man said, 'Who next?' The Prophet [ﷺ] said, **'Your mother.'** The man further said, 'Who is next?' The Prophet [ﷺ] said, **'Your mother.'** The man asked for the fourth time, 'Who next?'

The Prophet [ﷺ] said, '**Your father**'."[266] The Prophet [ﷺ] also said, **"Allāh has forbidden you to be undutiful to your mothers."**[267]

"There was a man named Jurayj and he was devoted to prayer. One day his mother called him while he was in prayer. She said, 'Jurayj it is your mother, so talk to her. 'She found him at the time absorbed in prayer, so he said [to himself]: 'O Lord, my mother [is calling me] [whereas I am absorbed] in my prayer. He opted for the Prayer. She [his mother] went back, then came again for the second time and said, 'O Jurayj, it is your mother calling you, so talk to me. He said, ' O Allāh, there is my mother also and my prayer, and he opted for the prayer. She said: O Allāh, this Jurayj is my son. I talk to him but he refuses to talk to me. O Allāh, don't bring death to him unless he has seen the prostitutes, and if she invoked for turmoil to afflict him, he would indeed become afflicted in some form of turmoil. There was a shepherd living nearby his temple. It so happened that a woman of that village came there and that shepherd committed fornication with her and she became pregnant and gave birth to a child. It was said to her: Whose child is this? She said: He is the child of the one who is living in this temple. So there came persons with hatchets and spades. They called Jurayj and he did not talk to them and they were about to demolish that temple that he saw them and he came to them and they said: Ask her [this woman] what she says. He smiled then touched the head of the child and said: Who is your father? He [the child] said: My father is the shepherd of the sheep, and when they heard this, they said: We are prepared to rebuild with gold and silver what we have demolished from your temple. He said: No, rebuild it with clay as it was before. He then went up [to his room and absorbed himself in prayer]"[268]

Therefore we need to pay special attention to our mothers, to the point that if one is performing a *Sunnah* prayer they should answer their mother if she calls.

---

[266] *Sahīh Al-Bukhārī*, [Eng. Trans. vol. 8 #2].

[267] *Sahīh Al-Bukhārī*, [Eng. Trans. vol. 8 #6].

[268] *Sahīh Muslim*, [Eng. Trans. vol. 4 #6187].

Your Father.

The Prophet [ﷺ] said:

"A son cannot repay what he owes his father unless he finds him in slavery then buys him and emancipates him." [269]

"The finest act of goodness is that a person should treat kindly the loved ones of his father." [270]

This refers to his father's friends. The Prophet [ﷺ] also said:

"Shall I not inform you of the biggest of the great sins?' We said, 'Yes, O Allāh's Messenger!' He said, 'To join partners in worship with Allāh; to be undutiful to one's parents.'" [271]

"A man asked the Prophet [ﷺ], 'What deeds are the best? The Prophet [ﷺ] said, '*To perform the [daily compulsory] prayers at their [early] stated fixed times; To be good and dutiful to one's own parents and to participate in Jihad in Allāh's cause."* [272]

Your Husband.

Since this overlaps it will be covered in depth under the chapter on ***nikāh*** [marriage].

Children.

If you are blessed with children, remember they are a loan to you from Allāh. He may recall them at any time, and whoever bears this with patience their reward is Paradise.[273] Additionally, they are the future generation of Muslims so we have to do our best in rearing them up and everything done for the sake of Allāh has its reward. It is a difficult task and children don't

---

[269] Sunan of Abū Daud, [Eng. Trans. vol.3 pg.1422. #5118]. Declared sahīh by Sheik Al-Albānī.

[270] *Sahīh Muslim*, [Eng. Trans. vol. 4 #6192].

[271] *Sahīh Al-Bukhārī*, [Eng. Trans. vol. 8 #7].

[272] *Sahīh Al-Bukhārī*, [Eng. Trans. vol. 9 #623].

[273] *Sahīh Al-Bukhārī*, [Eng. Trans. vol. 2. #340- #341].

come with instruction pamphlets and they have a wide range of needs and emotions that must be fulfilled. However within the Qur`ān and *Sunnah* we have some guidelines that when followed make the task easier by the will of Allāh. Remember, being a mother and wife is a full time job that is one of the most important in the world. How it came to be looked upon as less is only from those with a lack of Divine guidance who have little or no sense of morality. May Allāh keep us among the rightly guided, Āmīn.

Mercy:

She should be merciful to her children, kiss them and embrace them. The Prophet [ﷺ] used to kiss and smell his son Ibrāhīm[274] and he [ﷺ] used to say about his two grandsons, Al-Hasan and Al-Husayn [the children from his daughter Fātimah and son-in-law 'Alī Ibn Abī Tālib]:

"*They are my two sweet smelling flowers in this world.*"[275]

The Prophet [ﷺ] also said upon hearing the story of the lady who divided her last date, which she wanted for herself, between her two daughters,

"*Whoever is in charge of [put to test by] these daughters and treats them generously, then they will act as a shield for him from the [Hell] Fire.*"[276]

Once, when the Prophet [ﷺ] kissed Al-Hasan, Al-Aqra' Ibn Hābis At-Tamīmī was sitting near him and said upon seeing that,

"I have ten children and I have never kissed anyone of them, *'Allāh's Messenger [ﷺ] cast a look at him and said, 'Whoever is not merciful to others will not be treated mercifully.*"[277]

The Prophet made another remark over a similar incident [i.e., kissing male children] concerning a Bedouin:

"*I cannot put mercy in your heart after Allāh has taken it away.*"[278]

---

[274] *Sahīh Al-Bukhārī*, [Eng. Trans. vol. 8 #23]. Ibrāhīm died as an infant and the Prophet [ﷺ] did not leave any sons.

[275] *Sahīh Al-Bukhārī*, [Eng. Trans. vol. 8 #23].

[276] *Sahīh Al-Bukhārī*, [Eng. Trans. vol. 8 #24].

[277] *Sahīh Al-Bukhārī*, [Eng. Trans. vol. 8 #26].

[278] *Sahīh Al-Bukhārī*, [Eng. Trans. vol. 8 # 27].

Allāh's Messenger [ﷺ] said,

"Allāh divided Mercy into one hundred parts and He kept its ninety nine parts with Him and sent down its one part on the earth, and because of that, its one single part, His creations are Merciful to each other, so that even the mare lifts up its hoofs away from its baby animal, least it should trample on it."[279]

The gravity of the sin of killing one's children over lack of food or poverty.

Allāh said:

﴿ وَلَا تَقْتُلُوٓا۟ أَوْلَٰدَكُمْ خَشْيَةَ إِمْلَٰقٍ ۖ نَّحْنُ نَرْزُقُهُمْ وَإِيَّاكُمْ ۚ إِنَّ قَتْلَهُمْ كَانَ خِطْـًٔا كَبِيرًا ﴾

﴾ And kill not your children for fear of poverty. We shall provide for them as well as for you. Surely, the killing of them is a great sin.﴿ 17:31

Abdullah [ؓ] said:

"O Allāh's Messenger! Which sin is the greatest?' He said, *'To set up a rival unto Allāh, though He Alone created you.'* I said, 'What is next?' He said, *'To kill your son lest he should share your food with you.'* I further asked, 'What next?' He said, *'To commit illegal sexual intercourse with the wife of your neighbor.'* Then Allāh revealed as proof of the statement of the Prophet [ﷺ]: verse 25:68."[280]

She is responsible for their well-being.

This means looking after the children's needs like cleanliness, food, manners, education [this includes Islāmic education] and she makes sure they are comfortable. Every woman by the will of Allāh has the natural inclination to take care of her children and wants to do so by the will of Allāh. The Prophet [ﷺ] said:

"The lady is a guardian and is responsible for her husbands house and his offspring."[281]

---

[279] *Sahīh Al-Bukhārī*, [Eng. Trans. vol. 8 #29].

[280] *Sahīh Al-Bukhārī*, [Eng. Trans. Vol.8 #30].

[281] *Sahīh Al-Bukhārī*, [Eng. Trans. vol.7 #128]

"Order your children with salāh at the age of seven and beat them [about it] at the age of ten." [282]

"The best women are the riders of the camels and the righteous among the women of the Quraysh. They are the kindest women to their children in their childhood and more careful women of the property of their husbands." [283]

Other facts she should know that are related to children.

a) Pictures.

In this day and time it is almost impossible to find anything for children without pictures. Know, that a picture of any live creature is forbidden in Islām. And we have been ordered to deface any such picture found.

Ali Ibn Abī Tālib [ﷺ] said:

"Should I not send you on the same mission as Allāh's Messenger sent me? Do not leave an image without defacing it or a high grave without leveling it." And another narration from Habīb with the same chain said, "[do not leave] a picture without obliterating it." [284]

Some suggestions as to how to do so include; don't buy it, from utensils scrap it all off or at least in such a way that it is not complete i.e., removing the head of the body, cut of badges from clothing or try and remove the head. These are merely suggestions and it is better not to have them, however one does get gifts which are much needed or there simply isn't anything else, the rule again is fear Allāh as much as you can then do what you need to. *Diapers* almost always have them however the scholars say the diapers are not for honor they are for purposes that degrade and it is therefore permissible by the will of Allāh. Also the Prophet [ﷺ] said,

---

[282] Sunan Abū Daud, [Eng. Trans. Vol. 1 #4940] Declared *hasan sahīh* by *Shaykh* Al-Albānī.

[283] *Sahīh Al-Bukhārī*, [Eng. Trans. vol. 7 #19]

[284] *Sahīh Muslim*, [Eng. Trans. vol. 2 #2115]

"Angels [of mercy] do not enter a house in which there is a dog or there are pictures."[285]

His wife 'Ā`ishah [ﵺ] said,

"The Prophet [ﷺ] never used to leave in the house anything carrying images or crosses but he obliterated it."[286]

"The Messenger of Allāh [ﷺ] returned from a journey when I had placed a curtain of mine having pictures over [the door of] a chamber of mine. When the Messenger of Allāh [ﷺ] saw it he tore it and said, *'The people who will receive the severest punishment on the Day of Resurrection will be those who try to make the like of Allāh's creations'*: so we turned it [i.e., the curtain] into one or two cushions."[287]

So the pictures were cut in such a way that they were not animals anymore but pieces of the animal [the animal was said to have been a horse with wings].[288] This prohibition includes photographs taken for keepsakes or history; the scholars say in this day and time an identification picture is needed that is the only exception [i.e., passports or ID cards]. Also included in the *harām* [forbidden] are any kind of statues, pictures painted or drawn of any live creature of Allāh's.

b]Some answers on diapering and toilet training.

Your *wudū`*:

If you were in *wudū`* to begin with and you changed your child's diaper using cloth or baby wipes or anything between you and the baby, then your *wudū`* is not broken by the will of Allāh. Washing your hands for hygiene is all you have to do. *However,* if you directly touched the private parts of the child to wash them then your *wudū`* is broken. Because touching the privates of yourself or others with nothing in between breaks your *wudū`* according to some scholars [e.g. *Shaykh* 'Abdul Al-Muhsin Al-'Abbād]. The scholars who hold this position say the *hadīth* where a man asked whether

---

[285] *Sahīh Al-Bukhārī,* [Eng. Trans. Vol. 7 #833]

[286] *Sahīh Al-Bukhārī,* [Eng. Trans. vol. 7 #836].

[287] *Sahīh Al-Bukhārī,* [Eng. Trans. vol.7 #838].

[288] *Fath Al-Bāri`*, [vol. 10 pg. 401-402].

touching his private part without a cover broke his *wudū`* and the answer the Prophet [ﷺ] gave at the time was no as it was a part of his body, was abrogated by the *hadīth*, narrated by Busrah bint Safwān where the Prophet [ﷺ] said:

"He who touches his [sexual] organ should perform ablution"[289]

Imam *Al-Bukhārī* said it was the most authentic *hadīth* in this chapter [regarding the point]. Some scholars include the criterion that the touch has to be carrying lustful intention, however the previous group says it has nothing to do with lust, it is a matter of touching it with or without cover. I tend to agree as the *hadīth* is clear and a touch or kiss doesn't break *wudū`* [see *hadīth* on the Prophet [ﷺ] kissing his wives and leaving for prayer without second ablution]. Therefore the touch, lustful or not, as described in the *hadīth* is based simply on cover or no cover and Allāh the Exalted, knows best.

If the urine of a nursing child gets onto your clothing then in the case of a boy you simply pour or sprinkle water over it for purification. However, for a girl you must wash it off [the composition of the girl's urine is different from a boys]. Umm Qays bint Muhsin Narrates:

"I brought my young son who had not started eating [ordinary food] to Allāh's Messenger[ﷺ] who took him and made him sit on his lap. The child urinated on the garment of the Prophet [ﷺ] so he asked for water and poured it over the soiled area and did not wash it."[290]

The Prophet [ﷺ] also said,

"The urine of a female child should be washed thoroughly and the urine of a male child should be sprinkled over [with water]."[291]

---

289 Sunan of Abū Daud, [Eng. Trans. Vol.1 #181]. Declared *sahīh* by Sheik Al-Albānī.

290 *Sahīh Al-Bukhārī*, [Eng. Trans. vol. 1 #223].

291 Sunan of Abū Daud, [Eng. Trans. vol. 1 #375]. Declared *hasan sahīh* by Shaykh Al-Albānī.

Any stools on clothing must of course be completely washed off or the garment changed [for both male and female].

The house:

a) During toilet training the child might soil the house accidentally, if that happens [for wood, tiled, or carpeted floors] remove as much as possible then pour water [and soap if needed] over it and clean it. If it is a floor of soil [direct ground] then pour water over it for urine and for stools remove it and pour water [dirt once dry after this is purified]. The point is to remove the origin of the matter, to purify the spot. Once while the Prophet [ﷺ] was in the mosque, "A Bedouin came and passed urine in one corner of the Mosque. The people shouted at him but the Prophet [ﷺ] stopped them till he finished urinating. The Prophet [ﷺ] ordered them to spill a bucket of water over that place and they did so."[292] The floor of the mosque at that time was a dirt floor.

b) As for bedding, the companions used to put it in the sun to dry [mattresses]. Sheets may be treated as garments above, by the will of Allāh.

The rest of her family.

Allāh, the Almighty, said:

﴿ وَٱتَّقُوا۟ ٱللَّهَ ٱلَّذِى تَسَآءَلُونَ بِهِۦ وَٱلْأَرْحَامَ إِنَّ ٱللَّهَ كَانَ عَلَيْكُمْ رَقِيبًا ﴾

﴾ ...and fear Allāh through Whom you demand [your mutual rights], and [do not cut the relations of] the wombs [kinship]. Surely Allāh is Ever an All-Watcher over you.﴿ 4:1

﴿ وَٱعْبُدُوا۟ ٱللَّهَ وَلَا تُشْرِكُوا۟ بِهِۦ شَيْـًٔا وَبِٱلْوَٰلِدَيْنِ إِحْسَـٰنًا وَبِذِى ٱلْقُرْبَىٰ وَٱلْيَتَـٰمَىٰ
وَٱلْمَسَـٰكِينِ وَٱلْجَارِ ذِى ٱلْقُرْبَىٰ وَٱلْجَارِ ٱلْجُنُبِ وَٱلصَّاحِبِ بِٱلْجَنۢبِ وَٱبْنِ ٱلسَّبِيلِ
وَمَا مَلَكَتْ أَيْمَـٰنُكُمْ إِنَّ ٱللَّهَ لَا يُحِبُّ مَن كَانَ مُخْتَالًا فَخُورًا ٣٦ ﴾

---

[292] Sahīh Al-Bukhārī, [Eng. Trans. vol. 1 #221].

﴾ Worship Allāh and join none with Him [in worship]; and do good to parents, kinsfolk, orphans, Al-Miskīn [the poor], the neighbor who is near of kin, the neighbor who is a stranger, the companion by your side, the wayfarer [you meet], and those [slaves] whom your right hand possesses. Verily, Allāh does not like such as are proud and boastful.﴿ 4:36

The Prophet [ﷺ] said,

"The person who severs the bond of kinship will not enter Paradise."[293]

"He who likes that his sustenance should be expanded and his age may be lengthened should join the ties of kinship."[294]

Abū Hurayrah reported that a person said,

"Allāh's Messenger' I have relatives with whom I try to have a close relationship but they sever [this relation]. I treat them well, but they treat me ill. I am sweet to them but they are harsh toward me'. Upon this he [the Prophet [ﷺ]] said: *'If this is so as you say, then you in fact throw hot ashes [upon their faces] and there would always remain with you on behalf of Allāh [an angel to support you] who would keep you dominant over them so long as you adhere to this path [path of righteousness]."* [295]

According to some of the scholars, the order of rights of kinship in Islām is; Your children and wife, your parents, then your brothers and sisters, then your paternal uncles and aunts [father's side], then you maternal uncles and aunts [mother side] then other relatives. The Prophet [ﷺ] said when instructing someone on how to spend his money,

"Spend it on yourself, [i.e., your genuine needs] *and if anything is left, it should be spent on your family, and if anything is left [after meeting the needs of your family] it should be spent on relatives, and if anything is left from the family it should be spent like this, like this.'* And he was saying: In front of you, on your right and on your left."[296]

---

[293] Sahīh Al-Bukhārī, [Eng. Trans. vol. 8 #13].

[294] Sahīh Muslim, [Eng. Trans. vol.4 #6203].

[295] Sahīh Muslim [Eng. Trans. vol.4 # 6204].

[296] Sahīh Muslim, [Eng. Trans. vol.2 #2183]

There is also wisdom to be seen in rulings, like in inheritance the males get more, since in payments of blood money the paternal side is responsible for it [as such due respect for the responsibility and maintenance received is appropriate].

"A case was brought to the Prophet [ﷺ] and he gave judgment [the case was the unintentional murder by a woman of another pregnant woman] and he also decided that the *diyah* [blood money] of the woman is to be paid by her relative on the fathers side."[297]

Additionally where the woman is unmarried or divorced her father cares for her, if he is not alive, the responsibility goes to her brother, hence in inheritance the brother gets more. Regarding custody of children, the mother's sister is looked at in the in the same light as the mother, thus sometimes in case of the death of the parents the sister would get custody [if she is Muslim].

[297] *Sahīh Muslim*, [Eng. Trans. vol.3 #4168].

CHAPTER 10

NIKĀH [MARRIAGE]

The believing man and woman should get married as soon as they are ready and able. The majority of the scholars are of the opinion that it is *mustahabb* [beloved by Allāh] to do so.

Allāh the Almighty, said:

﴿ وَأَنكِحُوا الْأَيَامَىٰ مِنكُمْ وَالصَّالِحِينَ مِنْ عِبَادِكُمْ وَإِمَائِكُمْ إِن يَكُونُوا فُقَرَاءَ يُغْنِهِمُ اللَّهُ مِن فَضْلِهِ وَاللَّهُ وَاسِعٌ عَلِيمٌ ﴾

﴾ And marry those among you who are single [i.e., a man who has no wife and the woman who has no husband] and [also marry] the sālihūn [pious, fit and capable ones] of your [male] slaves and maid servants [female slaves]. If they be poor, Allāh will enrich them out of His Bounty. And Allāh is All-Sufficient for His creatures needs, All-Knowing [about the state of the people]. ﴿ 24:32

And His Prophet [ﷺ] said,

"O young people! Whoever among you can marry, should marry, because it helps him lower his gaze and guard his modesty [i.e., his private parts from committing illegal sexual intercourse etc.] and whoever is not able to marry should fast as fasting diminishes his sexual power."[298] In another version of the same *hadīth* in Imam Muslim's *Sahīh* collection there is the addition, "I lost no time in marrying."[299]

---

[298] *Sahīh Al-Bukhārī*, [Eng. Trans. vol.7 #4].

[299] *Sahīh Muslim* [Eng. Trans. vol. 2 #3234].

"Allāh's Messenger [ﷺ] used to command us to marry and severely forbid celibacy and say, *'Marry women who are prolific and loving, for I shall out number the prophets by you on the Day of Resurrection'.*" [300]

1) The age to do so.

Contrary to popular opinion especially in the west, there is no real age to 'wait' for marriage. What is amazing is that some western parents prefer their children to 'date' around and even provide opportunities and advice for 'safe sex' with whomever they wish. These parents get 'worried' if they perceive their child is not yet doing so if they feel they are now old enough!

These breeds a generation of twisted immoral people who find illegal sexual intercourse to be perfectly normal and marriage to be a burden and something to steer clear of. An average teenager in the west will be pushed out on a 'date' with a smile and a nod of encouragement. However, if that same teen came and informed their parent that they have found someone and they would like to get married, the parent is appalled, and depending on the personality of the parent the teen will be punished in some way, sometimes going to the 'law' of the land for help to stop this honorable deed!

On the contrary, the purpose of marriage is to provide comfort, love, security and create a legitimate family while satisfying in a legal manner the sexual needs of both spouses as Allāh created both male and female with this urge although the man may tend to be more driven in this aspect,

﴿ وَخُلِقَ ٱلْإِنسَـٰنُ ضَعِيفًا ﴾

﴿ And man was created weak [cannot be patient to leave sexual intercourse with woman] ﴾ 4:28

---

[300] Found in *Musnad* of Aḥmad declared *ṣaḥīḥ* by Ibn Ḥibbān also in *Sunan* of Abū Dāwud [Eng. Trans. vol.2 #2045]. Declared *ḥasan ṣaḥīḥ* by Sheik Al-Albānī.

Allāh will put love between their hearts. The Prophet [ﷺ] said to a young companion of his who had married a matron instead of someone close to his age [because he [ﷺ] knew the urges found in the human], *"Why didn't you marry a young girl so that you could sport with her and she could sport with you, or you could amuse her and she could amuse you?"*[301]

Allāh created us and placed certain qualities and desires in us, this is our nature. To follow the laws He sent us that perfectly fit our natures, is appropriate and obligatory. To fight the laws and put our own ideas and ideals in first position is futile. In other words, to try to make people pretend they don't need the love and comfort and satisfaction in a marriage, as opposed to illegal and artificial means of achieving what they try to deny exists in them, is ridiculous. For example, illegal sexual intercourse with numerous partners, human milk banks, human sperm banks [for those who feel men are not necessary yet the natural urge to have kids overwhelms them, or those who wish to produce 'genetically superior' kids etc.], going to a bar or restaurant to find 'company' because they don't want to go home to a empty apartment because of that natural urge for companionship of the opposite sex. All this is eliminated by the will of Allāh by marriage in Islām. Therefore an appropriate age is whenever they start gaining serious interest in the opposite sex.

"The Prophet [ﷺ] married ['Ā`ishah [رضي الله عنها]] when she was six years old and consummated his marriage when she was nine years old and then she remained with him for nine years [till his death]."[302]

'Ā`ishah was fifteen[303] years old when he [ﷺ] died, she was the most beloved of his wives to him and was one of the most learned female scholars ever at that age narrating a huge number of *hadīth* [from memory] at that age.

---

[301] Sahīh Muslim, [Eng. Trans. vol. 2 # 3460].

[302] Sahīh Al-Bukhārī [Eng. Trans. vol. 7 #65]

[303] Some say eighteen years of age.

2) Those whom it is not permissible to marry.

Allāh, the Exalted said:

﴿وَلَا تَنكِحُوا۟ ٱلْمُشْرِكَٰتِ حَتَّىٰ يُؤْمِنَّ ۚ وَلَأَمَةٌ مُّؤْمِنَةٌ خَيْرٌ مِّن مُّشْرِكَةٍ وَلَوْ
أَعْجَبَتْكُمْ ۗ وَلَا تُنكِحُوا۟ ٱلْمُشْرِكِينَ حَتَّىٰ يُؤْمِنُوا۟ ۚ وَلَعَبْدٌ مُّؤْمِنٌ خَيْرٌ مِّن مُّشْرِكٍ وَلَوْ
أَعْجَبَكُمْ ۗ أُو۟لَٰٓئِكَ يَدْعُونَ إِلَى ٱلنَّارِ ۖ وَٱللَّهُ يَدْعُوٓا۟ إِلَى ٱلْجَنَّةِ وَٱلْمَغْفِرَةِ بِإِذْنِهِۦ ۖ وَيُبَيِّنُ
ءَايَٰتِهِۦ لِلنَّاسِ لَعَلَّهُمْ يَتَذَكَّرُونَ ﴿٢٢١﴾﴾

﴿ ***And do not marry the mushrikāt [idolatresses, etc.] till they believe [worship Allāh Alone]. And indeed a slave woman who believes is better than a [free] mushrikah [idolatress], even though she pleases you. And give not [your daughters] in marriage to the mushrikūn till they believe [in Allāh Alone] and verily, a believing slave is better than a [free] mushrik, even though he pleases you.*** ﴾ *2:221*

﴿وَلَا تَنكِحُوا۟ مَا نَكَحَ ءَابَآؤُكُم مِّنَ ٱلنِّسَآءِ إِلَّا مَا قَدْ سَلَفَ ۚ إِنَّهُۥ كَانَ فَٰحِشَةً
وَمَقْتًا وَسَآءَ سَبِيلًا ﴿٢٢﴾ حُرِّمَتْ عَلَيْكُمْ أُمَّهَٰتُكُمْ وَبَنَاتُكُمْ وَأَخَوَٰتُكُمْ وَعَمَّٰتُكُمْ
وَخَٰلَٰتُكُمْ وَبَنَاتُ ٱلْأَخِ وَبَنَاتُ ٱلْأُخْتِ وَأُمَّهَٰتُكُمُ ٱلَّٰتِىٓ أَرْضَعْنَكُمْ وَأَخَوَٰتُكُم
مِّنَ ٱلرَّضَٰعَةِ وَأُمَّهَٰتُ نِسَآئِكُمْ وَرَبَٰٓئِبُكُمُ ٱلَّٰتِى فِى حُجُورِكُم مِّن نِّسَآئِكُمُ
ٱلَّٰتِى دَخَلْتُم بِهِنَّ فَإِن لَّمْ تَكُونُوا۟ دَخَلْتُم بِهِنَّ فَلَا جُنَاحَ عَلَيْكُمْ وَحَلَٰٓئِلُ
أَبْنَآئِكُمُ ٱلَّذِينَ مِنْ أَصْلَٰبِكُمْ وَأَن تَجْمَعُوا۟ بَيْنَ ٱلْأُخْتَيْنِ إِلَّا مَا قَدْ سَلَفَ ۗ إِنَّ
ٱللَّهَ كَانَ غَفُورًا رَّحِيمًا ﴿٢٣﴾﴾

﴿ ***And marry not women whom your fathers married, except what has already passed; indeed it was shameful and most hateful, and an evil way. Forbidden to you [for marriage] are: your mothers, your daughters, your sisters, your father's sisters, your mother's sisters, your brothers daughters, your sister's daughters, your foster mother who gave you suck, your foster milk-suckling sisters, your wives' mothers, your step-daughters under your guardianship, born of you wives to whom you have gone in-***

but there is no sin if you have not gone in to them [to marry their daughters], - the wives of your sons who [spring] from your loins, and two sisters at the same time, except what has already passed; verily, Allāh is Oft-Forgiving, Most Merciful. Also [forbidden are] women already married, except those [slaves] whom your right hand possess. Thus Allāh ordained for you. All others are lawful, provided you seek [them in marriage] with Mahr [bridal money given by the husband to the wife at the time of marriage] from your property, desiring chastity, not committing illegal sexual intercourse, so with those of whom you have enjoyed sexual relations, give them their Mahr as prescribed;﴾ 4:22-24

The sister just needs to replace the female with the male equivalent in the verses with the exception of, the man already married, as the man can have up to four wives at one time and the payment of *Mahr* as only men are required to do so. There is an opinion that it is permissible to marry stepdaughters or stepsons even if one has had relations with the parent because Allāh said, "...***who are under your guardianship.***" Therefore they say if the child was not under your guardianship it is permissible, However, and Allāh knows best, the correct opinion is that it is not lawful because the Prophet [ﷺ] had a step-daughter who was not under his guardianship and when it was proposed that he marry her he said it was not lawful.[304]

3) *Mahr* [dowry].

Allāh, the Almighty said:

﴿ وَءَاتُوا۟ ٱلنِّسَآءَ صَدُقَـٰتِهِنَّ نِحْلَةً ۚ فَإِن طِبْنَ لَكُمْ عَن شَىْءٍ مِّنْهُ نَفْسًا فَكُلُوهُ هَنِيٓـًٔا مَّرِيٓـًٔا ﴿٤﴾ ﴾

﴿ ***And give to the women [whom you marry] their Mahr [obligatory bridal-money given by the husband to his wife at the time of marriage] with a good heart; but if they, of their own good pleasure, remit any part of it to you, take it and enjoy it without fear of any harm [as Allāh has made it lawful].*** ﴾ **4:4**

[304] Sahīh Al-Bukhārī [Eng. Trans. vol. 7 #42]. [Details in both chapter and hadīth]

3) Disclosing marital secrets.

Allāh's Messenger [ﷺ] said:

"The most wicked among the people in the sight before Allāh on the Day of Judgment is the man who has intercourse with his wife and she with him, and then spreads her secrets." [320]

This holds true for the woman also. It shows the gravity of the sin of divulging marital secrets. Whatever happens between the man and wife is never to be discussed with anyone not your mother or best friend nor in passing conversation, in any manner.

4] Sodomy is strictly forbidden in Islām.

A man may approach his wife however he wishes but avoiding her anus. Abū Hurayrah [ؓ] said that the Prophet [ﷺ] said:

"He who has intercourse with his wife through her anus is accursed." [321]

And what is your chance of achieving Paradise with its Owner's Curse upon you? And Allāh Knows best.

5] The time spent with each wife [if a man has more than one].

i]If one marries a virgin or a matron;

"When anyone who already has a wife marries a virgin, he should stay with her for seven nights [and then turn to his other wife], but when anyone having a virgin with him [as his wife] marries a woman who has been previously married he should stay with her for three nights." [322]

---

[320] *Sahīh Muslim*, [Eng. Trans. vol.2 #3369]

[321] Sunan of Abū Daud [Engl. Trans. Vol.2 #2157 pg. 579]. Declared *hasan* by *Shaykh* Al-Albānī.

[322] *Sahīh Muslim*, [Eng. Trans. vol. 2 #3448]

The above *hadīth* counts from the day of the wedding [or whenever all parties involved agree on in case of the parties living in different countries etc.] the time division must be equal as seen in the next point, the reason behind this is to give the virgin time to get used to married life while the matron only has to get used to her new husband.

i] Sharing time equally between wives;

First, let us clarify the use of the word 'time' here. The man's time between *Fajr salāh* and *'Asr salāh* is his to work, provide and do as he deems necessary. He may visit all his wives and then the time after *'Asr* he retires to the house of the one whose night it is. Therefore it is the night i.e., *'Asr* to *Fajr* that is for the wife whose turn it is. He should only have sexual relations with whosever's turn it is but in case he did it with another wife in the day time it is not forbidden as the Prophet [ﷺ] used to go to all his wives in one day, however to avoid ill feelings it is best to avoid this. In addition. Allāh informed the Prophet [ﷺ] unlike the rest of the men in his Ummah, he did not have to observe the times however he was nevertheless equal to all his wives.

﴾ You [O Muhammad [ﷺ]] can post pone [the turn of] whom you will of them [your wives] and you may receive whom you will. And whomever you desire of those whom you have set aside [her turn temporarily] it is no sin on you [to receive her again], that is better; that they may be comforted not grieved.﴿ 33:51

Besides which, the Prophet [ﷺ] was said to have the strength of thirty men.

"Whenever the Prophet [ﷺ] finished his 'Asr prayer, he would enter upon his wives and stay with one of them."[323]

---

[323] *Sahīh Al-Bukhārī*, [Eng. Trans. vol.7 #143].

6] A wife may give her turn to another wife;

" Sawdah bint Zam'ah gave up her turn to me ['Ā`ishah] and so the Prophet [ﷺ] used to give me both my day and Sawdah's."[324]

7] Marriage under false pretexts;

This is in reference to the groom or guardian not informing the concerned parties of any defects [or the like]. In such a case divorce is permitted. If intercourse [sexual] took place she keeps the *Mahr* if not he should get it back and if he wishes to give her a gift he may. 'Umar Ibn Al-Khaṯṯāb [ﷺ] said,

" If any man marries a woman and after cohabitation with her finds that she is mad or affected with leprosy, she gets her *Mahr* [after he divorces her] for having intercourse with her and it is due to him from the one who has deceived him with her."[325]

8] If one spouse embraces Islām before the other;

If it is the husband who embraces Islām before his wife and his wife is either a Christian or Jew he may keep her or divorce her, as Allāh permitted the marriage of a Muslim male to a chaste woman of the book [Christian or Jew] in the verse. Note that she must be chaste and have the ability to want to stay as such protecting his and her honor:

﴿وَٱلْمُحْصَنَٰتُ مِنَ ٱلَّذِينَ أُوتُوا۟ ٱلْكِتَٰبَ مِن قَبْلِكُمْ ۝٥﴾

﴾ ***And a chaste woman from the people of the book [are lawful for you].*** ﴿ **5:5**

[324] Sahīh Al-Bukhārī, [Eng. Trans. vol. 7 #139].

[325] Sa'īd Ibn Mansūr, Mālik and Ibn Abī Shaybah reported it. Its narrators are said to be reliable by Al-Hāfidh Ibn Hajar Al-'Asqalānī.

However, if his wife is from any other religion or an outright pagan he must divorce her. This includes some so-called 'Muslim' sects [e.g. the Twelve Imamer Shiites[326]] that are not in the fold of Islām [as their innovations in the religion are so great]. This is in accordance with the verses of Allāh,

﴿ وَلَا تَنكِحُوا۟ ٱلْمُشْرِكَـٰتِ حَتَّىٰ يُؤْمِنَّ ۚ وَلَأَمَةٌ مُّؤْمِنَةٌ خَيْرٌ مِّن مُّشْرِكَةٍ وَلَوْ أَعْجَبَتْكُمْ ﴾

﴿ And do not marry the mushrikāt [idolatresses, etc.] till they believe [worship Allāh Alone]. And indeed a slave woman who believes is better than a [free] Mushrikah [idolatress], even though she pleases you.﴾ 2:221

﴿ وَلَا تُمْسِكُوا۟ بِعِصَمِ ٱلْكَوَافِرِ وَسْـَٔلُوا۟ مَآ أَنفَقْتُمْ ﴾

﴿ Likewise hold not the disbelieving women as wives, and ask for [the return of] that which you have spent [as Mahr]﴾ 60:10

If during her *'Iddah* [waiting] period she accepts Islām, he may take her back. If it is the wife who accepts Islām first then no matter what religion he is from he is not legal for her to stay married to. In fact, the simple fact that she is now a Muslim nullifies the marriage and she must commence her Iddah.

9] *Nikāh Al-Mut'ah* [Temporary Marriage];

This has been forbidden till the Day of Judgment.

"Allāh's Messenger [ﷺ] said, '*I had permitted to you the temporary marriage of women, but Allāh has prohibited you from that till the Day of Resurrection. So if anyone has a woman by temporary marriage he should let her go and do not take back any of your gifts from them*'."[327]

---

[326] *Rāfidah*- the name given to the twelve Imamer Shiites after they refused to follow Zayd Ibn 'Alī Ibn Hussein when he disapproved of their insult to the companions of the Prophet [ﷺ] especially the first of them Abū Bakr, 'Umar and 'Uthmān [ﷺ].

[327] *Sahīh Muslim*, [Eng. Trans. vol. 2. #3255].

10] *Shighār* contracts [exchange of family members in marriage instead of *Mahr*];

These are also prohibited,

"Allāh's Messenger [ﷺ] prohibited *Shighār* which means that a man gives his daughter in marriage on condition that the other gives his daughter to him in marriage without any dower being paid by either."[328]

Allāh the Exalted and His Messenger have informed us of the method by which marriage is to be contracted. This should neither be ignored nor should it be added to.

11] It is forbidden for a *muhrim* [one in the state of *Ihrām*] to marry or propose;

The Messenger of Allāh [ﷺ] said:

"A Muhrim should neither marry himself nor should he be got married to anyone, nor should he make the proposal of marriage."[329]

12] It is permissible to look at a woman before marrying her;

It is permissible to look at a woman's face or hands before marrying her [not her body]. The Prophet [ﷺ] asked a man who had married a woman:

"*Did you cast a glance at her?* He replied, 'No'. He [ﷺ] said, *'Go and cast a glance at her, for there is something in the eyes of the Ansār.*"[330]

In other circumstances it may be that he might see something to induce him to marry her or like in this case to make sure he wanted to marry her.

---

[328] *Sahīh Muslim*, [Eng. Trans. vol. 2 #3295].

[329] *Sahīh Muslim*, [Eng. Trans. vol. 2 #3280].

[330] *Sahīh Muslim*, [Eng. Trans. vol.2 #3314].

The Rights of the Spouses.

The Husband.

i] Obedience.

Allāh the All-Mighty, the Wise said,

﴿ ٱلرِّجَالُ قَوَّٰمُونَ عَلَى ٱلنِّسَآءِ بِمَا فَضَّلَ ٱللَّهُ بَعْضَهُمْ عَلَىٰ بَعْضٍ وَبِمَآ أَنفَقُوا۟ مِنْ أَمْوَٰلِهِمْ ۚ فَٱلصَّٰلِحَٰتُ قَٰنِتَٰتٌ حَٰفِظَٰتٌ لِّلْغَيْبِ بِمَا حَفِظَ ٱللَّهُ ﴾

﴾ Men are the protectors and maintainers of women, because Allāh has made one of them to excel the other, and because they spend [to support them] from their means. Therefore the righteous women are devoutly obedient [to Allāh and to their husbands] and guard in the husbands absence what Allāh orders them to guard [e.g. their chastity, their husbands property etc.]. ﴿ 4:34

She should obey her husband in everything except if he orders her to do something against the laws of Allāh or His Messenger [ﷺ], as there is no obedience to created beings in disobedience to the Creator [Allāh]. An example:

1. He asks for food or a book or to correct something in her behavior or worship, in this he is to be obeyed.

Another example:

2. He orders you to break fast in *Ramaḏān* [when you are not ill or traveling], or wear false hair, or remove your *ḫijāb* in the presence of non-*maḫram* males, in this he is not to be obeyed. We see this when the Prophet [ﷺ] was approached by a woman for a verdict.

"An Anṣārī woman gave her daughter in marriage and the hair of the latter started falling out. The Anṣārī woman came to the Prophet [ﷺ] and mentioned that to him and said, 'Her [my daughters] husband suggested that I should let her wear false hair.' The Prophet [ﷺ] said, ' *No, [don't do that] for Allāh sends His Curses upon such ladies who lengthen their hair artificially and there is no obedience to created things in disobedience to Allāh."* [331]

ii] The right to discipline his wife.

The rest of the above stated verse continues as follows,

﴿ وَٱلَّٰتِى تَخَافُونَ نُشُوزَهُنَّ فَعِظُوهُنَّ وَٱهْجُرُوهُنَّ فِى ٱلْمَضَاجِعِ وَٱضْرِبُوهُنَّ فَإِنْ أَطَعْنَكُمْ فَلَا تَبْغُوا۟ عَلَيْهِنَّ سَبِيلًا إِنَّ ٱللَّهَ كَانَ عَلِيًّا كَبِيرًا ﴾

﴿ As for those women on whose part you see ill-conduct admonish them [first], [next], refuse to share their beds, [and last] beat them [lightly, if it is useful], but if they return to obedience, seek not against them means [of annoyance]. Surely, Allāh is Ever Most High, Most Great.﴾ 4:34

a) First, he admonishes her. This is the first step that Allāh has ordered and it may not be overlooked. And this could be in the form of body language like a frown or silence or talking nicely about the problem or even angrily [loudly]. Most ladies respond to this, however if the woman ignores it then the next step ordered is taken.

b) He may then refuse to share her bed. In other words her sexual needs are not met and he may move to sleep in another room, or stay in the same room but not have sexual contact with her etc.

c) Finally, if it is deemed useful, he may beat her lightly. This needs to be clarified. Beating is to be done lightly only if it is deemed a useful solution to the problem as it may worsen the situation with no chance of reconciliation. Also, it may be that if the situation has reached this point, a divorce might be better and Allāh knows best. The Prophet [ﷺ] never used to beat his wives, children or slaves and in him is the best example. I urge the sisters to pay heed and not anger their husbands with such bad conduct for him to actually have to consider this last point. Some scholars of the *Salaf* are of the opinion that it is strictly forbidden to beat the women except for lewd conduct or such. Furthermore, it is forbidden

---

[331] *Sahīh Al-Bukhārī*, [Eng. Trans. vol. 7 #133].

to hit her severely that it would break a bone otherwise he would have to pay the penalty [of injuring another Muslim] and he may not hit her face.

"None of you should flog his wife as he flogs a slave then have sexual intercourse with her in the last part of the day." [332]

The Prophet [ﷺ] also said:
" *'Do not beat Allāh's handmaidens'*, but when 'Umar [ؓ] came to the Messenger of Allāh [ﷺ] and said, 'women have become emboldened towards their husbands', he [ﷺ] then gave permission to beat them. Then many women came round the family of the Prophet [ﷺ] complaining against their husbands. So the Prophet of Allāh [ﷺ] said, *'Many women have gone round Muhammad's family complaining about their husbands. They are not the best among you'*." [333]

iii] He has the right to fulfill his needs [sexual] with her whenever he pleases.

Allāh said,

﴿ نِسَآؤُكُمْ حَرْثٌ لَّكُمْ فَأْتُوا۟ حَرْثَكُمْ أَنَّىٰ شِئْتُمْ وَقَدِّمُوا۟ لِأَنفُسِكُمْ ۚ وَٱتَّقُوا۟ ٱللَّهَ وَٱعْلَمُوٓا۟ أَنَّكُم مُّلَٰقُوهُ ۗ وَبَشِّرِ ٱلْمُؤْمِنِينَ ﴿٢٢٣﴾ ﴾

﴾ Your wives are a tilth for you, so go to your tilth, when or how you will [have sexual relations with your wives in any manner you choose as long as it is in the vaginal opening and not the Anus as that is forbidden] ﴿ 2:223

﴿ وَخُلِقَ ٱلْإِنسَٰنُ ضَعِيفًا ﴾

﴾... and man was created weak [cannot be patient to leave sexual; intercourse with woman]. ﴿ 4:28

[332] *Sahīh Al-Bukhārī*, [Eng. Trans. vol. 7 #132].

[333] Sunan of Abū Daud, [Eng. Trans. vol. 2 #2141]. And declared *sahīh* by Sheik Al-Albānī.

His Prophet [ﷺ] said:

"If a man invites his wife to sleep with him and she refuses to come to him, then the angels send their curses on her till morning." [334]

Also, because of this right a woman may not fast supererogatory fasts without her husband's permission.

"A woman should not fast [optional fasts] except with her husbands permission if he is at home [staying with her]." [335]

If the woman is fasting it hampers her husbands ability to fulfils his desire with her hence since it is supererogatory she must ask his permission if he is at home [i.e., not traveling etc.]. This does not only refer to the night time for there is another ***hadīth*** that says even if she were occupied at the oven baking bread [or cooking] and he calls her, she must respond.[336]

iv] It is also from his rights that she never allows anyone in his house without his permission.

The Prophet [ﷺ] said about a wife:

" She should not allow anyone to enter his house except with his permission." [337]

In another ***hadīth***, she should not let anyone sit on his bed without his permission. This is in reference to enemies, or people he dislikes as they may be bad influences, or even that he wants to find no one other than his family when he returns for one reason or another.

---

[334] *Sahīh Al-Bukhārī*, [Eng. Trans. vol.7 #121].

[335] *Sahīh Al-Bukhārī*, [Eng. Trans. vol. 7 #120].

[336] *Sunan* of At-Tirmidhī #284. Declared *hasan sahīh gharīb* by *Shaykh* Al-Albānī.

[337] *Sahīh Al-Bukhārī*, [Eng. Trans. vol. 7 #123].

v] He may also ask her to see to the affairs of the house and children.

The Prophet [ﷺ] said:

"All of you are guardians and are responsible for your wards. The ruler is a guardian; The man is a guardian of his family. The lady is a guardian and is responsible for their husband's house and his offspring and so all of you are guardians and are responsible for your wards." [338]

vi] He also has the right to expect her to look attractive for him.

This includes obvious basic hygiene, like baths or brushing ones teeth, clipping nails, shaving the pubes and under arms as well as the other aspects like wearing attractive clothing and wearing perfume [at home only]. The Prophet [ﷺ] and his companions [ؓ] were returning from an expedition in this *hadīth*,

"Then we approached [Medina] and were going to enter [it], the Prophet [ﷺ] said, ' wait till you enter [your houses] at night [in the first part of the night] so that the ladies with unkempt hair may comb their hair, and those whose husbands have been absent [for a long time] may shave [their pubic hair]." [339]

vii] She should be grateful to him for all he does for her.

The Prophet [ﷺ] said:

" Then I saw the [Hell] Fire and I have never before, seen such a horrible sight as that and I saw the majority of it's dwellers were women! The people asked, 'O Allāh's Messenger, what is the reason for that?' He replied, '*Because of their ungratefulness.*' It was said, they disbelieve in Allāh [are they ungrateful to Allāh]?' He replied, '*They are not thankful to their husbands and are ungrateful for the favors done to them. Even if you do*

---

[338] *Sahīh Al-Bukhārī*, [Eng. Trans. vol. 7 #128].

[339] *Sahīh Al-Bukhārī* ,[Eng. Trans. vol. 7 #172].

good to one of them all your life, when she sees some harshness from you, she will say, 'I have never seen any good from you!'" [340]

The Rights of the Wife.

Allāh the Almighty, said,

﴿وَلَهُنَّ مِثْلُ ٱلَّذِى عَلَيْهِنَّ بِٱلْمَعْرُوفِ ۚ وَلِلرِّجَالِ عَلَيْهِنَّ دَرَجَةٌ ۗ وَٱللَّهُ عَزِيزٌ حَكِيمٌ ﴿٢٢٨﴾﴾

﴾ And they [women] have rights [over their husbands as regards living expenses etc.] similar [to those of their husbands] over them [as regards obedience and respect etc.] to what is reasonable, but men have a degree [of responsibility] over them. And Allāh is All-Mighty, All-Wise. ﴿ 2:228

A man asked the Prophet [ﷺ],

"What is the right of the wife of one of us over him? He [ﷺ] said: *'That you should give them food what you have for yourself, and clothe them by which you clothe yourself, and do not strike her on the face, do not revile her or separate yourself from her except in the house'.*" [341]

i] She has the right to expect protection and maintenance from him.

And Allāh the Exalted, said,

﴿ٱلرِّجَالُ قَوَّٰمُونَ عَلَى ٱلنِّسَآءِ بِمَا فَضَّلَ ٱللَّهُ بَعْضَهُمْ عَلَىٰ بَعْضٍ وَبِمَآ أَنفَقُوا۟ مِنْ أَمْوَٰلِهِمْ ۚ﴾

﴾ Men are the protectors and maintainers of women, because Allāh has made one of them to excel the other and because they spend [to support them] from their means. ﴿ 4:34

---

[340] *Sahīh Al-Bukhārī*, [Eng. Trans. vol. 7 #125].

[341] *Sunan* of Abū Dāwud, [Eng. Trans. Vol. 2 #2139]. Declared *hasan sahīh* by *Shaykh* Al-Albānī.

He should clothe, feed and house her as he does himself, and wherever the need arises, protect her from harm, and this includes the Hereafter [advice on the religion] or worldly affairs [actual bodily harm or insult]. This is the way of Islām. For this, she is grateful to her Lord [Allāh] and her husband. I might remind the sister that from his sense of protection will be his jealousy, she should not find it offensive, if she is indeed a believer.

ii] She has the right to expect mercy and kindness from him.

The Messenger of Allāh [ﷺ] said:

" Whoever believes in Allāh and the Last Day should not hurt [trouble] his neighbor. And I advise you to take care of women for they are created from a rib and the most crooked portion of the rib is the upper part; if you try to straighten it, it will break [divorce her] and if you leave it, it will remain crooked. So I urge you to take care of women." [342]

Women can be emotional thus irrational at times, they also have different views on subjects compared to men. However, they should both try to avoid points of argument, and he should be patient with her. Also, see the *hadīth* of Abū Zar' covered under point [v].

iii] She may expect him to converse and communicate with her.

The Prophet [ﷺ] used to converse with his wives and Ibn 'Umar said: "During the lifetime of the Prophet [ﷺ] we used to avoid chatting leisurely and freely with our wives lest some divine inspiration might be revealed concerning us. But when the Prophet [ﷺ] died we started chatting leisurely and freely [with them]." [343]

---

[342] *Sahīh Al-Bukhārī*, [Eng. Trans. vol. 7 #114].

[343] *Sahīh Al-Bukhārī*, [Eng. Trans. vol. 7 #115].

iv] She has the same rights for sexual gratification as he does.

Allāh the Exalted, said,

﴿أُحِلَّ لَكُمْ لَيْلَةَ ٱلصِّيَامِ ٱلرَّفَثُ إِلَىٰ نِسَآئِكُمْ هُنَّ لِبَاسٌ لَّكُمْ وَأَنتُمْ لِبَاسٌ لَّهُنَّ﴾

﴿ It is made lawful for you to have sexual relations with your wives on the night of As-Sawm [fasts]. They are a libās [i.e., body cover, or screen or sakan [i.e., you enjoy the pleasure of living with them see Tafsīr At-Tabarī] of verse7:189] for you dnd you are the same for them.﴾ 2:187

In the beginning, in Islām they were forbidden to have sexual intercourse with their spouses at all in the month of *Ramadān*, then Allāh revealed this verse.

v] She to has the right to expect him to look attractive for her.

He should also practice the basic hygiene necessary in Islām and should perfume himself and wear clean attractive clothing. At this point we shall cover the long *hadīth* of Abū Zar' to gain a better understanding of the points above and more. It should be noted that this *hadīth* describes a type of gathering before the coming of Islām and one should not discuss their husbands as such, as it involves backbiting them. 'Ā`ishah [ﷺ] the wife of the Prophet [ﷺ] narrated:

"Eleven women sat [at a place] and promised and contracted that they would not conceal anything of the news of their husbands. The first one said, 'My husband is like the meat of a lean weak camel which is kept on top of a mountain which is neither easy to climb, nor is the meat fat, so that one might put up with the trouble of fetching it'. The second one said, 'I shall not relate my husbands news for fear that I may not be able to finish his story, for if I describe him, I will mention all his defects and bad traits.' The third one said, ' My husband is a tall man; if I describe [and he hears of that] he will divorce me, and if I keep quiet, he will neither divorce me nor treat me as a wife.' The fourth one said, 'My husband is a moderate person like the night of Tihama which is neither hot nor cold. I am neither afraid of him nor am I discontented with him.' The fifth one said, 'My husband when entering [the house] is a leopard, and when going out is a lion. He does not ask about whatever is in the house.' The sixth one said, 'If my husband eats, he eats too much [leaving the dishes empty], and if he drinks he leaves nothing, and if he sleeps he sleeps alone [away from me] covered in garments and does not stretch his hands here and there so as to know how I fare [get along].' The seventh one said , ' My husband is a wrong doer or weak and foolish. All the defects are present in him. He may injure your head or body or both.' The eighth one said, 'My husband is soft to touch like a rabbit and smells like a Zarnab [a kind of good smelling grass].' The ninth one said, ' My husband is a tall generous man wearing a long strap for carrying his sword. His ashes are abundant and his house is near the people who would easily consult him.' The tenth one said, ' My husband is Mālik, and what is Mālik? Mālik is greater than whatever I say about him. [he is beyond and above all praises, which can come to mind. Most of his camels are kept at home [ready to be slaughtered for guests] and only a few are taken to the pastures. When the camels hear the sound of the lute [or tambourine] they realize that they are going to be slaughtered for the guests.' The eleventh one said, ' My husband is Abū Zar', and what is Abū Zar' [what should I say about him?]. He has given me many ornaments and my ears are heavily loaded with them and my arms have become fat [i.e., I have become fat]. And he has pleased me, and I have become so happy that I feel proud of myself. He found me with my family who were mere owners of sheep and living in poverty, and brought me to a respected family having horses and camels and threshing and purifying grain. Whatever I say, he does not rebuke or insult me. When I sleep, I sleep till late in the morning, and when I drink water [or milk] I drink my fill. The mother of Abū Zar', and what may one say in the praise of the mother of Abū Zar'? Her saddlebags were always full of provision and her house was spacious as for the son of Abū Zar', what may one say of the son of Abū Zar'? His bed is as narrow as an unsheathed sword and an arm of a kid [four months] satisfies his hunger. As for the daughter of Abū Zar', she is obedient to her father and to her mother. She has a fat well built body and that arouses the jealousy of her husband's other wife. As for the [maid] slave girl of Abū Zar', what may one say of the [maid] slave girl of Abū Zar'? She does not uncover our secrets but keeps them, and does not waste our provisions and does not leave the rubbish scattered everywhere in our house.' The eleventh lady added, 'one day it so happened that Abū Zar' went out at the time when the milk was being milked from the animals, and he saw a woman who had two sons like two leopards playing with her two breasts, [on seeing her] he divorced me and married her. There after I married a noble man who used to ride a fast tireless horse and keep a spear in his hand. He gave me many things and also a pair of every kind of livestock and said, ' eat [of this] •O Umm Zar' and give provision to your relatives.' She added 'Yet all of those things which my second husband gave me could not fill the smallest utensil of Abū Zar's.' 'Ā`ishah [ﷺ] then said, *"Allāh's Messenger[ﷺ] said to me, 'I am to you as Abū Zar' was to his wife Umm Zar'."*[344]

Notice which one the Prophet [ﷺ] likened himself to for his behavior. As for the meanings meant in some of the descriptions:

(a) Her husband was badly behaved, worthless, arrogant and miserly.

(b) She compares her husband with a leopard, which is well known for being shy, harmless and fond of too much sleep. She compares him with a lion when he is out for fighting. Besides, he does not interfere in the home affairs e.g. he does not ask her how much she spends, nor does he criticizes any fault he may notice.

(c) He is noble and brave.

(d) He is so generous that he always makes fires for his guests to entertain them, hence the abundant ashes.

(e) He lives near to the people so he is always at hand to solve their problems and help them in hardships and give them good advice.

(f) They were rich farmers- Her husband took her out of poverty into prosperity.

(g) She was well off and generous.

(h) He was a slender man who ate little.

(i) She was trustworthy, careful and clean.

---

[344] *Sahīh Al-Bukhārī*, [Eng. Trans. vol. 7 #117].

Another right that both the husband and wife share is the right to have children.

Allāh the [Only] Originator, the Creator, said in His Book:

﴿فَٱلْـَٔـٰنَ بَـٰشِرُوهُنَّ وَٱبْتَغُوا۟ مَا كَتَبَ ٱللَّهُ لَكُمْ﴾

﴿So now have sexual relations with them and seek that which Allāh has ordained for you [offspring],﴾ 2:187

Neither spouse may partake in any birth control method without real reason and without approval of the other spouse. The Prophet [ﷺ] said:

"Seek to have offspring, seek to have offspring!"[345]

A man came to the Prophet [ﷺ] and said:

"I have found a woman of rank and beauty, but she does not give birth to children. Should I marry her?' He said, '**No**'. He came again to him, but he prohibited him. He came to him a third time, and he [the Prophet [ﷺ]] said: *"Marry women who are loving and very prolific, for I shall out number the peoples by you."*[346]

- ***Summary***:

- To get married both parties may have representatives however the man can represent himself but the woman needs a *walī* or guardian to act on her behalf. Preferably this should be a male from her family, however if no Muslim male exists to help her.she may approach the Imam of her local *Masjid* to act on her behalf.
- Once suitable parties [future spouses [acceptable to the bride and groom to be]] have been located then a contract must be drawn up including the *Mahr* [dowry] agreed upon and then it is signed by witnesses.
- At this point, they are legally married; a Wedding banquet should be held as soon as they are able. [See Chapter 5 under 'Special occasions' for detail on the banquet]

---

345 Sahīh *Al-Bukhārī*, [Eng. Trans. vol.7 #174].

346 Sunan of Abū Dāwud. [Eng. Trans.Vol.2 #2045]. Declared *hasan sahīh* by *Shaykh* Al-Albānī.

CHAPTER 11

TALĀQ [DIVORCE]

Allāh the Exalted, the Wise, said:

﴿يَٰٓأَيُّهَا ٱلنَّبِيُّ إِذَا طَلَّقۡتُمُ ٱلنِّسَآءَ فَطَلِّقُوهُنَّ لِعِدَّتِهِنَّ وَأَحۡصُواْ ٱلۡعِدَّةَۖ وَٱتَّقُواْ ٱللَّهَ
رَبَّكُمۡۖ لَا تُخۡرِجُوهُنَّ مِنۢ بُيُوتِهِنَّ وَلَا يَخۡرُجۡنَ إِلَّآ أَن يَأۡتِينَ بِفَٰحِشَةٖ مُّبَيِّنَةٖۚ وَتِلۡكَ
حُدُودُ ٱللَّهِۚ وَمَن يَتَعَدَّ حُدُودَ ٱللَّهِ فَقَدۡ ظَلَمَ نَفۡسَهُۥۚ لَا تَدۡرِي لَعَلَّ ٱللَّهَ يُحۡدِثُ بَعۡدَ ذَٰلِكَ
أَمۡرٗا ١ فَإِذَا بَلَغۡنَ أَجَلَهُنَّ فَأَمۡسِكُوهُنَّ بِمَعۡرُوفٍ أَوۡ فَارِقُوهُنَّ بِمَعۡرُوفٖ وَأَشۡهِدُواْ
ذَوَيۡ عَدۡلٖ مِّنكُمۡ وَأَقِيمُواْ ٱلشَّهَٰدَةَ لِلَّهِۚ ذَٰلِكُمۡ يُوعَظُ بِهِۦ مَن كَانَ يُؤۡمِنُ بِٱللَّهِ
وَٱلۡيَوۡمِ ٱلۡأٓخِرِۚ وَمَن يَتَّقِ ٱللَّهَ يَجۡعَل لَّهُۥ مَخۡرَجٗا ٢﴾

﴿ When you divorce women, divorce them at their 'Iddah [prescribed periods] and count [accurately] their Iddah. And fear Allāh your Lord [O Muslims]...Then when they are about to attain their term appointed, either take them back in a good manner or part with them in a good manner. And take as witnesses two just persons from among you [Muslims]...﴾
65:1-2.

This is a sad end but is legal in Islām as a way out of a failed marriage and Allāh has revealed an entire Sūrah [Chapter] in the Qur`ān devoted to it in addition to Āyāt [verses] in other Sūrahs. It is a serious institution and is not to be toyed with [used every time one wants to 'teach' her/or him a lesson or whenever they get angry.]. The woman may also ask for a divorce if necessary [*Khul'ah*]. She may not ask for one without good reason as Paradise is forbidden for one who asks her husband for one without good cause.

The *Sunnah* of Divorce.

1) First of all, the wife is not to be on her period.

She should be clean from her period.

"Ibn 'Umar [ﷺ] reported that he divorced his wife while she was menstruating during the lifetime of the Prophet [ﷺ]. 'Umar Ibn Al-Khaṯṯāb [ﷺ] asked Allāh's Messenger [ﷺ] about it, whereupon Allāh's Messenger [ﷺ] said, "*Command him [Ibn 'Umar] to take her back [and keep her] and pronounce divorce when she is purified.*" [347]

2) She may only be divorced twice, after the third time she has to marry someone else and be divorced by him before her former husband can remarry her.

Allāh the Almighty said,

﴿ ٱلطَّلَـٰقُ مَرَّتَانِ ۖ فَإِمْسَاكٌۢ بِمَعْرُوفٍ أَوْ تَسْرِيحٌۢ بِإِحْسَـٰنٍ ۗ وَلَا يَحِلُّ لَكُمْ أَن تَأْخُذُوا۟ مِمَّآ ءَاتَيْتُمُوهُنَّ شَيْـًٔا ﴾

﴿ The divorce is twice, after that, either you retain her on reasonable terms or release her with kindness. And it is not lawful for you [men] to take back [from your wives] any of your Mahr, which you have given them. ﴾ 2:229

﴿ فَإِن طَلَّقَهَا فَلَا تَحِلُّ لَهُۥ مِنۢ بَعْدُ حَتَّىٰ تَنكِحَ زَوْجًا غَيْرَهُۥ ۗ فَإِن طَلَّقَهَا فَلَا جُنَاحَ عَلَيْهِمَآ أَن يَتَرَاجَعَآ إِن ظَنَّآ أَن يُقِيمَا حُدُودَ ٱللَّهِ ۗ وَتِلْكَ حُدُودُ ٱللَّهِ يُبَيِّنُهَا لِقَوْمٍ يَعْلَمُونَ ﴿٢٣٠﴾ وَإِذَا طَلَّقْتُمُ ٱلنِّسَآءَ فَبَلَغْنَ أَجَلَهُنَّ فَأَمْسِكُوهُنَّ بِمَعْرُوفٍ أَوْ سَرِّحُوهُنَّ بِمَعْرُوفٍ ۚ وَلَا تُمْسِكُوهُنَّ ضِرَارًا لِّتَعْتَدُوا۟ ۚ وَمَن يَفْعَلْ ذَٰلِكَ فَقَدْ ظَلَمَ نَفْسَهُۥ ۚ وَلَا تَتَّخِذُوٓا۟

---

[347] *Sahīh Muslim*, [Eng. Trans. vol. 2 #3473].

ءَايَـٰتِ ٱللَّهِ هُزُوًا ۚ وَٱذْكُرُوا۟ نِعْمَتَ ٱللَّهِ عَلَيْكُمْ وَمَآ أَنزَلَ عَلَيْكُم مِّنَ ٱلْكِتَـٰبِ وَٱلْحِكْمَةِ

يَعِظُكُم بِهِۦ ۚ وَٱتَّقُوا۟ ٱللَّهَ وَٱعْلَمُوٓا۟ أَنَّ ٱللَّهَ بِكُلِّ شَىْءٍ عَلِيمٌ ﴿٢٣١﴾

﴾ And if he has divorced her [the third time], then she is not lawful unto him thereafter until she has married another husband. Then, if the other husband divorces her, it is no sin on both of them that they reunite, provided they feel they can keep the limits ordained by Allāh.﴿ 2:230

One divorce is described below; the divorce is not to be pronounced three times all together, as this is a violation of the laws of Allāh and His Messenger. Allāh further says,

﴿ وَإِذَا طَلَّقْتُمُ ٱلنِّسَآءَ فَبَلَغْنَ أَجَلَهُنَّ فَأَمْسِكُوهُنَّ بِمَعْرُوفٍ أَوْ سَرِّحُوهُنَّ بِمَعْرُوفٍ

وَلَا تُمْسِكُوهُنَّ ضِرَارًا لِّتَعْتَدُوا۟ ۚ وَمَن يَفْعَلْ ذَٰلِكَ فَقَدْ ظَلَمَ نَفْسَهُۥ ۚ وَلَا تَتَّخِذُوٓا۟

ءَايَـٰتِ ٱللَّهِ هُزُوًا ۚ وَٱذْكُرُوا۟ نِعْمَتَ ٱللَّهِ عَلَيْكُمْ وَمَآ أَنزَلَ عَلَيْكُم مِّنَ ٱلْكِتَـٰبِ وَٱلْحِكْمَةِ

يَعِظُكُم بِهِۦ ۚ وَٱتَّقُوا۟ ٱللَّهَ وَٱعْلَمُوٓا۟ أَنَّ ٱللَّهَ بِكُلِّ شَىْءٍ عَلِيمٌ ﴾

﴾ And when you have divorced women ...But do not take them back to hurt them, and whoever does that, then he has wronged himself. And treat not the Verses [laws] of Allāh as a jest, but remember Allāh's Favors on you [Islām], and that which He has sent down to you of the Book [Qur`ān] and Al-Hikmah [the Prophet [ﷺ] Sunnah-Islāmic Jurisprudence] whereby He instructs you. And fear Allāh, and know that Allāh is All-Aware of Everything.﴿ 2:231

3] After the one pronouncement of divorce, he has the choice to return to her during the three the prescribed period, if this time elapses he can only return to her with a new marriage contract. If however, it were the third time, he is prohibited from returning to her.

The Prophet [ﷺ] said about Ibn 'Umar:

"Command him to take her back until she is pure and then enters the second menses and then becomes pure. Then either divorce her or retain her."[348]

The divorce should only be pronounced when the sister is pure [not menstruating]. Her husband says: "you are divorced" [or the equivalent] and then she starts her Iddah [waiting period], which lasts for three consecutive menstrual periods. If he has not returned to her during her *'Iddah* then he can only take her back with a new marriage contract. If he has relations with her during her Iddah, that nullifies his intention of divorce, it also counts as one divorce. In Islām divorce is only twice [i.e., doing the above actions [two periods each] twice] after the third time he cannot take her back until she marries someone else and he divorces her [i.e., has a normal marriage including sexual relations]. It is explicitly forbidden for a man to marry a woman with the intention of making her legal for her first husband, he should be marrying her with the intention of keeping her as his wife.

Other Facts She Should Know.

1] Her Iddah [waiting period].

Allāh the Exalted the Mighty said,

﴿ وَٱلۡمُطَلَّقَٰتُ يَتَرَبَّصۡنَ بِأَنفُسِهِنَّ ثَلَٰثَةَ قُرُوٓءٖۚ وَلَا يَحِلُّ لَهُنَّ أَن يَكۡتُمۡنَ مَا خَلَقَ ٱللَّهُ فِيٓ أَرۡحَامِهِنَّ إِن كُنَّ يُؤۡمِنَّ بِٱللَّهِ وَٱلۡيَوۡمِ ٱلۡأٓخِرِۚ وَبُعُولَتُهُنَّ أَحَقُّ بِرَدِّهِنَّ فِي ذَٰلِكَ إِنۡ أَرَادُوٓاْ إِصۡلَٰحٗاۚ وَلَهُنَّ مِثۡلُ ٱلَّذِي عَلَيۡهِنَّ بِٱلۡمَعۡرُوفِۚ وَلِلرِّجَالِ عَلَيۡهِنَّ دَرَجَةٞۗ وَٱللَّهُ عَزِيزٌ حَكِيمٌ ﴾

﴿ And divorced women shall wait [as regards their marriage] for three menstrual periods, and it is not lawful for them to conceal what Allāh has created in their wombs, if they believe in Allāh and the Last Day. And

---

[348] *Sahīh Muslim* [Eng. Trans. vol. 2 #3480].

their husband's have more right to take them back in that period, if they wish for reconciliation... ***2:228.***

﴿ وَأُوْلَٰتُ ٱلْأَحْمَالِ أَجَلُهُنَّ أَن يَضَعْنَ حَمْلَهُنَّ ﴾

And those of your women as have passed the age of monthly courses, for them the Iddah, if you have doubt, is three months; and for those who have no courses [[immature] their Iddah is three months likewise, except in the case of death]. ***65:4***

She commences her waiting period;

a) Immediately after her husband pronounces the divorce. The waiting period ends either when he returns to her, or after the end of her third period he divorces her.

b) Also at the confirmation of the death of her husband. This period will end after four months and ten days, the length of the morning period for the loss of a husband [the death of anyone else has a morning period of three days only]. The Prophet of Allāh [ﷺ] said:

" It is not lawful for a lady who believes in Allāh and the Last Day to mourn for a dead person for more than three days unless he is her husband for whom she should mourn for four months and ten days."[349]

She may pass this period in the house of her husband or in the house where she receives the news of her husband's death and the latter opinion was held by two of the righteous Caliphs ['Umar and 'Uthmān] among others. During this period she may not beautify herself i.e., using *kuhl*[350], perfume, saffron and related cosmetics nor may she where bright attractive clothing and she should not leave the house except for an emergency like a visit to the hospital [for real need].

---

[349] *Sahīh Al-Bukhārī*, [Eng. Trans. vol. 7 Chapter 46. #251].

[350] *Kuhl* a black substance used as eyeliner.

c] For those women who are pregnant, her Iddah ends [if her husband died or she is of those whom divorce is pronounced] when she delivers regardless of whether it is in one day or nine months. After which she may remarry even when she is still bleeding but her husband cannot have relations with her till she is purified.

﴿ وَٱلَّٰٓـِٔي يَئِسۡنَ مِنَ ٱلۡمَحِيضِ مِن نِّسَآئِكُمۡ إِنِ ٱرۡتَبۡتُمۡ فَعِدَّتُهُنَّ ثَلَٰثَةُ أَشۡهُرٖ وَٱلَّٰٓـِٔي
لَمۡ يَحِضۡنَۚ وَأُوْلَٰتُ ٱلۡأَحۡمَالِ أَجَلُهُنَّ أَن يَضَعۡنَ حَمۡلَهُنَّۚ ﴿٤﴾ ﴾

﴾ And for those who are pregnant [whether they are divorced or their husband's are dead], their Iddah is until they lay down their burden; ﴿ 65:4

2] During the Iddah [for the one who has been divorced by her husband one or two times] she is to remain in the house of the husband and he must continue to provide for her.

Allāh the Exalted said:

﴿ لَا تُخۡرِجُوهُنَّ مِنۢ بُيُوتِهِنَّ وَلَا يَخۡرُجۡنَ إِلَّآ أَن يَأۡتِينَ بِفَٰحِشَةٖ مُّبَيِّنَةٖۚ ﴿١﴾ ﴾

﴾... turn them not out of their [husband's] homes nor shall they [themselves] leave, except in case they are guilty of some open illegal sexual intercourse.﴿ 65:1

﴿ أَسۡكِنُوهُنَّ مِنۡ حَيۡثُ سَكَنتُم مِّن وُجۡدِكُمۡ وَلَا تُضَآرُّوهُنَّ لِتُضَيِّقُواْ عَلَيۡهِنَّۚ وَإِن
كُنَّ أُوْلَٰتِ حَمۡلٖ فَأَنفِقُواْ عَلَيۡهِنَّ حَتَّىٰ يَضَعۡنَ حَمۡلَهُنَّۚ فَإِنۡ أَرۡضَعۡنَ لَكُمۡ فَـَٔاتُوهُنَّ أُجُورَهُنَّ
وَأۡتَمِرُواْ بَيۡنَكُم بِمَعۡرُوفٖۖ وَإِن تَعَاسَرۡتُمۡ فَسَتُرۡضِعُ لَهُۥٓ أُخۡرَىٰ ﴿٦﴾ لِيُنفِقۡ ذُو سَعَةٖ
مِّن سَعَتِهِۦۖ وَمَن قُدِرَ عَلَيۡهِ رِزۡقُهُۥ فَلۡيُنفِقۡ مِمَّآ ءَاتَىٰهُ ٱللَّهُۚ لَا يُكَلِّفُ ٱللَّهُ نَفۡسًا إِلَّا مَآ
ءَاتَىٰهَاۚ سَيَجۡعَلُ ٱللَّهُ بَعۡدَ عُسۡرٖ يُسۡرٗا ﴿٧﴾ ﴾

﴾ Lodge them [the divorced women] where you dwell, according to your means, and do not harm them so as to straighten them [that they are obliged to leave your house]. And if they are pregnant, then spend on

them till they lay down their burden. And if they give suck to the children for you, give them their due payment, and let each of you accept the advice of the other in a just way. But if you make difficulties for one another some other woman may give suck for him. Let the rich man spend according to his means; and the man whose resources are restricted, let him spend according to what Allāh has given him.*}** ***65:6-7

3) Divorce before [sexual] relations have taken place.

This applies to both before and after *Mahr* has been agreed upon. Allāh said:

﴿ لَّا جُنَاحَ عَلَيْكُمْ إِن طَلَّقْتُمُ ٱلنِّسَآءَ مَا لَمْ تَمَسُّوهُنَّ أَوْ تَفْرِضُوا۟ لَهُنَّ فَرِيضَةً ۚ
وَمَتِّعُوهُنَّ عَلَى ٱلْمُوسِعِ قَدَرُهُۥ وَعَلَى ٱلْمُقْتِرِ قَدَرُهُۥ مَتَٰعًۢا بِٱلْمَعْرُوفِ ۖ حَقًّا عَلَى
ٱلْمُحْسِنِينَ ﴿٢٣٦﴾ ﴾

{ There is no sin on you, if you divorce women while you have not yet touched them [had relations], nor appointed unto them their Mahr. But bestow on them [a suitable gift], the rich according to his means and the poor according to his means, a gift of reasonable amount is a duty on the doers of good.} ***2:236***

﴿ وَإِن طَلَّقْتُمُوهُنَّ مِن قَبْلِ أَن تَمَسُّوهُنَّ فَنِصْفُ فَروَقَدْ مَا فَرَضْتُمْ إِلَّآ يَعْفُوا
عُقْدَةُ ٱلنِّكَاحِ ۚ وَأَن تَعْفُوٓا۟ أَقْرَبُ لِلتَّقْوَىٰ ۚ وَلَا تَنسَوُا۟ ٱلْفَضْلَ بَيْنَكُمْ ۚ إِنَّ ٱللَّهَ
بِمَا تَعْمَلُونَ بَصِيرٌ ﴿٢٣٧﴾ ﴾

{ And if you divorce them before you have touched them, and you have appointed unto them the Mahr, then pay half of the [Mahr], unless they [the women] agree to forgo it, or he [the husband], in whose hands the marriage is, agrees to forgo and give her full appointed Mahr. And to forgo and give [her the full Mahr] is nearer to Taqwā [piety, righteousness]. And do not forget liberality between yourselves.} ***2:237***

4) ***Al-Khul'ah*. [separation from the wife for compensation]**

This is where the woman asks her husband for a divorce and agrees to return her *Mahr* [dowry] in exchange. She should have a valid reason for doing so as the odor of Paradise is forbidden for the one who asks for a divorce without a strong reason.[351] A woman came to the Prophet [ﷺ] and said:

> "O Allāh's Messenger, I do not find fault with Thābit Ibn Qays in respect of character or religion, but I, being a Muslim dislike to behave in an un-Islāmic manner.' Allāh's Messenger [ﷺ] asked her, ' *Will you give him back his garden?'* And she replied, ' Yes'. So Allāh's Messenger [ﷺ] said to him, *'Accept the garden and divorce her once.*"[352]

It was reported by Ibn Mājah that 'Amr Ibn Shu'ayb [from his father] said. "Thābit Ibn Qais was ugly and his wife said, 'Were it not for the fear of Allāh, when he entered my presence I would spit on his face.'"

5) ***Adh-Dhihār*** **[the making of a vow to stay away from one's wife i.e., making her unlawful for himself] and related topics.**

This is where the man would say to his wife, 'You are like the back of my mother to me' meaning unlawful. This would be said out of anger and the wife would be left in a hanging state [as to the state of her marriage]. And Allāh the Exalted the Mighty said:

﴿ ٱلَّذِينَ يُظَٰهِرُونَ مِنكُم مِّن نِّسَآئِهِم مَّا هُنَّ أُمَّهَٰتِهِمْۖ إِنْ أُمَّهَٰتُهُمْ إِلَّا ٱلَّٰٓـِٔي
وَلَدْنَهُمْۚ وَإِنَّهُمْ لَيَقُولُونَ مُنكَرًا مِّنَ ٱلْقَوْلِ وَزُورًاۚ وَإِنَّ ٱللَّهَ لَعَفُوٌّ غَفُورٌ ﴿٢﴾
وَٱلَّذِينَ يُظَٰهِرُونَ مِن نِّسَآئِهِمْ ثُمَّ يَعُودُونَ لِمَا قَالُوا۟ فَتَحْرِيرُ رَقَبَةٍ مِّن قَبْلِ أَن
يَتَمَآسَّاۚ ذَٰلِكُمْ تُوعَظُونَ بِهِۦۚ وَٱللَّهُ بِمَا تَعْمَلُونَ خَبِيرٌ ﴿٣﴾ فَمَن لَّمْ يَجِدْ فَصِيَامُ

---

[351] *Sunan* of Abū Dāwud, [Eng. Trans. vol. 2 #2218] Declared sahīh by *Shaykh* Al-Albānī.

[352] Sahīh *Al-Bukhārī*, [Eng. Trans. vol. 7 #197].

شَهْرَيْنِ مُتَتَابِعَيْنِ مِن قَبْلِ أَن يَتَمَاسَّا فَمَن لَّمْ يَسْتَطِعْ فَإِطْعَامُ سِتِّينَ مِسْكِينًا
ذَٰلِكَ لِتُؤْمِنُوا بِاللَّهِ وَرَسُولِهِ وَتِلْكَ حُدُودُ اللَّهِ وَلِلْكَافِرِينَ عَذَابٌ أَلِيمٌ ﴿٤﴾

﴾ Those among you who make their wives unlawful to them by [dhihār] they cannot be like their mothers. None can be like their mothers except those who gave them birth. And verily, they utter an ill word and a lie. And verily, Allāh is Oft-Pardoning, Oft-Forgiving. And those who make unlawful to themselves their wives by dhihār and wish to free themselves from what they uttered; [the penalty] in that case is the freeing of a slave before they touch each other. This is an admonition to you [so that you may not repeat such an ill thing]. And Allāh is All-Aware of what you do. And he who finds not [the money for freeing a slave] must fast two consecutive months before they touch each other. And he, who is unable to do so, should feed sixty masākīn [poor people]. That is in order that you may have perfect Faith in Allāh and His Messenger. These are the limits set by Allāh. And for disbelievers, there is a painful torment.﴿ 58:2-4

The wife is always lawful for her husband and neither one of them can change this right except for her privates during her menses or sexual intercourse during the daytime in *Ramadān* or while in Ihram, or if it is the third divorce,. So when the husband makes such an oath he has disobeyed Allāh and His Messenger [ﷺ] and must pay the penalty. Likewise, he should not make any other such oath of abstention [from her]; except for disciplinary purposes, the duration of which may not exceed four months and at the end of this period or less [whatever time he stipulated but no more than four months] he should return to her or divorce her. In the time ignorance, the people would stay away from their wives for one or two years and Allāh appointed a period of no more than four months[353]. Ibn 'Umar [رضي الله عنه] narrated " When a period of four months elapses, the one who swears to stay away from his wife must be made to return to her or divorce her, and the divorce is not valid until the husband pronounces it." And Allāh the Almighty said:

---

[353] Sūrah Al-Baqarah: 226.

﴿ وَسَرِّحُوهُنَّ سَرَاحًا جَمِيلًا ﴾

﴿ And set them free [divorce the women] in a handsome manner.﴾ 33:49.

Therefore, it is agreed amongst the scholars that it is the man who pronounces the divorce.

6) *Al-Li'ān* [invoking the curse of Allāh by the spouses on themselves in the case of unproven adultery].

The husband has the right to use *Li'ān.* A woman is not entitled to maintenance after this. Once the accusation has been made, if it is revoked then the accuser will be punished for slander [80 lashes with a whip and his/or her word will not be accepted as witness]. And if it is true the liar will be punished in the next world for making a false oath in the Name of Allāh and the adultery.

Allāh the Almighty said,

﴿ وَٱلَّذِينَ يَرْمُونَ أَزْوَٰجَهُمْ وَلَمْ يَكُن لَّهُمْ شُهَدَآءُ إِلَّآ أَنفُسُهُمْ فَشَهَٰدَةُ أَحَدِهِمْ أَرْبَعُ شَهَٰدَٰتٍۭ بِٱللَّهِ إِنَّهُۥ لَمِنَ ٱلصَّٰدِقِينَ ۝٦ وَٱلْخَٰمِسَةُ أَنَّ لَعْنَتَ ٱللَّهِ عَلَيْهِ إِن كَانَ مِنَ ٱلْكَٰذِبِينَ ۝٧ وَيَدْرَؤُا۟ عَنْهَا ٱلْعَذَابَ أَن تَشْهَدَ أَرْبَعَ شَهَٰدَٰتٍۭ بِٱللَّهِ إِنَّهُۥ لَمِنَ ٱلْكَٰذِبِينَ ۝٨ وَٱلْخَٰمِسَةَ أَنَّ غَضَبَ ٱللَّهِ عَلَيْهَآ إِن كَانَ مِنَ ٱلصَّٰدِقِينَ ۝٩ ﴾

﴿ And for those who accuse their wives, but have no witnesses except themselves, let the testimony of one of them be four testimonies [i.e., four times] by Allāh that he is one of those who speak the truth. And the fifth [testimony should be] the invoking of the Curse of Allāh on him if he be of those who tell a lie [against her]. But he shall avert the punishment [of stoning to death] from her, if she bears witness four times by Allāh, that he [her husband] is telling a lie. And the fifth [testimony] should be that the Wrath of Allāh be upon her if he [her husband] speaks the truth. And the fifth [testimony] [should be] the invoking of the curse of Allāh on him if he be of those who tell a lie [against her]. But it shall avert the punishment [of stoning to death] from her, if she bears witness four times

by Allāh, that he [her husband] is telling a lie. And the fifth [testimony] should be that the Wrath of Allāh be upon her if he [her husband] speaks the truth. **24:6-9**

Ibn 'Umar [ﷺ] when asked about *Li'ān* by Sa'īd Ibn Jubayr [the narrator of the *hadīth*] said: "The first one who asked about it was so and so. He said, 'O Allāh's Messenger, tell me if one of us finds his wife committing adultery what should he do? If he talks he would talk about a grievous affair, and if he keeps silent it is also [something great] [which he cannot afford to do].' Allāh's Messenger [ﷺ] kept quiet [for some time]. After that time he [that very person] came to him and said: 'I have been involved in that very case about which I had asked you." Allāh the Exalted and Majestic then revealed the verses of Sūrah Nūr: "*Those who accuse their wives.*" And he [the Prophet ﷺ] recited them to him and admonished him, and exerted him and informed him that the torment of the world is less painful than the torment of the Hereafter. He said, 'No, by Him Who sent you with the Truth, I did not tell a lie against her. He [the Prophet ﷺ] then called her [the accused] and admonished her, and exhorted her, and informed her that the torment of this world is less painful than the torment of the Hereafter. She said, 'No, by Him Who sent you with the Truth, he is a lair. [It was] the man who started the swearing of oath and he swore in the name of Allāh four times that he was among the truthful, and at the fifth turn he said,' Let the curse of Allāh be upon me if I am among the liars. Then the woman was called and she swore four times in the name of Allāh that he [her husband] was among the liars, and at the fifth time she swore, 'Let the curse of Allāh be upon me if he were among the truthful'. He [the Prophet ﷺ] then effected separation between the two."

And in another *hadīth*, Ibn 'Umar also mentioned that the Prophet [ﷺ] said to them [the invokers]: "*Your account is with Allāh. One of you must be a liar. You have no right over this woman.*' He said, 'Messenger of Allāh, what about my wealth [dower]? He said, '*You have no claim to wealth. If you tell the truth, it is the recompense for your having had the right to intercourse with her, and if you tell a lie against her it is still more remote from you than she is.*"[354]

After this, the Prophet asked that she should be observed to see the features of the child she bears i.e., to see if it resembled her former husband or the man she was accused of adultery with. She had in fact lied and the child she bore resembled the man she had committed adultery with. The children from *Li'ān* are attributed to the mother only.

7) On suspected paternity.

It is upon the woman to be honest and the man not to be highly suspicious [without reason], A man came to the Prophet [ﷺ] and said: "My wife has given birth to a black son. He [ﷺ] said, '*Have you any camels?*' He said, 'They are red'. He asked, '*Is there a dusky one amongst them?*' He replied, 'Some of them are dusky.' He asked, '*How do you think they have come about?*' He replied, 'This may be a strain to which they reverted.' He said, '*And perhaps this is a strain to which the child has reverted.*" [355]

8) Guardianship of children in divorce.

The woman has more right to retain the children [if she is Muslim] unless she remarries then the man may demand them. A woman said: "Messenger of Allāh, my womb is a vessel to this son of mine, my breasts, a water skin for him, and my lap a guard for him, yet his father has divorced me, and wants to take him away from me.' The Messenger of Allāh [ﷺ] said, '*You have more right to him as long as you do not marry.*"[356]

---

[354] *Sahīh Muslim*, [Eng. Trans. vol. 2 #3556 and #3557 respectively.]

[355] *Sunan* of Abū Dāwud [Eng. Trans. vol.2 #2253]. Declared *sahīh* by *Shaykh* Al-Albānī.

[356] *Sunan* of Abū Dāwud [Eng. Trans. vol. 2 #2269]. Declared *hasan* by *Shaykh* Al-Albānī.

And in another *hadīth* the choice was given to the child by the Prophet [ﷺ] to pick either of his parents and he chose his mother. The child was about seven years of age.[357]

Also in the case of an orphan with no parents alive the maternal aunt gets custody, assuming she is Muslim. The Prophet [ﷺ] said:

"The maternal aunt is like the mother."[358]

Otherwise, if the mother is dead or insane or a non-Muslim the father has more right to the children first. The same applies to a divorce where one parent accepts Islām and the other does not the child goes to whichever parent is Muslim.

"Rāfi' Ibn Sinān [ﷺ] narrated that he accepted Islām but his wife refused to accept it. The Prophet [ﷺ] then made the mother sit down to a side and the father to another side and made the daughter sit down between them. She [the daughter] then inclined to her mother, the Prophet [ﷺ] then said: *"O Allāh! Guide her."* The daughter then inclined towards her father and he took her."[359]

However the man is responsible for the expenses of the children in any case [i.e., food, clothing].

---

[357] *Sunan* of Abū Dāwud [Eng. Trans. vol.2 #2270]. Declared *sahīh* by Sheik Al-Albānī.

[358] *Sunan* of Abū Dāwud [Eng. Trans. vol.2 #2273]. Declared *sahīh* by *Shaykh* Al-Albānī.

[359] *Sunan* of Abū Dāwud [Eng. Trans. vol.2 #2236]. Declared *sahīh* by *Shaykh* Al-Albānī.

CHAPTER 12

THE FOOD FOR THE BELIEVERS

Allāh the Exalted the Mighty said:

﴿ يَـٰٓأَيُّهَا ٱلنَّاسُ كُلُوا۟ مِمَّا فِى ٱلْأَرْضِ حَلَـٰلًا طَيِّبًا وَلَا تَتَّبِعُوا۟ خُطُوَٰتِ ٱلشَّيْطَـٰنِ ۚ إِنَّهُۥ
لَكُمْ عَدُوٌّ مُّبِينٌ ﴿١٦٨﴾ ﴾

﴾ O Mankind! Eat of that which is lawful and good on earth, and follow not the footsteps of Shaytān [Satan]. Verily, he is to you an open enemy.﴿
2:168

﴿ إِنَّمَا حَرَّمَ عَلَيْكُمُ ٱلْمَيْتَةَ وَٱلدَّمَ وَلَحْمَ ٱلْخِنزِيرِ وَمَآ أُهِلَّ بِهِۦ لِغَيْرِ ٱللَّهِ ﴾

﴾ He has forbidden to you only the maytah [dead animals], and blood and the flesh of swine, and that which is slaughtered as a sacrifice for other than Allāh [or that has been slaughtered for Idols, etc. on which Allāh's name has not been mentioned while slaughtering].﴿ 2:173

﴿ يَـٰٓأَيُّهَا ٱلَّذِينَ ءَامَنُوٓا۟ إِنَّمَا ٱلْخَمْرُ وَٱلْمَيْسِرُ وَٱلْأَنصَابُ وَٱلْأَزْلَـٰمُ رِجْسٌ مِّنْ عَمَلِ
ٱلشَّيْطَـٰنِ فَٱجْتَنِبُوهُ لَعَلَّكُمْ تُفْلِحُونَ ﴿٩٠﴾ ﴾

﴾ O you who believe! Intoxicants [all kinds of alcoholic drinks or illegal drugs], gambling, Al-Ansāb and Al-Azlām [arrow for luck or decision] are an abomination of Shaytān's [Satan] handiwork. So avoid [strictly all] that [abomination] in order that you may be successful.﴿ 5:90

This is easy by the will of Allāh, then Allāh the Exalted also said:

﴿ فَمَنِ ٱضْطُرَّ غَيْرَ بَاغٍ وَلَا عَادٍ فَلَآ إِثْمَ عَلَيْهِ ۚ إِنَّ ٱللَّهَ غَفُورٌ رَّحِيمٌ ﴿١٧٣﴾ ﴾

﴾...But if one is forced by necessity without willful disobedience nor transgressing due limits then there is no sin on him. Truly, Allāh is oft forgiving, Most Merciful.﴿ 2:173

This means you avoid it fearing Allāh and if by accident you consumed it thinking it was something else, or if you were forced either by starvation or by enemies with a threat of death or bodily harm to you or to another Muslim. However the least amount necessary for survival is to be consumed with loathing in your heart knowing it is *haram*. And Allāh knows best.

Other Facts She Should Know.

1) The food of the people of the Book [Jews and Christians].

Allāh the Almighty said:

﴿ ٱلْيَوْمَ أُحِلَّ لَكُمُ ٱلطَّيِّبَٰتُ ۖ وَطَعَامُ ٱلَّذِينَ أُوتُوا۟ ٱلْكِتَٰبَ حِلٌّ لَّكُمْ وَطَعَامُكُمْ حِلٌّ
لَّهُمْ ۖ وَٱلْمُحْصَنَٰتُ مِنَ ٱلْمُؤْمِنَٰتِ وَٱلْمُحْصَنَٰتُ مِنَ ٱلَّذِينَ أُوتُوا۟ ٱلْكِتَٰبَ مِن قَبْلِكُمْ
إِذَآ ءَاتَيْتُمُوهُنَّ أُجُورَهُنَّ مُحْصِنِينَ غَيْرَ مُسَٰفِحِينَ وَلَا مُتَّخِذِىٓ أَخْدَانٍ ۗ وَمَن يَكْفُرْ
بِٱلْإِيمَٰنِ فَقَدْ حَبِطَ عَمَلُهُۥ وَهُوَ فِى ٱلْءَاخِرَةِ مِنَ ٱلْخَٰسِرِينَ ﴿٥﴾ ﴾

﴾ Made lawful to you this day are At-Tayyibāt [all kinds of halāl [lawful] foods, which Allāh has made lawful [meat of slaughtered animals, milk products, fats, vegetables, fruits etc.]]. The food [slaughtered cattle, edible animals etc.] of the people of the scripture [Jews and Christians] is lawful to you and yours is lawful to them. ﴿ 5:5

And He warns us:

﴿ وَلَا تَأْكُلُوا۟ مِمَّا لَمْ يُذْكَرِ ٱسْمُ ٱللَّهِ عَلَيْهِ وَإِنَّهُۥ لَفِسْقٌ ۗ وَإِنَّ ٱلشَّيَٰطِينَ لَيُوحُونَ
إِلَىٰٓ أَوْلِيَآئِهِمْ لِيُجَٰدِلُوكُمْ ۖ وَإِنْ أَطَعْتُمُوهُمْ إِنَّكُمْ لَمُشْرِكُونَ ﴿١٢١﴾ ﴾

﴾ Eat not [O Believers] of that [meat] on which Allāh's name has not been pronounced [at the time of slaughter] for sure it is a fisq [a sin and disobedience of Allāh]. And certainly, the Shayātīn [devils] do inspire their friends [from mankind] to dispute with you, and if you obey them [by making dead animals lawful] then you would indeed be mushrikūn

[polytheists] [because they [devils and their friends] made lawful to you to eat that which Allāh has made unlawful to eat and you obeyed them considering it lawful to eat and by so doing you worshipped them, and to worship others besides Allāh is polytheism]. ﴾ ***6:121***

In a *hadīth*, 'Adī Ibn Hātim said:

"O Allāh's Messenger! They do not worship them [i.e., their Rabbis and Monks].' Allāh's Messenger said: *"They certainly do. They [Rabbis and Monks] made lawful things as unlawful and unlawful things as lawful, and they [i.e., Jews and Christians] followed them; and by doing so, they really worshipped them."*[360]

So beware! You may fall under the verse of Allāh:

﴿ وَمَا يُؤْمِنُ أَكْثَرُهُم بِٱللَّهِ إِلَّا وَهُم مُّشْرِكُونَ ﴾

﴾ ***And most of them believe not in Allāh except that they attribute partners unto Him [i.e., polytheists]*** ﴾ ***12:106***

Therefore, depending on what country you live in you must avoid the food of pagans while at the same time be careful of the food of the people of the Book, making sure that it does not contain pork or alcohol.

2] Hunting.

It is forbidden in the state of Ihram [pilgrims]. Allāh the Exalted, said:

﴿ يَـٰٓأَيُّهَا ٱلَّذِينَ ءَامَنُوٓا۟ أَوْفُوا۟ بِٱلْعُقُودِ ۚ أُحِلَّتْ لَكُم بَهِيمَةُ ٱلْأَنْعَـٰمِ إِلَّا مَا يُتْلَىٰ عَلَيْكُمْ غَيْرَ مُحِلِّى ٱلصَّيْدِ وَأَنتُمْ حُرُمٌ ۗ إِنَّ ٱللَّهَ يَحْكُمُ مَا يُرِيدُ ﴾

﴾ ***Lawful to you [for food] are all beasts of cattle except that which will be announced to you [here in], game [also] being unlawful when you assume Ihram for Hajj or 'Umrah verily. Allāh commands that which He wills.*** ﴾ ***5:1***

Animals may be used to hunt i.e., Dogs or Falcons.

---

[360] *Tafsīr At-Tabarī*, vol.10 pg. 114. *Hadīth* in Ahmad and At-Tirmidhī who said it was *hasan gharīb*.

﴿ وَمَا عَلَّمْتُم مِّنَ ٱلْجَوَارِحِ مُكَلِّبِينَ تُعَلِّمُونَهُنَّ مِمَّا عَلَّمَكُمُ ٱللَّهُ فَكُلُوا۟ مِمَّآ أَمْسَكْنَ عَلَيْكُمْ وَٱذْكُرُوا۟ ٱسْمَ ٱللَّهِ عَلَيْهِ وَٱتَّقُوا۟ ٱللَّهَ إِنَّ ٱللَّهَ سَرِيعُ ٱلْحِسَابِ ﴾

﴾ ...And those beasts and birds of prey which you have trained as hounds training and teaching them [to catch] in the manner directed to you by Allāh, so eat what they catch for you, but mention Allāh's name upon it, and fear Allāh verily Allāh is swift in reckoning.﴿ 5:4

His Messenger [ﷺ] clarifies this further for us.

"If you let loose your trained hounds after a game, mention the name of Allāh, then you can eat what the hounds catch for you, even they killed the game. But you should not eat of it if the hound has eaten of it, for then it is likely that the hound has caught the game for itself. And if other hounds join your hound in hunting the game, then do not eat of it."[361]

3] Animals of the water whether dead or alive.

Allāh the Glorious, the Merciful said:

﴿ أُحِلَّ لَكُمْ صَيْدُ ٱلْبَحْرِ وَطَعَامُهُۥ مَتَـٰعًا لَّكُمْ وَلِلسَّيَّارَةِ ﴾

﴾ Lawful to you is [the pursuit of] water game and its use for food for the benefit of yourselves and those who travel.﴿ 5:96

﴿ وَمَا يَسْتَوِى ٱلْبَحْرَانِ هَـٰذَا عَذْبٌ فُرَاتٌ سَآئِغٌ شَرَابُهُۥ وَهَـٰذَا مِلْحٌ أُجَاجٌ وَمِن كُلٍّ تَأْكُلُونَ لَحْمًا طَرِيًّا وَتَسْتَخْرِجُونَ حِلْيَةً تَلْبَسُونَهَا وَتَرَى ٱلْفُلْكَ فِيهِ مَوَاخِرَ لِتَبْتَغُوا۟ مِن فَضْلِهِۦ وَلَعَلَّكُمْ تَشْكُرُونَ ﴾

﴾ And the two seas [kinds of water] are not alike, this is sweet and pleasant to drink, and that is salt and bitter. And from them both you eat fresh tender meat [fish], and derive the ornaments that you wear. ﴿ 35:12

---

[361] Sahīh Al-Bukhārī, [Eng. Trans. vol. 7 Chapter 7. #392].

Abū Bakr [ﷺ] said, floating fish is lawful to eat.
'Umar Ibn Al-Khattāb [ﷺ] said, The sea game means what is fished, and its food means what the sea throws [on its shore].
Ibn 'Abbās [ﷺ] said, The sea food means the dead fish except what you regard as unclean [i.e., rotten or poisoned etc.].
Shurayh said, every sea animal is regarded as slaughtered.
Al-Hasan does not see any harm in eating tortoises.[362]

4] Fanged beasts of prey and birds with talons.

"Allāh's Messenger [ﷺ] prohibited the eating of all fanged beasts of prey, and all the birds with talons."[363]

5] Meat cut from live animals.

" Allāh's Messenger [ﷺ] said, *'Whatever [portion] is cut off from an animal when it is live is dead meat'."*[364] [i.e., dead meat is unlawful to eat.]

6] Black cumin [nigella or black seed].

Allāh's Messenger [ﷺ] said:
"There is healing in black cumin for all diseases except death."[365]

There are different ways to use black seed depending on the diseases e.g. one may take a spoonful with water every day or use its oil etc.

---

[362] *Sahīh Al-Bukhārī* [Eng. Trans. vol. 7 Chapter 12. Pg. 292]
[363] *Sahīh Muslim* [Eng. Trans. vol. 3 #4754]
[364] *Sunan* of At-Tirmidhī, and Imām At-Tirmidhī said it is *hasan gharīb*.
[365] *Sahīh Al-Bukhārī*, [Eng. Trans. Vol. 7 Chapter 7. #592].

7] Dates.

Allāh said to Maryam the mother of 'Isā [ﷺ] after his birth:

﴿ وَهُزِّىٓ إِلَيْكِ بِجِذْعِ ٱلنَّخْلَةِ تُسَٰقِطْ عَلَيْكِ رُطَبًا جَنِيًّا ﴾

﴿And shake the trunk of the date palm tree towards you, it will let fall fresh ripe dates upon you.﴾ 19:25

The Prophet [ﷺ] said:

"He who ate seven 'Ajwah [a type of good Medina dates] dates in the morning, poison and magic will not harm him on that day." [366]

"A family which has dates will not be hungry." [367]

"The Messenger of Allāh [ﷺ] used to break his fast before praying with some fresh dates; but if there were no fresh dates, he had a few dry dates, and if there were no dry dates, he took some mouthfuls of water." [368]

8] Garlic and Onions.

The smell is offensive and it is forbidden to eat these raw and go to the *masjid*. The Messenger of Allāh [ﷺ] said:

"Whoever has eaten garlic or onion should keep away from us [or should keep away from our mosque]." [369]

Abū Ayyūb Al-Ansārī prepared food with garlic and sent it to the Prophet [ﷺ] who did not eat it. So he went to the Prophet [ﷺ] distressed for this reason.

---

[366] *Sahīh Muslim*, [Eng. Trans. vol. 3 #5081].

[367] *Sahīh Muslim*, [Eng. Trans. vol. 3 #5078.]

[368] *Sunan* of Abū Dāwud; [Eng. Trans. Vol.2 Chapter 787. #2349]. Declared *hasan sahīh* by *Shaykh* Al-Albānī.

[369] *Sahīh Al-Bukhārī*, [Eng. Trans. vol. 7 Chapter 50. #363].

"He asked, "Is it forbidden?" But the Prophet [ﷺ] said, *"No,[it is not forbidden] but I do not like it,'* and he [Abū Ayyūb] said, 'I also do not like what you do not like. He [Abū Ayyūb] said, [the Prophet [ﷺ] did not eat garlic] as he was visited [by Angels] who brought him the Message of Allāh."[370]

[i.e., he had distinguished individuals to talk to].

9] Vinegar

Jābir [رضي الله عنه] narrated that the **Prophet [ﷺ]** said:

"What a good condiment vinegar is!"[371]

However vinegar produced from wine is ***harām*** [forbidden]. When asked about vinegar from wine the Prophet [ﷺ] said: *"No. [it is prohibited]"*[372]

10] Honey.

Allāh the Almighty, the Exalted, said:

﴿ وَأَوْحَىٰ رَبُّكَ إِلَى ٱلنَّحْلِ أَنِ ٱتَّخِذِى مِنَ ٱلْجِبَالِ بُيُوتًا وَمِنَ ٱلشَّجَرِ وَمِمَّا يَعْرِشُونَ ۝٦٨ ثُمَّ كُلِى مِن كُلِّ ٱلثَّمَرَٰتِ فَٱسْلُكِى سُبُلَ رَبِّكِ ذُلُلًا ۚ يَخْرُجُ مِنۢ بُطُونِهَا شَرَابٌ مُّخْتَلِفٌ أَلْوَٰنُهُۥ فِيهِ شِفَآءٌ لِّلنَّاسِ ۗ إِنَّ فِى ذَٰلِكَ لَءَايَةً لِّقَوْمٍ يَتَفَكَّرُونَ ﴾

﴿ And your Lord inspired the bee saying: "Take your habitations in the mountains and in the trees and in what they erect. Then eat of all the fruits and follow the ways your Lord made easy [for you].' There comes from their bellies a drink of varying color wherein is healing for man.﴾ 16:68-69.

---

[370] *Sahīh Muslim*, [Eng. Trans. vol. 3 #5099].

[371] *Sunan* of Abū Dāwud, [Eng. Trans. Vol. 3 Chapter 1443. #3811]. Declared *sahīh* by *Shaykh* Al-Albānī.

[372] *Sahīh Muslim*, [Eng. Trans. vol.3 #4891].

"Allāh's Messenger [ﷺ] used to love sweet edible things and honey."[373]

The Prophet [ﷺ] said:

"If there is any healing in your medicines, then it is in cupping, a gulp of honey or branding with fire [cauterization] that suits the ailment, but I don't like to be [cauterized] branded with fire."[374]

A man came to the Prophet [ﷺ] and said: "My brother has some abdominal trouble.' The Prophet [ﷺ] said, *'Let him drink honey'*. The man came for the second time and the Prophet [ﷺ] said to him, *'Let him drink honey.'* He came for the third time the Prophet [ﷺ] said, *'Let him drink honey.'* He returned again and said, 'I have done that.' The Prophet [ﷺ] said, *'Allāh has said the truth, but your brothers abdomen has told a lie. Let him drink honey.'*"[375]

11] Truffles [used in candies, soups etc. and it grows without any human effort it is a kind of fungus referred to as 'Manna' at times].

The Prophet [ﷺ] said:

"Truffles are a kind of Manna which Allāh the Glorious and Exalted, sent down upon the people of Israel and its juice is a medicine for the eyes."[376]

12] Locusts.

They are lawful as seen in the following *hadīth*.

"We participated with the Prophet [ﷺ] in six or seven *ghazawāt* [battles which the Prophet [ﷺ] was heading], and we used to eat locusts with him."[377]

---

[373] *Sahīh Al-Bukhārī*, [Eng. Trans. vol. 7 Chapter 33. #342].

[374] *Sahīh Al-Bukhārī*, [Eng. Trans. vol. 7 Chapter 4. #587]

[375] *Sahīh Al-Bukhārī*, [Eng. Trans. vol.7 Chapter 4. #588].

[376] *Sahīh Muslim*, [Eng. Trans. vol.3 pg.1129].

13] Domestic Asses and Horses.

Horses may be eaten but Asses are forbidden.

"On the Day of Khaybar, Allāh's Messenger [ﷺ] forbade the flesh of domestic asses but permitted horse flesh."[378]

14] Sand Lizards.

They may be eaten by those who wish as it was served on the table spread of the Prophet [ﷺ] who did not eat it but he did not prohibit it.

"I do not eat [lizard], but I do not prohibit it's eating."[379]

15] Zebra.

It is permissible as seen in the following ***hadīth***. Narrated Abū Qatādah [ﷺ] in part of a longer ***hadīth*** regarding the Zebra:

"The Prophet [ﷺ] said, *'That was a meal Allāh fed you with.'* [It is also said that the Prophet [ﷺ] said, *'Have you got something of its meat?'* ."[380]

16] Hyena.

There are two opinions I know of amongst our scholars some [like Ibn 'Abbās [ﷺ] and Ash-Shāfi'ī] say it is edible citing the *hadīth*:

"I asked Jābir [ﷺ], ' Is Hyena a game?' He replied, 'Yes'. I asked, 'Did Allāh's Messenger [ﷺ] say that?' He replied, 'Yes'."[381]

While the others [At-Tahāwī and Imam Mālik] say it is unlawful as it eats human flesh and therefore even digs up graves..It also might be considered

---

377 *Sahīh Al-Bukhārī*, [Eng. Trans.vol.7 Chapter 13. #403].

378 *Sahīh Al-Bukhārī*, [Eng. Trans. vol. 7 Chapter 28. #433].

379 *Sahīh Al-Bukhārī*, [Eng. Trans. vol.7 Chapter 33. #445].

380 *Sahīh Al-Bukhārī*, [Eng. Trans. vol. 4 #163]

381 *Sunan* of Abū Dāwud, [Eng. Trans. Vol. 3 #3792]. Declared *sahīh* by *Shaykh* Al-Albānī.

an beast of pray as it attacks when hungry enough and it has fangs and, "Allāh's Messenger [ﷺ] forbade the eating of meat of beasts that have fangs."[382] Allāh knows best.

17] Frogs

It is not considered lawful as per the *hadīth* upon 'Abd Ar-Rahmān Ibn 'Uthmān Al-Qurashī [ﷺ]:

"A physician consulted Allāh's Messenger [ﷺ] about extracting medicine from frogs and he prohibited killing them."[383]

18] Cats [Domestic]

Its sale is disapproved of and it is unlawful [as they are animals of prey] to eat cats. And one should be kind to them. The Prophet [ﷺ] said: *"A lady was punished because of a cat which she had imprisoned till it died. She entered the [Hell] Fire because of it, she neither gave it food nor water as she imprisoned it, nor set it free to eat from the vermin of the earth."* [384]

"I asked Jābir [ﷺ] about the price of a dog and a cat he said; 'Allāh's Messenger [ﷺ] disapproved of that.'"[385]

The Prophet [ﷺ] said about the cat:

"It is not unclean but one of those who intermingle with you."[386]

---

[382] *Sahīh Al-Bukhārī* [Eng. Trans. vol. 7 Chapter 29. #438].

[383] *Musnad* of Imam Ahmad. [*sahīh* by Al-Hākim]

[384] *Sahīh Al-Bukhārī*, [Eng. Trans. vol.4 Chapter 46. #689.]

[385] *Sahīh Muslim*, [Eng. Trans. vol. 3 #3808]

[386] *Sunan* of Abū Dāwud, [Eng. Trans. vol.1 pg.19 #75]. Declared *hasan sahīh* by *Shaykh* Al-Albānī.

19] Dogs

They are only to be kept for hunting or guarding [sheep, property etc.]. They may neither be kept as pets nor eaten.

"The Prophet [ﷺ] said, *'Whoever keeps a dog which is neither a watch dog nor a hunting dog, will get a daily deduction of two qirāṯ [a twentieth or twenty fourth of a dīnār], from his good deeds.'"*[387]

What will be left of your good deeds at your death? They are also considered impure. The Prophet [ﷺ] said:

"The cleansing of the utensil belonging to one of you, after it has been licked by a dog is to wash it seven times, using soil the first time." [388]

Another version of this *ḥadīth* includes the wording; *"he should spill the contents."*

20] The prohibition of eating any animal that feeds on filth nor are we allowed to drink its milk.

Ibn 'Umar [رضي الله عنه] narrates that:

"The Prophet [ﷺ] prohibited eating the animal which feeds on filth and drinking its milk." [389]

Drink.

With the exception of Alcohol [in any amount] [and milk from animals that feed on filth] and blood, all drinks, juice, milk, water etc. are *ḥalāl* [lawful], as seen in the commands of Allāh and His Messenger [ﷺ]. Allāh the Exalted the Wise said:

﴿ يَسْـَٔلُونَكَ عَنِ ٱلْخَمْرِ وَٱلْمَيْسِرِ ۖ قُلْ فِيهِمَآ إِثْمٌ كَبِيرٌ وَمَنَٰفِعُ لِلنَّاسِ وَإِثْمُهُمَآ أَكْبَرُ مِن نَّفْعِهِمَا ﴿٢١٩﴾ ﴾

---

[387] *Saḥīḥ Al-Bukhārī*, [Eng. Trans. Vol.7 Chapter 6. #389].

[388] *Saḥīḥ Muslim*, [Eng. Trans.vol.1 #550 and 546. Pgs. 166-167].

[389] *Sunan* of Abu Dāwud. [Eng. Trans. Vol.3 #3776]. Declared *saḥīḥ* by *Shaykh* Al-Albānī.

﴾ They ask you [O Muhammad ﷺ] concerning alcoholic drink and gambling. Say: ' In them is great sin, and [some] benefit for men, but the sin of them is greater than their benefit.﴿ 2:219

This verse was abrogated [nullified or cancelled] by the verse:

﴿ يَٰٓأَيُّهَا ٱلَّذِينَ ءَامَنُوٓا۟ إِنَّمَا ٱلْخَمْرُ وَٱلْمَيْسِرُ وَٱلْأَنصَابُ وَٱلْأَزْلَٰمُ رِجْسٌ مِّنْ
عَمَلِ ٱلشَّيْطَٰنِ فَٱجْتَنِبُوهُ لَعَلَّكُمْ تُفْلِحُونَ ۝٩٠ إِنَّمَا يُرِيدُ ٱلشَّيْطَٰنُ أَن يُوقِعَ
بَيْنَكُمُ ٱلْعَدَٰوَةَ وَٱلْبَغْضَآءَ فِى ٱلْخَمْرِ وَٱلْمَيْسِرِ وَيَصُدَّكُمْ عَن ذِكْرِ ٱللَّهِ وَعَنِ
ٱلصَّلَوٰةِ ۖ فَهَلْ أَنتُم مُّنتَهُونَ ۝٩١ ﴾

﴾ O you who believe! Intoxicants, and gambling, and Al-Ansāb, and Al-Azlām [arrows for luck or decision] are an abomination of Shaytān's [Satan] handiwork. So avoid [strictly all] that [abomination] in order that you may be successful. Shaytān wants only to excite enmity and hatred between you with intoxicants and gambling, and hinder you from the remembrance of Allāh and salāh. So will you not abstain?﴿ 5:90-91.

And His Prophet [ﷺ] said:

"Every intoxicant is khamr [wine] and every intoxicant is forbidden. If anyone drinks wine [an intoxicant] Allāh will not accept prayer from him for forty days, but if he repents, Allāh will accept his repentance. If he repeats it a fourth time, it is binding on Allāh that He will give him tīnah Al-Khabāl to drink.' He was asked, 'What is *tīnah Al-Khabāl* O Messenger of Allāh?' He replied, *'Discharge of wounds flowing from the inhabitants of Hell. If anyone serves it to a minor who does not distinguish between the lawful and the unlawful, it is binding on Allāh that He will give him [the server] the discharge of wounds flowing from the discharge of wounds flowing from the inhabitants of Hell to drink.'"*[390]

---

[390] *Sunan* of Abū Dāwud, [Eng. Trans. Vol.3 Chapter 1386. #3672]. Declared *sahīh* by *Shaykh* Al-Albānī.

"If a large amount of anything causes intoxication, a small amount of its is prohibited."[391]

He [ﷺ] also said:

"A person at the time of drinking an alcoholic drink is not a believer."[392]

And:

"From among the portents of the Hour are general ignorance [about religious affairs] will prevail, [religious] knowledge will decrease, illegal sexual intercourse will prevail, alcoholic drinks will be drunk [in abundance], men will decrease and women will increase so much that for every fifty women there will be one man to look after them."[393]

May Allāh the Exalted keep us far from such evil, Āmīn.

Alcohol in cosmetics.

There are two opinions, one being it is *haram* to use, citing the verse, ***"Intoxicants...are an abomination..."5:90*** therefore concluding that it must be is *najis*, meaning impure. This opinion is held by the majority of the scholars including As-Shāfi'ī and Imam Ahmad, whereas other scholars say that while it is *harām* to consume internally, it is a pure substance on its own, these include As-San'ānī. And Ibn Abbās [ﷺ] said, that the word *rijs* here can be used for both 'anger' and 'impurities'. The English translations carry *rijs* here to mean *abomination* and may be closer to anger as a result of its consumption, and Allāh knows best. However, those using this argument say, the origin of things is pure unless otherwise specified as all things *harām* are not impure like gold for men whereas all things that are impure are *harām* e.g. pork. And therefore it is permissible to use in cosmetics i.e., perfumes and such. As we have not been informed that it is an impure substance but rather its effects on the body as far as memory etc. are the main reasons given. One must choose for one's self, only Allāh knows better.

---

[391] *Sunan* of Abū Dāwud, [Eng. Trans. Vol.3 Chapter 1386. #3673]. Declared *hasan sahīh* by *Shaykh* Al-Albānī.

[392] *Sahīh Al-Bukhārī*, [Eng. Trans. vol.7 Chapter 1. #484].

[393] *Sahīh Al-Bukhārī*, [Eng. Trans. vol.7 Chapter 1. #483].

CHAPTER 13

TAWBAH [REPENTANCE]

Allāh the Oft-Forgiving said:

﴿ وَءَاخَرُونَ ٱعْتَرَفُوا۟ بِذُنُوبِهِمْ خَلَطُوا۟ عَمَلًا صَٰلِحًا وَءَاخَرَ سَيِّئًا عَسَى ٱللَّهُ أَن
يَتُوبَ عَلَيْهِمْ إِنَّ ٱللَّهَ غَفُورٌ رَّحِيمٌ ﴿١٠٢﴾ ﴾

﴾ And [there are] others who have acknowledged their sins, they have mixed a deed that was righteous with another that was evil. Perhaps Allāh will turn to them in forgiveness. Surely, Allāh is Oft-Forgiving, Most Merciful.﴿ 9:102

﴿ أَلَمْ يَعْلَمُوٓا۟ أَنَّ ٱللَّهَ هُوَ يَقْبَلُ ٱلتَّوْبَةَ عَنْ عِبَادِهِۦ وَيَأْخُذُ ٱلصَّدَقَٰتِ وَأَنَّ ٱللَّهَ
هُوَ ٱلتَّوَّابُ ٱلرَّحِيمُ ﴿١٠٤﴾ ﴾

﴾ Know they not that Allāh accepts repentance from His slaves and takes the sadaqah [alms, charity], and that Allāh Alone is the One Who forgives and accepts repentance, Most Merciful?﴿ 9:104

Allāh the Most Merciful, the Majestic loves for His slaves to repent [with remorse] and is pleased with it.

> *"Allāh is more pleased with the repentance of His slave at the time he repents to Him than if one of you was on his camel in the desert but it escaped from him and upon it was his food and drink. He then gave up looking for it, came to a tree and laid down in its shade. While he was feeling sad about his camel it suddenly appeared, standing before him. So he took its nose string and said in his extreme joy: 'O Allāh You are my slave and I am Your Lord'; by mistake due to his happiness."*[394]

---

[394] *Sahīh Muslim*, [Eng. Trans. vol. 4 # 6618]

There are some things one should be aware of however.

You have to be a Muslim.

Allāh the Almighty said:

﴿ وَمَن يَبْتَغِ غَيْرَ ٱلْإِسْلَٰمِ دِينًا فَلَن يُقْبَلَ مِنْهُ وَهُوَ فِى ٱلْءَاخِرَةِ مِنَ ٱلْخَٰسِرِينَ ﴾

﴾ And whoever seeks a religion other than Islām, it will never be accepted of him, and in the Hereafter he will be one of the losers.﴿ 3:85

﴿ وَلَيْسَتِ ٱلتَّوْبَةُ لِلَّذِينَ يَعْمَلُونَ ٱلسَّيِّـَٔاتِ حَتَّىٰٓ إِذَا حَضَرَ أَحَدَهُمُ ٱلْمَوْتُ
قَالَ إِنِّى تُبْتُ ٱلْـَٔـٰنَ وَلَا ٱلَّذِينَ يَمُوتُونَ وَهُمْ كُفَّارٌ ۚ أُو۟لَـٰٓئِكَ أَعْتَدْنَا لَهُمْ
عَذَابًا أَلِيمًا ﴿١٨﴾ ﴾

﴾ And of no effect is the repentance of those who ... nor those who die while they are disbelievers. For them we have prepared a painful torment.﴿ 4:18

﴿ وَإِذَا جَآءَكَ ٱلَّذِينَ يُؤْمِنُونَ بِـَٔايَـٰتِنَا فَقُلْ سَلَـٰمٌ عَلَيْكُمْ ۖ كَتَبَ رَبُّكُمْ عَلَىٰ
نَفْسِهِ ٱلرَّحْمَةَ ۖ أَنَّهُۥ مَنْ عَمِلَ مِنكُمْ سُوٓءًۢا بِجَهَـٰلَةٍ ثُمَّ تَابَ مِنۢ بَعْدِهِۦ وَأَصْلَحَ
فَأَنَّهُۥ غَفُورٌ رَّحِيمٌ ﴿٥٤﴾ ﴾

﴾ When those who believe in Our Āyāt [proofs, evidences verses signs etc.] come to you say, Salām 'Alaykum Your Lord has written mercy for Himself, so that, if any of you does evil in ignorance and thereafter repents and does righteous good deeds [by obeying Allāh] then surely He is Oft-Forgiving, Most Merciful.﴿ 6:54

One shouldn't wait till death is about to overtake them.

Allāh the Exalted said:

﴿ وَلَيْسَتِ ٱلتَّوْبَةُ لِلَّذِينَ يَعْمَلُونَ ٱلسَّيِّـَٔاتِ حَتَّىٰٓ إِذَا حَضَرَ أَحَدَهُمُ ٱلْمَوْتُ قَالَ إِنِّى تُبْتُ ٱلْـَٔـٰنَ وَلَا ٱلَّذِينَ يَمُوتُونَ وَهُمْ كُفَّارٌ ۚ أُو۟لَـٰٓئِكَ أَعْتَدْنَا لَهُمْ عَذَابًا أَلِيمًا ﴿١٨﴾ ﴾

﴿ And of no effect is the repentance of those who continue to do evil deeds until death faces one of them and he says: 'Now I repent' nor of those who die while they are disbeliever's for them We have prepared a painful torment.﴾ 4:18

You should not expose your sins.

The Prophet [ﷺ] said:

"Everyone of my Ummah is excused except the one who does not conceal."[395]

A man came to the Messenger of Allāh [ﷺ] and said:
"I sported with a woman [did something less than fornication e.g. touched or kissed] in the outskirts of Medina, and I have committed an offence short of fornication [touching or kissing]. Here I am [before you], kindly deliver verdict about me which you deem fit.' 'Umar [رضي الله عنه] said: 'Allāh concealed your fault. You had better conceal it also. Allāh's Messenger [ﷺ] however, gave no reply to him. The man stood up and went away and Allāh's Messenger [ﷺ] sent a person after him to call him and he recited this verse:

﴿ وَأَقِمِ ٱلصَّلَوٰةَ طَرَفَىِ ٱلنَّهَارِ وَزُلَفًا مِّنَ ٱلَّيْلِ ۚ إِنَّ ٱلْحَسَنَـٰتِ يُذْهِبْنَ ٱلسَّيِّـَٔاتِ ۚ ذَٰلِكَ ذِكْرَىٰ لِلذَّٰكِرِينَ ﴿١١٤﴾ ﴾

[395] Ahmad 1/402-3 Declared *hasan* by Shaykh Al-Albānī.

﴿ And observe prayer at the ends of the day and in the first hours of the night [the five salāh]. Surely, good deeds take away evil deeds [small sins]. That is a reminder for the mindful. ﴾ 11:114

A person from amongst the people said, 'Allāh's Messenger does it concern this man only? Thereupon he [ﷺ] said, *"No, but the people at large [his Ummah]."*[396]

You should beware of your minor sins.

The Prophet [ﷺ] said about the minor sins: *"Beware of the minor sins. They are added upon a person until they will destroy him, like a person who was in the waterless desert then came a group of people. A man came with a piece of wood then another came with a piece of wood until they had collected enough to start a fire to cook with what they had put on it."*[397]

One should not ignore their minor sins thinking they can't harm them. The Prophet Muhammad [ﷺ] said: *"Had the non-believer known of all the Mercy which is in the Hands of Allāh, he would not loose hope of entering Paradise, had the believer known of all the punishment which is present with Allāh, he would not consider himself safe from the Fire of Hell."*[398]

For a believer to be safe they should live between fear and hope from Allāh, we should be afraid of the Fire.

---

[396] *Sahīh Muslim* [Eng. Trans. vol.4 #6658]

[397] *Musnad* of Imām Ahmad [vol.1 pg. 402-403] and declared *hasan* by Al-Albānī.

[398] *Sahīh Al-Bukhārī*, [Eng. Trans. vol.8 #476]

The Merit of repentance and the proof that accepting Islām is an expiation of sins.

﴿ يَـٰٓأَيُّهَا ٱلَّذِينَ ءَامَنُوا۟ تُوبُوٓا۟ إِلَى ٱللَّهِ تَوْبَةً نَّصُوحًا عَسَىٰ رَبُّكُمْ أَن يُكَفِّرَ عَنكُمْ سَيِّـَٔاتِكُمْ وَيُدْخِلَكُمْ جَنَّـٰتٍ تَجْرِى مِن تَحْتِهَا ٱلْأَنْهَـٰرُ يَوْمَ لَا يُخْزِى ٱللَّهُ ٱلنَّبِىَّ وَٱلَّذِينَ ءَامَنُوا۟ مَعَهُۥ ۖ نُورُهُمْ يَسْعَىٰ بَيْنَ أَيْدِيهِمْ وَبِأَيْمَـٰنِهِمْ يَقُولُونَ رَبَّنَآ أَتْمِمْ لَنَا نُورَنَا وَٱغْفِرْ لَنَآ ۖ إِنَّكَ عَلَىٰ كُلِّ شَىْءٍ قَدِيرٌ ۝٨ ﴾

﴿ O you who believe! Turn to Allāh with sincere repentance! It maybe that your Lord will remit you of your sins and admit you into Gardens under which rivers flow [Paradise]- the day which Allāh will not disgrace the Prophet and those who believe with him. And their Light will run forward before them and[with their records -Books of deeds]in their right hands. They will say: 'Our Lord! Keep perfect our Light for us [and do not put it off till we cross over the Sirāt [a slippery bridge over Hell] safely] and grant us forgiveness. Verily, You are able to do all things.﴾
66:8

Upon accepting Islām your previous sins are forgiven and your good deeds are brought in with you, provided, that you leave your evil deeds behind and embark on good deeds. Hakīm Ibn Hizām [ﷺ] said to the Prophet [ﷺ]:

"Before embracing Islām I used to do good deeds like give in charity, slave-manumitting, and keeping good relations with kith and kin. Shall I be rewarded for those deeds?' The Prophet [ﷺ] said, *"You became Muslim with all those good deeds."* [without loosing them]."[399]

[399] *Sahīh Muslim*, [Eng. Trans. Vol. 1 #223].

Narrated Ibn 'Abbās:

"Some pagans who committed murders in great numbers and committed illegal sexual intercourse excessively, came to Muhammad [ﷺ] and said, 'O Muhammad! Whatever you say and invite people to is good: but we wish that you could inform us weather we can make an expiation for our past evil deeds."[400] Then Allāh revealed the verses:

﴿ قُلْ يَـٰعِبَادِىَ ٱلَّذِينَ أَسْرَفُوا۟ عَلَىٰٓ أَنفُسِهِمْ لَا تَقْنَطُوا۟ مِن رَّحْمَةِ ٱللَّهِ ۚ إِنَّ ٱللَّهَ يَغْفِرُ ٱلذُّنُوبَ جَمِيعًا ۚ إِنَّهُۥ هُوَ ٱلْغَفُورُ ٱلرَّحِيمُ ﴾

﴾ Say: 'O My slaves who have transgressed against themselves. Despair not of the Mercy of Allāh: Verily Allāh forgives sins. Truly He is Oft-Forgiving, Most Merciful.﴿ 39:53

They wanted to accept Islām but were worried about their past sins. The Prophet [ﷺ] said to 'Amr Ibn Al-'Ās when he voiced the same fears,

"Verily Islām wipes away what was before it."[401]

"If a person embraces Islām sincerely, then Allāh shall forgive all his past sins, and after that starts the settlement of accounts: the reward of his good deeds will be ten to seven hundred times for each good deed and an evil deed will be recorded as it is unless Allāh forgives it."[402]

However, being the children of Adam [ﷺ] we still sin after Islām, it is in our nature but we must repent and abstain. The Prophet [ﷺ] said:

"If you were not to commit sin, Allāh would sweep you out of existence and He would replace you by those people who would commit sin and seek forgiveness from Allāh, and He would forgive them."[403]

This *hadīth* is not to encourage wrongdoers, but rather to give hope and encourage repentance.

---

[400] *Sahīh Al-Bukhārī*, [Eng. Trans. vol. 6 Chapter251. #334].

[401] Ahmad in *Musnad* of *Ash-Shami'īn* #17145.

[402] *Sahīh Al-Bukhārī*, [Eng. Trans. vol.1 Chapter 32 #40].

[403] *Sahīh Muslim*, [Eng. Trans. Vol. 4 #6622].

The outcome of our sins.

Allāh said:

﴿ كَلَّا ۖ بَلْ ۜ رَانَ عَلَىٰ قُلُوبِهِم مَّا كَانُوا يَكْسِبُونَ ﴾

﴾ Nay but on their hearts is the rusting for that which they have earned. ﴿
83:14

His Prophet Mu<u>h</u>ammad [ﷺ] explains this further for us.

" When the believer sins a black spot is put on his heart. If he repents, and refrains and seeks forgiveness his heart is cleaned from it. If he does more [sins] it increases until it takes over his heart."[404]

The door of repentance is open, use it.

Ibn 'Abbās [ﷺ] related that the Quraysh said to the Prophet [ﷺ]: 'Call upon your Lord for us to turn Mount As-<u>S</u>afā into gold and then we will believe you. He said, **"Will you do so?"** they said, 'Yes'. So he made a supplication and Jibrā`īl [ﷺ] came to him and said, 'Your Lord sends Salām to you and said if you like He will turn As-Safā into gold and if anyone from them then disbelieves after that I will punish him with a punishment that no one has ever been punished with in the world or if you like the doors of repentance and Mercy will be opened for them.' He replied, **"Rather the doors of repentance and Mercy."**[405]

The Prophet [ﷺ] also said, *"He [Allāh] will continue to accept repentance until the sun rises from the opposite direction."*[406]

The love of the Prophet [ﷺ] for his *ummah* made him choose the door of repentance for us. We should use it before death comes or the sun rises from the West, the only two things stopping a believer from having their sins forgiven! [The exception being those two Muslims not speaking to each other because of an argument until the make up].

---

[404] A<u>h</u>mad 2/297. Declared *<u>h</u>asan* by *Shaykh* Al-Albānī.

[405] A<u>h</u>mad 1/242,345. Declared *<u>h</u>asan* by Al-Mundhirī in *At-Targhīb wa At-Tarhīb*.

[406] *<u>Sahīh</u> Muslim*, [Eng. Trans. Vol.4 #6644].

CHAPTER 14

DEATH AND THE GRAVE

Allāh the Exalted the Mighty, said:

﴿ كَيْفَ تَكْفُرُونَ بِٱللَّهِ وَكُنتُمْ أَمْوَٰتًا فَأَحْيَٰكُمْ ثُمَّ يُمِيتُكُمْ ثُمَّ يُحْيِيكُمْ ثُمَّ إِلَيْهِ تُرْجَعُونَ ﴿٢٨﴾ ﴾

﴾ ***How can you disbelieve in Allāh? Seeing that you were dead and he gave you life. Then He will give you death, then again will bring you to life [on the Day of Resurrection] and then unto Him you will return.*** ﴿ *2:28.*

Death.

The first death is that nothingness before conception and the second at some point after birth. Death is inevitable, it only happens to you once and you cannot return to the present life. What you can do is try to prepare for the next life as you leave everything behind in this life except for three things. Firstly, you take with you to the next world your deeds, good and bad. Secondly, any charity you left that continues [i.e., you take the constant rewards] for example a tree that man or beast eats from or a well where the people use its water. And finally, your children who are pious and do good deeds on your behalf e.g. fasting, *du'ā`*, charity or *Hajj* [the reward of these deeds].[407]

[407] *Sunan* of Abū Dāwud, [Eng. Trans. Vol.2 #2874]. Declared sahīh by *Shaykh* Al-Albānī.

Other facts to know.

The manner in which you die as an indication of your next life.

If Allāh recalls His slave while he is doing a good deed [jihad, reading Qur`ān, praying etc.] good is hoped for him. If his soul is recalled while he is engaged in evil [adultery, theft, murder, suicide drinking alcohol] that [evil] is what is feared for him. And Allāh the Exalted the Most Mighty took the people of old while they were in the midst of their wrongdoing [The 'Ād, Thamūd, Pharaoh etc.].

﴿ وَكَذَٰلِكَ أَخْذُ رَبِّكَ إِذَآ أَخَذَ ٱلْقُرَىٰ وَهِىَ ظَٰلِمَةٌ ۚ إِنَّ أَخْذَهُۥٓ أَلِيمٌ شَدِيدٌ ﴾

﴿ Such is the Seizure of your Lord when He seizes the [population of] the towns while they are doing wrong. Verily, His Seizure is painful and severe. ﴾ 11:102

Whereas the Prophets and their noble companions and such, were taken as Martyrs and while doing other such noble deeds and martyrs are in Paradise. And there are seven types of martyrdom, one who dies in: jihad, drowning, burning, a building falling on you, abdominal or internal complaint, and the woman who dies in child birth [the reward in hereafter is that of a martyr but they are not treated as such in this world.].[408] The Prophet [ﷺ] said: *"When Allāh intends good for a slave of His, He uses him for good.'* The companions asked, 'How does Allāh use him?' The Prophet [ﷺ] said: *"He enables him to do good deeds and makes it easy for him before his death then causes him to die while he is in that state of goodness."* [409]

---

[408] *Sunan* of Abū Dāwud, [Eng. Trans. vol.2 Chapter 1144. #3105]. Declared sahīh by *Shaykh* Al-Albānī.

[409] Narrated by Imām At-Tirmidhī who said that the *hadīth* was *hasan sahīh*. Also narrated by Al-Hākim who declared the *hadīth* to be sahīh and Adh-Dhahabī agreed with him. Also declared sahīh by *Shaykh* Al-Albānī.

Thus, remember the importance of doing good deeds as you never know exactly when or where you will be when Allāh recalls your soul. Know that it is not only your good deeds that will cause you to enter Paradise but also the Mercy of Allāh, so although we strive for good deeds we should do those we can do regularly. Allāh will say to those who are admitted to Paradise:

﴿ وَتِلْكَ ٱلْجَنَّةُ ٱلَّتِىٓ أُورِثْتُمُوهَا بِمَا كُنتُمْ تَعْمَلُونَ ﴿٧٢﴾ ﴾

﴿ This is the Paradise you have been made to inherit because of your deeds which you used to do [in the life of this world]. ﴾ 43:72

His Prophet [ﷺ] said: *"Do good deeds properly, sincerely and moderately, and receive good news because one's good deeds will not make him enter Paradise."* They asked, 'Even you, O Allāh's Messenger?' He said, *"Even I, unless and until Allāh bestows His pardon and Mercy on me."*[410]

We should not wish for death.

The Messenger of Allāh [ﷺ] said: " *None of you should wish for death for being afflicted with harm, but if he must wish he should say, 'O Allāh give me life as long as it is good for me and give me death if it is good for me.*"[411]

When death is close we should long to meet Allāh and not be afraid.

The Prophet of Allāh [ﷺ] said: *"Whoever loves the meeting with Allāh, Allāh loves the meeting with him; and whoever hates the meeting with Allāh, Allāh hates the meeting with him."*[412]

---

410 *Sahīh Al-Bukhārī*, [Eng. Trans. vol.8 Chapter 18. #470].

411 Sunan of Abū Daud, [Eng. Trans. vol.2 Chapter 1142. #3102]. Declared *sahīh* by *Shaykh* Al-Albānī.

412 *Sahīh Al-Bukhārī*, [Eng. Trans. vol. 8 Chapter 41. #514]

When the wife of the Prophet, 'Ā`ishah [ﷺ], asked who would love death, the Prophet [ﷺ] explained it refers to the time when they are informed after their death of their affairs with Allāh [i.e., the good news for a believer that Allāh is pleased with them and the bad news for the disbeliever]. We should hope for the Mercy of Allāh, as it is vast. His Prophet Muhammad [ﷺ] informed us that: *"Had the non-believer known of all the Mercy which is in the Hands of Allāh, he would not loose hope of entering Paradise, and had the believer known of all the Punishment which is present with Allāh, he would not consider himself safe from the Hell-Fire.'*[413]

This is in spite of the fact that Allāh has already promised the Hell-Fire to the disbelievers.

The lifespan of the Muslims.

"The lifespan of those in my Ummah is sixty to seventy years. And a very few of them will exceed this span."[414]

The final moments.

The dying person should say as the last words "La ilāha illa Allāh" [None has the right to be worshipped but Allāh]. And those around them should gently remind them to say it. Allāh's Messenger [ﷺ]said: *"Recite to those of you who are dying, 'There is no god but Allāh".*[415]

"Urge those of you who are on their death beds to say 'La ilāha illa Allāh' for verily, whoever's last words are 'La ilāha illa Allāh' will eventually enter Paradise even if he has to go through [before that] whatever [punishment] he has to go through."[416]

---

[413] *Sahīh Al-Bukhārī*, [Eng. Trans. vol.8 Chapter 19. #476].

[414] Narrated by At-Tirmidhī who said this *hadīth* is *hasan gharīb* and declared *hasan* by *Shaykh* Al-Albānī.

[415] *Sunan* of Abū Dāwud, [Eng. Trans. Vol. 2 #3111]. Declared *sahīh* by *Shaykh* Al-Albānī.

[416] Narrated by Ibn Hibbān in his *Sahīh* and declared authentic by *Shaykh* Al-Albānī.

Upon actual death.

The eyes of the dead should be shut, the family and friends should be patient and say as the Prophet [ﷺ] asked us to:

"We belong to Allāh and to Him we shall return. O Allāh reward me for my affliction and give me something better than it in exchange for it."[417]

It should be said by a Muslim when afflicted by any calamity and Umm Salamah [ﷺ] narrates she said it on the death of her husband and she was then married to the Prophet [ﷺ] after that [i.e., given the best of husbands]. The Prophet [ﷺ] said: *"When the soul is taken, the sight follows it."*[418]

The body should be covered, with a cloth, from prying eyes and food should be prepared for the family of the deceased.

The body should be covered so prying eyes do not come just to examine the changes in the body. "When the Prophet [ﷺ] died, he was covered with a Yemeni wrapper."[419] And the Prophet [ﷺ] said on the death of Ja'far [ﷺ]: *"Prepare food for the family of Ja'far for there came upon them an incident which has engaged them."*[420]

We have been forbidden to weep and wail loudly.

'Abdullāh Ibn 'Umar [ﷺ] said that Sa'd Ibn 'Ubādah [ﷺ] complained of illness. The Messenger of Allāh [ﷺ] came to visit him and he was accompanied by 'Abd Ar-Rahmān Ibn 'Awf, Sa'd Ibn Abī Waqqās and 'Abdullāh Ibn Mas'ūd. As he entered [his room] he found him in a swoon. Upon this he said: *"Has he died?"* They said, ' Messenger of Allāh it is not so.' The Messenger of Allāh [ﷺ] wept. When the people saw Allāh's Messenger [ﷺ] weeping they also began to weep. He said, *"Listen, Allāh*

---

[417] *Sahīh Muslim*, [Eng. Trans. Vol.2 #1999].

[418] *Sahīh Muslim*, [Eng. Trans. vol. 2 #2003].

[419] *Sahīh Muslim* [Eng. Trans. vol. 2 .#2056]

[420] *Sunan* of Abū Dāwud, [Eng. Trans. vol.2 #3126]. Declared *hasan* by *Shaykh* Al-Albānī.

does not punish for the tears that the eye sheds or the grief the heart feels, but he punishes for this [pointing to his tongue] or He may show mercy.'[421]

In the times of ignorance, the people [women] took up professional wailing for the dead. The people would upon a death, tear their hair and clothing wailing loudly etc. Islām forbade this.

The body should be washed and shrouded by trustworthy people.

The washing of the body is to be done by those who will keep the dignity and secrets of the deceased. They then commence washing the right side starting with the parts of the body over which *wuḏū`* is performed [ablution].[422] They are to be washed an odd number of times using camphor or the like in the last time.[423] The man should be shrouded in three pieces of cloth and the woman in five. The shroud should be of good quality and preferably white.[424]

The funeral prayer and procession.

One should try to attend both the funeral prayer and funeral. The Prophet [ﷺ] said: *"Whoever attends the funeral procession till he offers the funeral prayer for it, will get reward equal to one qirāṯ, and whoever accompanies it for the burial, will get a reward equal to two qirāṯ." It was asked, 'What are two qirāṯs?' He replied, "like two huge mountains.'*[425]

It is strongly recommended that women do not attend the actual burial as they are very emotional and in some countries it is prohibited. Umm 'Aṯiyyah narrated: "We were forbidden to follow the bier, but it was not

[421] *Saḥīḥ Muslim*, [Eng. Trans. vol.2 #2010].

[422] *Saḥīḥ Muslim*, [Eng. Trans. Vol.2 #2048].

[423] *Saḥīḥ Muslim*, [Eng. Trans. vol. 2 #2046].

[424] *Sunan* of Abū Dāwud, [Eng. Trans. vol.2 # 3142/ 3145]. Both declared *saḥīḥ* by *Shaykh* Al-Albānī.

[425] *Saḥīḥ Al-Bukhārī*, [Eng. Trans. vol.2. #410].

made absolute on us."[426] Therefore provided she is not going to behave in an unIslāmic manner [wailing etc.] she may go as she has to remember where she is going to be just like her male counterparts. The bigger the congregation [assembled for the prayer] the better. *"If a company of Muslims numbering one hundred pray over a dead person, all of them interceding for him, their intercession will be accepted.'*[427] And in another version, *"forty men"*.

The death of children.

"When a child of a servant of Allāh passes away, Allāh says to the angels, 'Did you take the Soul of my servants child?' They say, 'Yes!' He the Almighty says, 'Did you take away the apple of my servant's eye?' They say, 'Yes.' He the Almighty says, 'What did my servant say at this?' They say, 'He praised you and said, 'To Allāh we belong and to him we return.'[we are for Allāh and to him is our return] At this Allāh will say: 'Build for my servant a mansion in Paradise and call it the House of Praise." [428]

Muslim children who die before puberty [sinless] are in Paradise, "When Ibrāhīm the son of the Prophet [ﷺ] died the Prophet [ﷺ] said: *'There is a wet nurse for him in Paradise."* [429] And he [ﷺ] also said: *"Any Muslim whose three children died before the age of puberty will be granted Paradise by Allāh because of His Mercy to them."* [430] And in another narration a woman asked about two children and the answer was the same. As for children of the disbelievers the Prophet [ﷺ] answered: *"Since Allāh created them, He knows what kind of deeds they would have done."*[431]

---

[426] *Sahīh Muslim*, [Eng. Trans. vol. 2 #2039].

[427] *Sahīh Muslim*, [Eng. Trans.vol.2 #2071].

[428] Narrated by At-Tirmidhī declared *hasan* by *Shaykh* Al-Albānī.

[429] *Sahīh Al-Bukhārī*, [Eng. Trans. vol.2 #464].

[430] *Sahīh Al-Bukhārī*, [Eng. Trans. vol. 2 #463].

[431] *Sahīh Al-Bukhārī*,[Eng. Trans. Vol. 2 #465].

The death of a pregnant woman.

Some scholars [e.g. *Shaykh* Al-'Uthaymīn [432]] are of the opinion that if the child in the woman is capable of life outside then it may be surgically removed and her body sewn back up. However if the child is not capable of this or is dead then it will be buried along with its mother. If the mother was a non-Muslim she should not be buried in a Muslim [433] or Christian cemetery. Ahmad supports this opinion citing that a disbelieving woman cannot be buried in a Muslim cemetery as they would suffer from her punishment and she cannot be buried in a Christian cemetery, as the Muslim foetus will suffer from the disbelievers punishments.

The Grave.

It should be level, no mausoleum or cement structure may be built over it.

Tombstones and the like are not to be placed at the grave. "I heard the Messenger of Allāh [ﷺ] commanding us to level the grave."[434] "Allāh's Messenger [ﷺ] forbade that the graves should be plastered, or that they be used as sitting places [for the people], or a building should be built over them."[435]

The inside of it.

A niche may be made in it [on the side or middle], that may then be covered with bricks [to keep the body from rolling back],[436] and it should be deep enough that animals can not dig the body out. The body is to be placed

[432] *Natural Blood of Women*, by *Shaykh* Al-'Uthaymīn, pg 31.

[433] Fatwā by the *Lajnah* in *Compiled Legal Rulings of the Permanent Committī for Scholarly Research and Legal Rulings [* vol. 10 pg. 6].

[434] *Sahīh Muslim* [Eng. Trans. vol. 2 #2114].

[435] *Sahīh Muslim*, [Eng. Trans. vol. 2 #2116].

[436] *Sahīh Muslim*, [Eng. Trans. vol.2 #2112].

inside on its right side facing the *Qiblah* [Ka'bah] [bricks behind it]. And the grave then covered with soil.

We are forbidden to pray towards a grave, or offer sacrifices on it.

We may not pray to Allāh facing a grave, and it is even more repugnant to pray facing the grave while praying to the dead body in it for anything. Praying to the dead person is major *shirk* [polytheism] and the reward for it is the Hell-Fire this is because all worship is for Allāh alone and prayer or *du'ā`s*, and sacrifice are worship. Allāh said:

﴿ قُلْ إِنَّ صَلَاتِي وَنُسُكِي وَمَحْيَايَ وَمَمَاتِي لِلَّهِ رَبِّ ٱلْعَٰلَمِينَ ﴿١٦٢﴾ ﴾

﴾ Say [O Muhammad ﷺ]: Verily, my salāh, my sacrifice, my living and my dying are for Allāh, the Lord of the 'Ālamīn [mankind Jinn and all that exists]. ﴿ 6:162

The Messenger of Allāh [ﷺ] said: *"Do not pray facing towards the graves and do not sit on them."*[437] *"There is no slaughtering [of animals on graves] in Islām."*[438]

What happens to the person after the people leave the graveside.

Everyone will be crushed in their grave, for the believers it will be for a moment and for the disbelievers they will stay as such. Abdullah Ibn 'Umar narrates that the Prophet [ﷺ] said:

"This is [Sa'd Ibn Mu'ādh] for whom the Throne of Allāh moved. The doors of heaven were opened for him and seventy thousand angels took part in his funeral prayer. [His] grave was compressed and later on was expanded for him"[439]

---

[437] *Sahīh Muslim*,[Eng. Trans. vol.2 #2122].

[438] *Sunan* of Abū Dāwud, [Eng. Trans. vol.2 #3216]. Declared *sahīh* by *Shaykh* Al-Albānī.

[439] *Al-Bukhārī*, [Eng. Trans. Vol. 5 pg. 94]. Also narrated by Imām An-Nasā`ī in his *Sunan*.

"When a deceased person is laid in his grave, he hears the footsteps of the people as they go away. If he is a believer, the Prayer will stand by his head, the fasting will go to his right, alms to his left, and all other good deeds of charity, and kindness to relations and good behaviour will be by his feet. The deceased will be questioned by angels at his head. The Prayer will say, 'There is no entrance through me'. Then he will be questioned by his right side where fasting will say, 'There is no entrance through me'. Then he will be questioned by his left side where charity will say, 'There is no entrance through me.' Then he will be questioned by his feet where the good acts of voluntary charity, kindness to relations and good behaviour will say, 'There is no entrance through me.' Then they will say to him, 'Get up'. The sun will appear to him and begin to set. Then they will ask, 'This man who was among you what do you say about him? What is your testimony about him,' the man will say, ' Let me pray'. The angels will say, 'You will pray'. Answer our question, What do you think about this man who was among you? What do you say concerning him? What do you testify concerning him?' The deceased will say, 'I bear witness that Muhammad was the Messenger of Allāh who brought the truth from Allāh. The deceased will be told, 'According to this you lived and died and according to this you will be resurrected if Allāh wills." Then the door to Paradise will be opened for him. He will be told, 'This is your place in Paradise and what Allāh has prepared for you.' At this the desire and happiness of the deceased will increase. His grave will be enlarged seventy arm lengths and his grave will be lit up. His body will change to his original form and his spirit will be placed in a bird dangling by the trees of Paradise in a nice breeze'. The Prophet [ﷺ] added ' That is what is meant by the statement of Allāh, 'Allāh will establish in strength those who believe with the Word that stands firm, in this world and in the Hereafter.' He also mentioned the disbeliever and said, *his grave will be compressed, so that his ribs will be crushed together."*[440] And in another narration *" But a non-believer or a hypocrite will say to the angels, 'I do not know, but I used to say what the people used to say!' It will be said to him, 'Neither did you know nor did you take the*

[440] *Fiqh us-Sunnah,* [Eng. Trans. Vol. 4 pg.92-93] Origin in *Musnad* of Imām Ahmad and also narrated by Abū Hātim.

guidance [by reciting the Qur`ān]'. Then he will be hit with an iron hammer between his two ears, and he will cry and that cry will be heard by whatever approaches him except human beings." [441]

Some of the events in the grave and reasons for punishment [for Muslims as well] in the grave.

The Questioning.

Allāh the Exalted, said:

﴿ يُثَبِّتُ ٱللَّهُ ٱلَّذِينَ ءَامَنُواْ بِٱلْقَوْلِ ٱلثَّابِتِ فِى ٱلْحَيَوٰةِ ٱلدُّنْيَا وَفِى ٱلْءَاخِرَةِ وَيُضِلُّ ٱللَّهُ ٱلظَّٰلِمِينَ وَيَفْعَلُ ٱللَّهُ مَا يَشَآءُ ﴿٢٧﴾ ﴾

﴾ Allāh will keep firm those who believe, with the word that stands firm in this world, and in the Hereafter. ﴿ 14:27

This is in reference to the ability of the believer to answer the questions asked in the grave, Allāh gives them the firmness. The questions the angels ask are: 'Who is your Lord?' 'What is your religion?' And 'What do you say about this man?' as seen in the previous *hadīth*. Whereas for the disbeliever Allāh said:

﴿ وَمَنْ أَظْلَمُ مِمَّنِ ٱفْتَرَىٰ عَلَى ٱللَّهِ كَذِبًا أَوْ قَالَ أُوحِىَ إِلَىَّ وَلَمْ يُوحَ إِلَيْهِ شَىْءٌ وَمَن قَالَ سَأُنزِلُ مِثْلَ مَآ أَنزَلَ ٱللَّهُ وَلَوْ تَرَىٰٓ إِذِ ٱلظَّٰلِمُونَ فِى غَمَرَٰتِ ٱلْمَوْتِ وَٱلْمَلَٰٓئِكَةُ بَاسِطُوٓاْ أَيْدِيهِمْ أَخْرِجُوٓاْ أَنفُسَكُمُ ٱلْيَوْمَ تُجْزَوْنَ عَذَابَ ٱلْهُونِ بِمَا كُنتُمْ تَقُولُونَ عَلَى ٱللَّهِ غَيْرَ ٱلْحَقِّ وَكُنتُمْ عَنْ ءَايَٰتِهِۦ تَسْتَكْبِرُونَ ﴾

﴾...And if you could but see, when the dhālimūn [polytheists and wrong doers], are in the agonies of death while the angels are stretching their hands out, [saying]:'Deliver your souls! This day you shall be recompensed with the torment of degradation because of what you used to

---

[441] *Sahīh Al-Bukhārī*, [Eng. Trans. vol.2 #422]

utter against Allāh other than the truth. And you used to reject His Āyāt [proofs, verses, signs, evidences, revelations, etc.] with disrespect.❳ *6:93*

Proof of the Punishment in the grave.

"'Ā`ishah said that a Jewess came to her and mentioned the torture of the grave, saying to her, 'May Allāh protect you from the punishment of the grave.' 'Ā`ishah then asked the Prophet [ﷺ] about the punishment in the grave. He said, *' Yes [there is] punishment in the grave.' 'Ā`ishah [رضي الله عنها] added, 'After that I never saw Allāh's Messenger[ﷺ] but seeking refuge with Allāh from the punishment in the grave in every prayer he prayed."* [442] Once the Prophet [ﷺ] went out after sunset and heard a dreadful voice, and said, *"The Jews are being punished in their graves."* [443]

Backbiting [or slander] and not protecting oneself from urine.

The Prophet [ﷺ] once passed by two graves and said, *"They [in the graves] are being tortured and not for a great thing to avoid.'* And then added, *'Yes, they are being punished for a big sin, for one of them used to go about with calumnies while the other never saved himself from being soiled with his urine."* [444]

Not helping the oppressed and being negligent in ablution.

Ibn Mas'ūd narrated that the Prophet [ﷺ] said: *"A person was ordered to be lashed a hundred times in his grave. He continuously asked Allāh to decrease his punishment until only one lash remained. His grave was totally filled with fire. When the fire was removed he regained consciousness and asked, 'Why was I lashed?' He was told "You offered a*

---

[442] Sahīh *Al-Bukhārī.* [Eng. Trans. Vol.2 #454]

[443] Sahīh *Al-Bukhārī.* [Eng. Trans. Vol.2 #457]

[444] Sahīh *Al-Bukhārī.* [Eng. Trans. Vol.2 #460]

prayer once without proper purification, and you passed by an oppressed person but you did not help him." [445]

Other reasons.

The Prophet [ﷺ] said: *"But I had seen a dream last night that two men came to me, caught hold of my hands, and took me to the Sacred land [Jerusalem]. There I saw a person sitting and another standing with an iron hook in his hand pushing it inside the mouth of the former till it reached the jaw bone, and then tore off one side of his cheek, and then did the same with the other side; in the mean time the first side of his cheek became normal again and then he repeated the same operation again. I said: 'What is this?' They told me to proceed on and we went on till we came to a man lying flat on his back, and another man standing at his head carrying a stone or a piece of rock, and crushing the head of the lying man, with that stone. Whenever he struck him, the stone rolled away. The man went to pick it up and by the time he returned to him, the crushed head had returned to its normal state and the man came back and stuck him again [and so on]. I said: 'Who is this?' They told me to proceed on; so we proceeded on and passed by a hole like an oven; with a narrow top and wide bottom, and the fire was kindling underneath that hole. Whenever the flame of fire went up, the people were lifted up to such an extent that they were about to get out of it, and whenever the fire got quieter, the people went down into it, and there were naked men and women in it. I said: 'Who is this?' They told me to proceed on. So we proceeded on till we reached a river of blood and a man was in it, and another man was standing at its bank with stones in front of him, facing the man standing in the river. Whenever the man in the river wanted to come out, the other one threw a stone in his mouth and caused him to retreat to his original position; and so whenever he wanted to come out the other would throw a stone in his mouth, and he would retreat to his original position. I asked: 'What is this?' They told me to proceed on and so we did so till we reached a well flourished green garden having a huge tree and near its root was sitting an old man with some children...I said to them*

---

[445] *Fiqh us-Sunnah,* [Eng. Trans. Vol.4 pg. 95]. Origin narrated by At-Tahāwī.

[my two companions], 'You have made me ramble all the night. Tell me all about that I have seen.' They said, 'As for the one whose cheek you saw being torn away, he was a liar and he used to tell lies, and the people would report those lies on his authority till they would spread all over the world. So he will be punished like that till the Day of Resurrection. The one whose head you saw being crushed is one whom Allāh had given the knowledge of Qur`ān [by heart] but he used to sleep at night [i.e., did not recite it then] and he did not use to act upon it [i.e., its orders]] by day; and so this punishment will go on until the Day of Resurrection. And those you saw in the hole [like an oven] were adulterers. And those you saw in the river of blood were those dealing in ribā [interest, usury]. And the old man you saw was Abraham and the little children around him were the offspring of the people. And the one who was kindling the fire was Mālik, the gate keeper of the Hell-Fire...'[446]

[446] *Sahīh Al-Bukhārī*, [Eng. Trans. Vol.2 pgs 263-265]

CHAPTER 15

DISCRIPTIONS OF PARADISE AND HELL

Paradise.

Allāh the Almighty, the Most Majestic said:

﴿ يَٰٓأَيُّهَا ٱلَّذِينَ ءَامَنُوا۟ ٱتَّقُوا۟ ٱللَّهَ وَٱبْتَغُوٓا۟ إِلَيْهِ ٱلْوَسِيلَةَ وَجَٰهِدُوا۟ فِى سَبِيلِهِۦ لَعَلَّكُمْ تُفْلِحُونَ ﴿٣٥﴾ ﴾

﴾ O mankind! Verily the promise of Allāh is true. So let not this present life deceive you, and let not the chief deceiver [Satan] deceive you about Allāh.﴿ *35:5*

﴿ وَسِيقَ ٱلَّذِينَ ٱتَّقَوْا۟ رَبَّهُمْ إِلَى ٱلْجَنَّةِ زُمَرًا حَتَّىٰٓ إِذَا جَآءُوهَا وَفُتِحَتْ أَبْوَٰبُهَا وَقَالَ لَهُمْ خَزَنَتُهَا سَلَٰمٌ عَلَيْكُمْ طِبْتُمْ فَٱدْخُلُوهَا خَٰلِدِينَ ﴿٧٣﴾ وَقَالُوا۟ ٱلْحَمْدُ لِلَّهِ ٱلَّذِى صَدَقَنَا وَعْدَهُۥ وَأَوْرَثَنَا ٱلْأَرْضَ نَتَبَوَّأُ مِنَ ٱلْجَنَّةِ حَيْثُ نَشَآءُ فَنِعْمَ أَجْرُ ٱلْعَٰمِلِينَ ﴿٧٤﴾ ﴾

﴾ And those who kept their duty to their Lord will be led to Paradise in groups, till, when they reach it, and its gates will be opened [before their arrival for their reception] and its keepers will say: Salām 'Alaykum [peace be upon you]! You have done well, so enter here to abide therein. And they will say: 'All the praises and thanks are to Allāh Who has fulfilled His Promise to us and has made us inherit [this] land. We can dwell in paradise where we will, how excellent a reward for the [pious, good] workers!﴿ *39:73-74.*

And who will attain it.

Allāh the Exalted said:

﴿ إِنَّ ٱلَّذِينَ ءَامَنُوا۟ وَعَمِلُوا۟ ٱلصَّٰلِحَٰتِ كَانَتْ لَهُمْ جَنَّٰتُ ٱلْفِرْدَوْسِ نُزُلًا ﴿١٠٧﴾
خَٰلِدِينَ فِيهَا لَا يَبْغُونَ عَنْهَا حِوَلًا ﴿١٠٨﴾ ﴾

﴾ Verily those who believe [in the Oneness of Allāh-Islāmic monotheism] and do righteous deeds, shall have the gardens of Al-Firdaws [Paradise] for their entertainment.﴿ 18:107

His Prophet [ﷺ] said: *"Paradise is surrounded by hardships and the Hell-Fire is surrounded by temptations [passions, lusts etc.]"* [447] *"He who said, 'There is no god but Allāh, He is one and there is no associate with Him, that Muhammad is His servant and His Messenger, and that 'Īsā is His servant and the son of his maidservant and he ['Īsā] is His Word which He communicated to Maryam and is His spirit, that Paradise is a fact and Hell is a fact,' Allāh would make him [who affirms these truths] enter Paradise through whichever of its eight doors he would like."* [448]

Some of its descriptions.

Allāh the Mighty, the Raiser [from death], the Just, describes [in His Book] [some aspects of] His Paradise.

The clothing of its inhabitants.

﴿ وَيَلْبَسُونَ ثِيَابًا خُضْرًا مِّن سُندُسٍ ﴾

﴾... they will wear green garments of fine and thick silk ...﴿ 18:31

﴿ يُحَلَّوْنَ فِيهَا مِنْ أَسَاوِرَ مِن ذَهَبٍ وَلُؤْلُؤًا وَلِبَاسُهُمْ فِيهَا حَرِيرٌ ﴾

﴾... wherein they will be adorned with bracelets of gold and pearls and their garments therein will be of silk. ﴿ 22:23

---

[447] *Sahīh Muslim*, [Eng. Trans. vol.4 #6778].

[448] *Sahīh Muslim*, [Eng. Trans. vol. 1 #43].

The food of its inhabitants.

﴿ وَأَمْدَدْنَٰهُم بِفَٰكِهَةٍ وَلَحْمٍ مِّمَّا يَشْتَهُونَ ﴿٢٢﴾ ﴾

﴾ And We shall provide them with fruit and meat such as they desire. ﴿ 52:22

The drink of its inhabitants.

﴿ يُطَافُ عَلَيْهِم بِكَأْسٍ مِّن مَّعِينٍ ﴿٤٥﴾ بَيْضَآءَ لَذَّةٍ لِّلشَّٰرِبِينَ ﴿٤٦﴾ لَا فِيهَا غَوْلٌ
وَلَا هُمْ عَنْهَا يُنزَفُونَ ﴿٤٧﴾ ﴾

﴾ Round them will be passed a cup of pure wine; white and delicious to the drinkers, Neither will they have Ghoul [any kind of hurt, abdominal pain, headache, sin etc.] from that, nor will they suffer intoxication therefrom. ﴿ 37:45-7

﴿ مَّثَلُ ٱلْجَنَّةِ ٱلَّتِى وُعِدَ ٱلْمُتَّقُونَ ۖ فِيهَآ أَنْهَٰرٌ مِّن مَّآءٍ غَيْرِ ءَاسِنٍ وَأَنْهَٰرٌ مِّن لَّبَنٍ
لَّمْ يَتَغَيَّرْ طَعْمُهُۥ وَأَنْهَٰرٌ مِّنْ خَمْرٍ لَّذَّةٍ لِّلشَّٰرِبِينَ وَأَنْهَٰرٌ مِّنْ عَسَلٍ مُّصَفًّى ۖ وَلَهُمْ
فِيهَا مِن كُلِّ ٱلثَّمَرَٰتِ وَمَغْفِرَةٌ مِّن رَّبِّهِمْ ۖ كَمَنْ هُوَ خَٰلِدٌ فِى ٱلنَّارِ وَسُقُوا۟ مَآءً حَمِيمًا
فَقَطَّعَ أَمْعَآءَهُمْ ﴿١٥﴾ ﴾

﴾ The description of Paradise which the muttaqūn [pious] have been promised [is that] in it are rivers of water the taste and smell of which are never changed, rivers of milk of which the taste never changes, rivers of wine delicious to those who drink, and rivers of clarified honey [clear and pure] ... ﴿ 47:15

﴿ وَيُطَافُ عَلَيْهِم بِـَٔانِيَةٍ مِّن فِضَّةٍ وَأَكْوَابٍ كَانَتْ قَوَارِيرَا۠ ﴿١٥﴾ قَوَارِيرَا۟ مِن فِضَّةٍ
قَدَّرُوهَا تَقْدِيرًا ﴿١٦﴾ وَيُسْقَوْنَ فِيهَا كَأْسًا كَانَ مِزَاجُهَا زَنجَبِيلًا ﴿١٧﴾ ﴾

﴾ And amongst them will be passed round vessels of silver and cups of crystal- Crystal clear made of silver. They will determine the measure thereof [according to their wishes]. And they will be given to drink there a cup [of wine] mixed with Zanjabīl [ginger]. ﴿ 76:15-17

﴿ يُطَافُ عَلَيْهِم بِصِحَافٍ مِّن ذَهَبٍ وَأَكْوَابٍ وَفِيهَا مَا تَشْتَهِيهِ ٱلْأَنفُسُ وَتَلَذُّ ٱلْأَعْيُنُ وَأَنتُمْ فِيهَا خَٰلِدُونَ ﴿٧١﴾ ﴾

﴾ Trays of gold and cups will be passed around them, [therein will be] all that one's inner self could desire, all that the eyes could delight in, and you will abide there in forever.﴿ *43:71*

On spouses for the inhabitants.

For the men:

﴿ كَذَٰلِكَ وَزَوَّجْنَٰهُم بِحُورٍ عِينٍ ﴿٥٤﴾ ﴾

﴾ And We shall marry them to Hūr 'Ayn [female fare ones] with wide lovely eyes.﴿ *44:54*

﴿ وَعِندَهُمْ قَٰصِرَٰتُ ٱلطَّرْفِ عِينٌ ﴿٤٨﴾ كَأَنَّهُنَّ بَيْضٌ مَّكْنُونٌ ﴿٤٩﴾ ﴾

﴾ And beside them will be Qasirāh At-Tarf [chaste females restraining their glances, desiring none except their husbands]...[delicate and pure] as if they were [hidden] eggs [well] preserved.﴿ *37:48-49*

﴿ وَأَزْوَٰجٌ مُّطَهَّرَةٌ ﴾

﴾ and wives that are mutahharah [purified mates or wives] [i.e., they will have no menses, urine or stools etc.].﴿ *3:15*

Hūr 'Ayn are very fair females created by Allāh as such, not from the offspring of Adam [ﷺ] with intense black irises of the eyes and intense white sclera's.

For the women:

This is a matter that only Allāh has the exact answer to. However some scholars said that female believers who go to Paradise will marry the same spouse she had on earth if he made it to Paradise except that he will have only the best of his qualities. If not [he didn't make it or she wasn't married] she will be given a suitable other, said to also be from the same creation as the *Hūr 'Ayn* by the will of Allāh. She will also be more beautiful than the *Hūr 'Ayn.* This [marriage] is a matter scholars have differed on however, a companion of the Prophet [ﷺ] is noted to have said to his wife that he would like for her not to remarry [after his death] as he wanted them to be married in Paradise. This and the following *hadīth* is why some of our scholars say the last husband she had is the one she will have in Paradise [however if she had more than one it is also said she would be able to choose and Allāh knows best]. In part of a longer *hadīth* narrated by Abū Maryam about the afflictions happening at that time Al-Hasan [ﷺ] said: *"Ā`ishah has moved to Al-Basrah. By Allāh! She is the wife of your Prophet [ﷺ] in this world and in the Hereafter. But Allāh has put you to test whether you will obey Him or her."*[449]

Other comforts for the inhabitants.

﴿ لَهُمْ دَارُ ٱلسَّلَـٰمِ عِندَ رَبِّهِمْ ۖ وَهُوَ وَلِيُّهُم بِمَا كَانُوا۟ يَعْمَلُونَ ﴿١٢٧﴾ ﴾

﴾ For them will be the home of peace [Paradise] with their Lord. And He will be their Walī [Helper and Protector] because of what they used to do. ﴿ 6:127

﴿ لَا يَذُوقُونَ فِيهَا ٱلْمَوْتَ إِلَّا ٱلْمَوْتَةَ ٱلْأُولَىٰ ﴾

﴾ They will never taste death therein, ﴿ 44:56

﴿ لَا يَمَسُّهُمْ فِيهَا نَصَبٌ وَمَا هُم مِّنْهَا بِمُخْرَجِينَ ﴿٤٨﴾ ﴾

﴾ No sense of fatigue shall touch them, nor shall they [ever] be asked to leave it. ﴿ 15:48

﴿ لَّا تَسْمَعُ فِيهَا لَـٰغِيَةً ﴿١١﴾ ﴾

﴾ Where they shall neither hear harmful speech nor falsehood, ﴿ 88:11

﴿ مُّتَّكِـِٔينَ فِيهَا عَلَى ٱلْأَرَآئِكِ ۖ لَا يَرَوْنَ فِيهَا شَمْسًا وَلَا زَمْهَرِيرًا ﴿١٣﴾ ﴾

﴾ Reclining on raised thrones, they will see there neither the excessive heat of the sun nor excessive bitter cold, [as in Paradise there is no sun and no moon], ﴿ 76:13

﴿ وَنَزَعْنَا مَا فِى صُدُورِهِم مِّنْ غِلٍّ تَجْرِى مِن تَحْتِهِمُ ٱلْأَنْهَـٰرُ ۖ

[449] *Sahīh Al-Bukhārī*, [Eng. Trans. Vol.9 pg. 171].

﴾ ***And We shall remove from their breasts any [mutual] hatred or sense of injury [as in this world].*** ﴿ ***7:43***

﴿ مُتَّكِـِٔينَ عَلَىٰ فُرُشٍۭ بَطَآئِنُهَا مِنْ إِسْتَبْرَقٍ وَجَنَى ٱلْجَنَّتَيْنِ دَانٍ ﴿٥٤﴾ ﴾

﴾ ***Reclining upon couches lined with silk brocade, and the fruits of two gardens will be at hand.*** ﴿ ***55:54***

﴿ وَزَرَابِىُّ مَبْثُوثَةٌ ﴿١٦﴾ ﴾

﴾ ***And rich carpets all spread out.*** ﴿ ***88:16***

﴿ لَٰكِنِ ٱلَّذِينَ ٱتَّقَوْا۟ رَبَّهُمْ لَهُمْ غُرَفٌ مِّن فَوْقِهَا غُرَفٌ مَّبْنِيَّةٌ تَجْرِى مِن تَحْتِهَا
ٱلْأَنْهَٰرُ وَعْدَ ٱللَّهِ لَا يُخْلِفُ ٱللَّهُ ٱلْمِيعَادَ ﴿٢٠﴾ ﴾

﴾ ***But for those who fear their Lord [Allāh] and keep their duty to Him, for them are built lofty rooms, one above the another under which rivers flow. [This is] the Promise of Allāh: and Allāh does not fail in [His] Promise.*** ﴿ ***39:20***

﴿ وَعَدَ ٱللَّهُ ٱلْمُؤْمِنِينَ وَٱلْمُؤْمِنَٰتِ جَنَّٰتٍ تَجْرِى مِن تَحْتِهَا ٱلْأَنْهَٰرُ خَٰلِدِينَ
فِيهَا وَمَسَٰكِنَ طَيِّبَةً فِى جَنَّٰتِ عَدْنٍ وَرِضْوَٰنٌ مِّنَ ٱللَّهِ أَكْبَرُ ذَٰلِكَ هُوَ ٱلْفَوْزُ
ٱلْعَظِيمُ ﴿٧٢﴾ ﴾

﴾ ***Allāh has promised the believers-men and women- gardens under which rivers flow to dwell therein forever, and beautiful mansions in Gardens of Eden. But the greatest bliss is the Good Pleasure of Allāh. That is the supreme success.*** ﴿ ***9:72***

Miscellaneous *hadīths* on Paradise.

"The first group [of people] who will enter Paradise will be [glittering] like the moon on a full moon night. They will neither spit therein, nor blow their noses therein nor relieve nature. Their utensils will be of gold and their combs of gold and silver, in their censers the aloes wood will be used, and their sweat will smell like musk. Every one of them will have two wives; the marrow of the bones of the wives legs will be seen through the flesh out of excessive beauty. They [the inhabitants] will neither have difference or

enmity [hatred] among themselves and their hearts will be as one heart, and they will be glorifying Allāh in the morning and afternoon.'[450]

"He who would get into Paradise would get in the form of Adam [ﷺ], his length being sixty cubits, then the people who followed him continued to diminish in size up to this day.'[451]

"In Paradise there is a street to which they [i.e., the inhabitants] would come every Friday. The north wind will blow and would scatter fragrance on their faces and on their clothes and would add to their beauty and loveliness, and then they would go back to their families and their family would say to them, 'By Allāh, you have increased in beauty and loveliness after leaving us, and they would say: 'By Allāh, you have also increased in beauty and loveliness after us."[452]

" The inmates of Paradise would see the inmates of the apartments over them just as you see the shining planets which remain in the eastern and western horizon because of the superiority that some have over others. They said, 'Allāh's Messenger would these abodes of the Messengers, others besides them, not be able to reach?' He said, Yes they will, by Him, in Whose Hand is my life, those who believe in Allāh and acknowledge the Truth, will reach them."[i.e., the pious would be able to visit and live near the Prophets they used to love in this world] [453]

"There is a tree in Paradise [so huge] that a fast [or trained] rider may travel for a hundred years without being able to cross it.'[454]

"I stood at the gate of Paradise and saw that the majority of the people who had entered it were poor people, while the rich were forbidden [to enter along with the poor, because they were waiting the reckoning of their accounts." [455]

---

[450] Sahīh *Al-Bukhārī*, [Eng. Trans. vol.4 #468].

[451] Sahīh *Muslim*, [Eng. Trans. vol. 4 #6809].

[452] Sahīh *Muslim*, [Eng. Trans. vol. 4 #6792].

[453] Sahīh *Muslim*, [Eng. Trans. vol. 4 #6790].

[454] Sahīh *Al-Bukhārī*, [Eng. Trans. vol.8 #559 c].

[455] Sahīh *Al-Bukhārī*, [Eng. Trans. vol.8 #555].

Hell.

Who will enter it?

Allāh the Most Mighty, the Judge said in His Book:

﴿ وَالَّذِينَ كَذَّبُوا بِآيَاتِنَا وَاسْتَكْبَرُوا عَنْهَا أُولَٰئِكَ أَصْحَابُ النَّارِ هُمْ فِيهَا
خَالِدُونَ ﴿٣٦﴾ ﴾

﴾ But those who reject our Āyāt [proofs, evidences, verses, signs, revelations etc.] and treat them with arrogance, they are the dwellers of the [Hell] Fire, they will abide therein forever.﴿ 7:36

﴿ فَأَنذَرْتُكُمْ نَارًا تَلَظَّىٰ ﴿١٤﴾ لَا يَصْلَاهَا إِلَّا الْأَشْقَى ﴿١٥﴾ الَّذِي كَذَّبَ وَتَوَلَّىٰ
﴿١٦﴾ وَسَيُجَنَّبُهَا الْأَتْقَى ﴿١٧﴾ ﴾

﴾ Therefore I have warned you of a Fire blazing fiercely [Hell], None shall enter it except the most wretched who denies and turns away. And the muttaqūn [pious] will be far removed from it [Hell]. ﴿ 92:14-17

﴿ إِنَّ الَّذِينَ كَفَرُوا مِنْ أَهْلِ الْكِتَابِ وَالْمُشْرِكِينَ فِي نَارِ جَهَنَّمَ خَالِدِينَ فِيهَا
أُولَٰئِكَ هُمْ شَرُّ الْبَرِيَّةِ ﴿٦﴾ ﴾

﴾ Verily those who disbelieve [in the religion of Islām, the Qur`ān and Prophet Muhammad ﷺ] from among the people of the Scripture [Jews and Christians] and Mushrikūn [polytheists, pagans, idolaters] will abide in the Fire of Hell. They are the worst of creatures.﴿ 98:6.

﴿ وَالَّذِينَ كَفَرُوا لَهُمْ نَارُ جَهَنَّمَ لَا يُقْضَىٰ عَلَيْهِمْ فَيَمُوتُوا وَلَا يُخَفَّفُ عَنْهُم
مِّنْ عَذَابِهَا كَذَٰلِكَ نَجْزِي كُلَّ كَفُورٍ ﴿٣٦﴾ ﴾

﴾ But those who disbelieve [in the Oneness of Allāh-Islāmic Monotheism], for them will be the Fire of Hell. Neither will it have a complete killing

***effect on them so that they die, nor shall its torment be lightened for them. Thus do We requite every disbeliever!* ❯ 35:36**

Clothing for its inhabitants.

﴿ فَٱلَّذِينَ كَفَرُوا۟ قُطِّعَتْ لَهُمْ ثِيَابٌ مِّن نَّارٍ يُصَبُّ مِن فَوْقِ رُءُوسِهِمُ ٱلْحَمِيمُ ﴿١٩﴾ يُصْهَرُ بِهِۦ مَا فِى بُطُونِهِمْ وَٱلْجُلُودُ ﴾

❮ *... then as for those who disbelieved, garments of fire will be cut out for them, boiling water will be poured down over their heads. With it will melt what is within their bellies, as well as their skins.* ❯ 22:19-20

Food and drink for its inhabitants.

﴿ إِنَّا جَعَلْنَٰهَا فِتْنَةً لِّلظَّٰلِمِينَ ﴿٦٣﴾ إِنَّهَا شَجَرَةٌ تَخْرُجُ فِىٓ أَصْلِ ٱلْجَحِيمِ ﴿٦٤﴾ طَلْعُهَا كَأَنَّهُۥ رُءُوسُ ٱلشَّيَٰطِينِ ﴿٦٥﴾ فَإِنَّهُمْ لَءَاكِلُونَ مِنْهَا فَمَالِـُٔونَ مِنْهَا ٱلْبُطُونَ ﴿٦٦﴾ ثُمَّ إِنَّ لَهُمْ عَلَيْهَا لَشَوْبًا مِّنْ حَمِيمٍ ﴿٦٧﴾ ثُمَّ إِنَّ مَرْجِعَهُمْ لَإِلَى ٱلْجَحِيمِ ﴾

❮ *Truly we have made it [i.e., Zaqqūm tree] a trial for the dhālimūn [polytheists, disbelievers, wrongdoers]. Verily, it is a tree that springs out of the bottom of the Hell-Fire, The shoots of its fruit stalks are like the heads of Shayāṯīn [devils]; Truly they will eat thereof and fill their bellies therewith. Then on top of that they will be given boiling water to drink so that it becomes a mixture [of boiling water and Zaqqūm in their bellies]. Then thereafter, verily their return is to the flaming fire of Hell.* ❯ 37:63-68.

﴿ فَمَالِـُٔونَ مِنْهَا ٱلْبُطُونَ ﴿٥٣﴾ فَشَٰرِبُونَ عَلَيْهِ مِنَ ٱلْحَمِيمِ ﴿٥٤﴾ فَشَٰرِبُونَ شُرْبَ ٱلْهِيمِ ﴾

❮ *Then you will fill your bellies therewith, And drink boiling water on top of it. And you will drink [that] like thirsty camels.* ❯ 56:53-55.

﴿ وَإِن يَسْتَغِيثُوا۟ يُغَاثُوا۟ بِمَآءٍ كَٱلْمُهْلِ يَشْوِى ٱلْوُجُوهَ ۚ بِئْسَ ٱلشَّرَابُ وَسَآءَتْ مُرْتَفَقًا ﴾

﴾...And if they ask for help [relief, water], they will be granted water like boiling oil, that will scald their faces.﴿ 18:29

﴿ لَّا يَذُوقُونَ فِيهَا بَرْدًا وَلَا شَرَابًا ﴿٢٤﴾ إِلَّا حَمِيمًا وَغَسَّاقًا ﴿٢٥﴾ ﴾

﴾ Nothing cool shall they taste therein nor any drink. Except boiling water, and dirty wound discharges. ﴿ 78:24-25.

Other punishments for its inhabitants [their only entertainment].

﴿ إِنَّ جَهَنَّمَ كَانَتْ مِرْصَادًا ﴿٢١﴾ لِّلطَّٰغِينَ مَـَٔابًا ﴿٢٢﴾ لَّٰبِثِينَ فِيهَآ أَحْقَابًا ﴿٢٣﴾ ﴾

﴾ Truly Hell is a place of ambush, a dwelling place for the Tāghīn [all those transgressing the limits set by Allāh, polytheists, disbelievers, hypocrites, sinners, criminals etc.]. They will abide therein for ages.﴿ 78:21-23.

﴿ إِنَّآ أَعْتَدْنَا لِلْكَٰفِرِينَ سَلَٰسِلَا۟ وَأَغْلَٰلًا وَسَعِيرًا ﴿٤﴾ ﴾

﴾ Verily we have prepared for the disbelievers iron chains, iron collars and a blazing fire.﴿ 76:4

﴿ لَهُمْ فِيهَا زَفِيرٌ وَهُمْ فِيهَا لَا يَسْمَعُونَ ﴿١٠٠﴾ ﴾

﴾ Therein breathing out deep sighs and roaring will be their portion, therein they will hear not.﴿ [456] *21:100*

﴿ وَلَهُم مَّقَٰمِعُ مِنْ حَدِيدٍ ﴿٢١﴾ كُلَّمَآ أَرَادُوٓا۟ أَن يَخْرُجُوا۟ مِنْهَا مِنْ غَمٍّ أُعِيدُوا۟ فِيهَا وَذُوقُوا۟ عَذَابَ ٱلْحَرِيقِ ﴿٢٢﴾ ﴾

---

[456] Ibn Mas'ūd when he recited this verse, he said, "When those [who are destined to remain in the Fire of Hell forever] will be thrown in the Hell-Fire, each of them will be put in a separate *tābūt* [box of fire with nails of fire] and he will not see anyone punished except himself." *Tafsīr Ibn Kathīr*, [vol.3 pg 192].

﴾ And for them are hooked rods of iron. Every time they seek to get away therefrom, from anguish, they will be driven back therein, and [it will be] said to them: 'Taste the torment of burning! ﴿ 22:21-2

Miscellaneous _hadīths_ on Hell.

"The fire which the sons of Adam [ﷺ] burn is only one seventieth part of the Fire of Hell." His companions said, 'By Allāh even ordinary fire would have been enough [to burn people].' There upon he said: *It is sixty nine parts in excess of [the heat of] fire in this world each of them being the equivalent to their heat."* [457]

"The molar tooth of an unbeliever or the canine teeth of an unbeliever will be like [Mount] Uhud and the thickness of his skin is like a three nights journey." [458] [To endure the torture].

"The distance of the two shoulders of the non believer in Hell will be a three days journey for a swift rider." [459]

"May I not inform you of the inmates of Hell-Fire? They are all proud, mean and haughty." [460]

"We were in the company of Allāh's Messenger [ﷺ] and we heard a terrible sound. Thereupon Allāh's Messenger [ﷺ] said, *'Do you know what that [sound] is this?'* We said, 'Allāh and His Messenger know best.' Whereupon he said, *that is a stone which was thrown seventy years before in Hell and has been constantly slipping down and now has reached its base.'* [461]

---

457 *Sahīh Muslim* [Eng. Trans. vol.4 #6811].

458 *Sahīh Muslim* [Eng. Trans. vol.4 #6831].

459 *Sahīh Muslim* [Eng. Trans. vol.4 #6832].

460 *Sahīh Muslim* [Eng. Trans. vol.4 #6835].

461 *Sahīh Muslim*, [Eng. Trans. vol. 4 #6813]

"And I stood at the gate of the Fire and found that the majority were women."[462]

Therefore it is easier to do the tasks that may be difficult when one thinks of the şeverity of the punishment. Sisters are advised to keep focused on the Hereafter and then choose options in life. Remember the Hereafter is eternal, here is another final *hadīth* to ponder over. The Prophet [ﷺ] said:

"Death would be brought on the Day of Resurrection in the form of a white-colored ram.[463] and in another narration, *"And it would increase the delight of the inmates of Paradise and it would increase the grief of the inmates of Hell-Fire."*

We seek refuge with Allāh from His Punishment with His Mercy. Āmīn. If Allāh wills you will be of those who take heed from the following verse.

﴿ وَذَرِ ٱلَّذِينَ ٱتَّخَذُواْ دِينَهُمۡ لَعِبٗا وَلَهۡوٗا وَغَرَّتۡهُمُ ٱلۡحَيَوٰةُ ٱلدُّنۡيَاۚ وَذَكِّرۡ بِهِۦٓ
أَن تُبۡسَلَ نَفۡسُۢ بِمَا كَسَبَتۡ لَيۡسَ لَهَا مِن دُونِ ٱللَّهِ وَلِيّٞ وَلَا شَفِيعٞ وَإِن
تَعۡدِلۡ كُلَّ عَدۡلٖ لَّا يُؤۡخَذۡ مِنۡهَآۗ أُوْلَٰٓئِكَ ٱلَّذِينَ أُبۡسِلُواْ بِمَا كَسَبُواْۖ لَهُمۡ شَرَابٞ
مِّنۡ حَمِيمٖ وَعَذَابٌ أَلِيمُۢ بِمَا كَانُواْ يَكۡفُرُونَ ٧٠ ﴾

❮ And leave alone those who take their religion as play and amusement, and whom the life of this world has deceived. But remind [them] with it [the Qur`ān] lest a person be given up to destruction for that which he has earned, when he will find for himself no protector or intercessor besides Allāh, and even if he offers every ransom, it will not be accepted from

---

[462] *Sahīh Al-Bukhārī*, [Eng. Trans. vol. 8 #555. The reasons have been covered before, ungratefulness to their husbands as one reason.]

[463] *Sahīh Muslim*, [Eng. Trans. vol. 4 #6827]

him. Such are they given up to destruction because of what they have earned. For them will be a drink of boiling water and a painful torment because they used to disbelieve. **❫ *6:70.***

﴿ وَٱذۡكُرُواْ ٱللَّهَ كَثِيرٗا لَّعَلَّكُمۡ تُفۡلِحُونَ ﴾

❪ Remember Allāh much that you may be successful❫ 62:10

May Allāh guide my family that they may find benefit in this book for this world and the hereafter, Āmīn.

Finished in Medina Munawwarah
By the mercy of Allāh, the Most High
On the 29th of Sha'bān 1418.

GLOSSARY

Adhān: The call to prayer of the Muslims.

Adab: Manners, behavior.

Al-Bait Al-Ma'mūr: Allāh's house in Paradise [equated with the *Ka'bah* in Makkah] it is over the seventh heaven.

Al-Ghurr Al-Muhajjalūn: Name given to the Muslims on the Day of Resurrection because the parts of their bodies that they used to wash in ablution will be shining.

Istihādah: The state in which a woman bleeds from her womb outside of her regular periods.

Khul'ah: The divorce whereby a wife parts from her husband by returning her *Mahr* [that that he gave to her].

Al-Lawh Al-Mahfūdh: The preserved tablet of Allāh where everything, which was to happen, was written down before creation, it is with Allāh above the heavens.

Li'ān: The oath taken by a husband and wife when he accuses her of illegal sexual intercourse without the proof [i.e., he may have witnessed it but he cannot produce four witnesses to testify to it nor does she confess]

Qadar: Divine Preordainment.

Al-Ulūhiyyah: A branch of the [three] branches of *Tawhīd*. It refers to the belief in the oneness in worship of Allāh Alone.

Nushrah: Seeking cure from the use of magic spells and incantations.

Ar-Rubūbiyyah: A branch of the [three] branches of *Tawhīd*. It refers to the belief in the Oneness in the Lordship of Allāh.

Tabarruj: The display of a woman's charms i.e., by not covering them or enhancing them for other than her husband.

At-Tiyarah: Bad omens.

Adh-Dhihār: The act of vowing to stay away from ones wife for a time period, making her unlawful to him.

'Aqīqah: The sacrifice of one or two sheep at the birth of a child to show gratitude to Allāh.
'Arsh: The Throne of Allāh.
Al-Asmā` wa As-Sifāt: A branch of the three branches of *Tawhīd.* It refers to the belief in the oneness of the names and characteristics of Allāh.
'Awrah: The private parts of your body. For a man it is between his navel and knees and for a woman her entire body [when in front of non-*mahram* men].
Bismillāh: In the name of Allāh.
Daff: A tambourine with no bells.
Da'wah: Call, invitation usually used to refer to the invitation to the religion of Allāh.
Dhikr: Remembrance of Allāh.
Du'ā`: Supplication or prayer.
'Īd Al-Adhā: It is the Muslims festival in the month of *Hajj*, which lasts for four days. A sacrifice is made [of an animal] to Allāh on the first day after the *'Īd* prayer.
'Īd Al-Fitr: The Muslims festival on the first day of Shawwāl lasting three days. It is on the first day after the end of fasting the month of *Ramadān.*
Fitnah: Troubles or problems.
Ghusl: A purifying bath taken by one in a state of major *hadath.* It is to be done in accordance with the *Sunnah* of the Prophet [ﷺ] and enables one to be in a state of ritual purity for worship.
Hadath: The passing of wind, urine, or stools [minor] or sexual discharge caused by intercourse or dreams [major] thus causing ritual impurity. Minor *hadath* necessitates ablution and major *hadath* necessitates a *Ghusl.*
***Hadīth*:** Statements or actions of the Prophet [ﷺ] or actions or sayings that he approved of by his family or companions.
Hayd: Menstruation.
Hajj: The pilgrimage to Makkah and a pillar of Islām.
Halāl: Lawful [things or actions according to the Islāmic *Sharī'ah*]
Al-Hamdulillāh: "All praise is for Allāh."
Harām: Unlawful [things or actions according to the Islāmic *Sharī'ah*]
Henna: A skin and hair dye.

Hijāb: The proper dress of a believing woman that adequately covers her aura in the presence of non-*mahram* men or anyone she feels will describe her to a person who should not know her appearance.

Husnā: Good [or good tidings]

'Iddah: The waiting period of a woman after death or divorce [before she may remarry]

Iftār: The meal after breaking fast.

Īmān: Faith

Injīl: The revelation sent with 'Īsā [Jesus the son of Mary].

Iqāmah: It is said immediately before the Prayer to inform of its start. The wording is the same as the *adhān* except lines repeated twice in the *adhān* are said only once in the *Iqāmah* with the exception of *Allāh Akbar*.

Islām: The religion of Monotheism sent with all the Prophets [ﷺ] and the final revelation was sent with Muhammad [ﷺ] the last of the Prophets.

Istighāthah: Seeking help from other than Allāh.

I'tikāf: Seclusion in a *masjid* for the sole purpose of worshipping Allāh, it has rules and guidelines.

Jāhiliyyah: Ignorance, usually referring to the ignorance due to lack of religious guidance before Islām.

Junub: The state of impurity caused by sexual intercourse or a wet dream.

Ka'bah: The house of Allāh in Makkah.

Kattam: A hair dye derived from a certain plant.

Khamr: Wine or alcoholic drinks.

Kuhl: A substance used as eyeliner by woman and also said to have healing properties and thus used for eye infections in by men too.

Kuffār: Those in the state of disbelief [in Allāh and His messenger and the Qur`ān as the last revelation].

Kursī: The footstool of Allāh.

Khutbah: A sermon or talk given by an Imam or religious leader to the rest of the Muslims [present].

Mahram: A person that one is not allowed to marry according to the *Sharī'ah* e.g. your parents.

Madhhab: A school of thought.

Musallā: The prayer area of a *masjid*.

Mushrikūn: Polytheist, Idolater disbeliever.

Nifās: The blood flowing out of the womb after the birth of a child [alive or dead].

Nikāh: Marriage.

Qadā`: Compensation for incorrect or skipped rituals in Islām.

Qiblah: The direction one turns to for prayer, facing the Ka'bah from anywhere in the world.

Qur`ān: The last revelation sent with Prophet Muhammad [ﷺ] from Allāh to all mankind and jinn.

Rak'ah: The part of the prayer, which consists of, one standing, one bowing and two prostration's.

Ruqyah: Recitation of verses from the Qur`ān for healing [physical or spiritual].

Sadaqah: Charity.

Salām 'Alaykum: The greeting of the Muslims, "May the peace of Allāh be upon you."

Sawm: Fasting.

Salāh: Prayer

Shighār: Exchange of family [female] members instead of paying *Mahr*. It is illegal in Islām.

Shaytān: Satan or the devil.

***Shirk*:** Polytheism.

Subhānallāh: "How perfect Allāh is!"

Subhānallāh wa bihamdih: " How perfect Allāh is and all praise is for Allāh."

Suhūr: A meal taken a few minutes before commencing fasting before dawn.

Sujūd As-Sahwah: Prostration of forgetfulness.

Sunnah: The ways of the Prophet [ﷺ] [deeds etc.] and that of his companions which he [ﷺ] found acceptable.

Talāq: Divorce.

Tawbah: Repentance.

Tawāf: Circumambulation of the Ka'bah.

Tawhīd: Islāmic Monotheism. [It has three divisions]

Tayammum: Ritual purification by use of soil, if water is unavailable or its use will cause harm.
Tawrāt: The revelation sent with Mūsā [ﷺ].
Wājib: Obligatory in Islām.
Walīmah: The wedding banquet.
Witr: An odd number of Rak'ah prayed after night prayers.
Zakāh : Obligatory charity.

Printed India